MARRIAGE IN THE EIGHTEENTH CENTURY ENGLISH NOVEL

MARRIAGE IN THE EIGHTEENTH CENTURY ENGLISH NOVEL

SARUP SINGH

MANOHAR
1995

ISBN 81-7304-124-5

First Published 1995

Published by
Ajay Kumar Jain
Manohar Publishers & Distributors
2/6, Ansari Road, Daryaganj
New Delhi - 110002

Lasertypeset by
A J Software Publishing Co. Pvt. Ltd.
305, Durga Chambers,
1333, D.B. Gupta Road,
Karol Bagh, New Delhi - 110005

Printed at
Print Perfect
A-6/1 Mayapuri
New Delhi 110064

For

Kalpana
Aruna
Ashok
and
Ajeet

Contents

Preface

This book is, in a sense, a sequel to my earlier book, *The Double Standard in Shakespeare and Related Essays: Changing Status of Women in 16th and 17th Century England* published in 1988. The changing status of women in 16th and 17th Century England inevitably led me to examine their status in 18th Century England. But the subject was too large and so I have chosen to confine myself to consider only one aspect of their lives, their status in marriage. I have further limited my area of concern to a few authors hoping that what these authors have to say reflects the temper of the age.

It will be noticed that this time my emphasis is on novel rather than on drama. The reason is obvious: in 18th century drama had declined in importance and literary evidence on a subject like marriage can more easily be found in the novel than in drama. Such evidence can, of course, be found in contemporary conduct books too, but they are more or less outside my field of study.

I begin with a discussion of Mary Astell's views on contemporary marriage. She is not a novelist but her *A Serious Proposal to the Ladies* and *Reflections Upon Marriage* are seminal works and they anticipate most of the trends in later writers. Her views have not lost their elelvance even today and she is in fact regarded by most critics as the first feminist in England. Defoe is writing more or less at the same time as Mary Astell and in some respects his thinking seems to have been influenced by her. But his views on marriage are often somewhat contradictory. His prose works are clearly like other conduct books in the period but in his novels, *Moll Flanders* and *Roxana*, he is wholly realistic and presents two women who use whatever method is available to them to survive in a difficult world. From Defoe, I go to Richardson for whom marriage is a sacred institution. I choose his first novel *Pamela* for discussion. Then I go to Fanny Burney who also regards marriage as the most important event in a woman's life but who finds most marriages in the age as mercenary and hostile to women's self-respect. I deal only with her first novel *Evelina* where too, as in *Pamela,* a girl has to struggle to achieve a happy marriage with the man of her choice.

After these four chapters, I go to Jane Austen. I devote two chapters to her, one to discuss problems of young women with small fortune, and the second chapter I devote to the larger question of marriage in Jane Austen.

It may be noticed that I have chosen to discuss a novel by a very minor writer, Susan Ferrier, who though a contemporary of Jane Austen, hardly figures in the history of the novel but since she gave her novel the title '*Marriage*', I was tempted to choose it for discussion. I am glad to say that I did so for, in its own way, it throws significant light on contemporary marriages. I have put this chapter before the two chapters on Jane Austen merely to ensure that it does not interfere with my main emphasis on Jane Austen.

This book was written during my stay in Gandhinagar. Two persons in Gujarat who were specially helpful to me at various stages are Professor V.Y. Kantak and Professor G.N. Devi of the Baroda University. I have great respect for Professor Kantak's mature wisdom and I have often gone to him for advice. Professor Devi is a younger person but a perceptive scholar. He has a bright future before him.

In Delhi, Dr. Amrik Singh has been available to me for advice throughout this period. I greatly value his knowledge and judgement and have been in constant touch with him during the preparation of the book. Another person to whom I am greatly indebted is Ms Naz Siddiqi of the British Council Library in New Delhi without whose help it would have been very difficult for me to write a book like this. She has been supplying me whatever books I have needed and has kept me in touch with the latest material available in the British Council Libraries in India or abroad. I should also mention Mr. H.C. Jain of the South Campus Library in the University of Delhi who too has been of immense help to me. Apart from providing books or articles available in the Delhi University Library he has also kept me in touch with relevant material on the subject elsewhere in India.

Gandhinagar, January 1995. Sarup Singh

Chapter I

Mary Astell's *Some Reflections Upon Marriage*

Mary Astell's *Some Reflections Upon Marriage* appeared in 1700. Since it contained some 'Bold Truths' and challenged some of the contemporary assumptions regarding man-woman relationship, she added an appendix to its last edition (1730). In this, she explained that she had no intention to 'stir up sedition of any sort' nor did she imagine that she had 'in any way undermine[d] the Masculine Empire or blow[n] the Trumpet of Rebellion to the Moiety of Mankind'[1] (p.96). She had merely stated that though women were often inferior to men on account of their 'want of Learning' (p.96), she saw no reason why they should accept 'the *Natural Inferiority*' (Italics Mary Astell's) of their sex as a 'Self-evident and Fundamental Truth' (p.97). She indeed rejected the whole idea of 'the natural Inferiority of either sex' and stated that 'The Relation between the two Sexes is mutual, and the Dependence reciprocal' (p.102). She regretted that men did not accept this reciprocal basis of man-woman relationship and in fact demanded from women total submision. Her complaint is that even though English men had fought a Civil War in order to achieve freedom from the arbitrary power of the King, none amongst them had cared to give the slightest thought to the problems of women who too needed to be freed from the arbitrary power of tyrannical husbands. She is angry that neither Milton nor any other 'advocates of Resistance' took notice of the plight of the 'poor *Female Slaves*' in seventeenth century England (Italics Mary Astell's) (pp.34-5). She is indignant at this general indifference and callousness of men to women's problems and asks with some sharpness:

> ... if absolute Sovereignty be not necessary in a State, how comes it be so in a Family? Or if in a Family why not in a State; since no Reason can be alleged for the one that will not hold strongly for the other? .... if Arbitrary Power is evil in it self, and an improper Method of Governing Rational and Free Agents, it aught not to be practis'd any where; nor is it less, but rather more mischievous in Families than in Kingdoms, by how much 100,000 Tyrants are worse than one. (pp. 106-107).

And then in a tone that challenges Hobbes' assumptions about feminine sensibility, she raises the question: '*If all Men are born Free*, how is it that all Women are born Slaves?' (p. 107) (Italics Mary Astell's).

Women are not, of course, born slaves but, broadly speaking, two factors tend to make them so - their lack of education and the institution of marriage, more particularly as it existed in seventeenth century England. These two factors are so intimately connected in Mary Astell's mind that whether she writes on marriage or on education, she cannot look at them separately. In her most important piece of writing, *A Serious Proposal to the Ladies for the Advancement of Their True and Greatest Interest* (Part I, 1694 and Part II, 1697), she is not concerned with the question of marriage as such and yet many of her ideas about woman's status in marriage also find a place in it.

Her avowed aim in *A Serious Proposal* is to convince her contemporaries that women are rational creatures and they need as rigorous an intellectual training as men. But in her society there was hardly any suitable provision for the education of girls. Rich parents could, of course, appoint tutors for their daughters but otherwise no institutions existed where girls could be taught Latin which was the key to all knowledge during the period. Such education was available only in Grammar Schools or the two Universities but girls were debarred from joining Grammar Schools and Universities were in any case completely out of bounds for them.

Mary Astell is convinced that education alone can save women from the indignity of being treated as 'cheap and contemptible'.[2] (p.1). Unfortunately the superficial and often demeaning culture of the Restoration period had done grave damage to women's 'concept of self'. They had often been treated as mere sex objects and most of them had happily accepted this role. Astell warns them not to degrade themselves by running after the title of being 'Wits' but cultivate wisdom which is far more important in life than 'the forth of flashy wit'. (p. 15). She wants to 'Raise' them 'above the Vulgar by something more truly illustrious, than a sounding Title or a great Estate'. Her ambition is to 'excite in [women] a generous *Emulation to excel in the best things*, and not in such Trifles as every mean person who has but Money enough may purchase'. (p.1) (Italics mine). To achieve this high goal, she wants the education of women to be of a high quality. She believes that 'Ignorance is the cause of most Feminine Vices' (p. 7) and regards 'Wisdom and Virtue' as the two most important attributes of a woman. Her proposal to set up a 'Monastery' (p. 14) is intended to cultivate precisely these two attributes in women. The Monastery was intended to serve not only as a place of '*Religious Retirement*' (Italics Mary Astell's) (p. 14) for the 'Daughters of Gentlemen' (p. 36) but also as an institution of 'Learned Education'. (p. 37).

The two purposes for which the monastery was to be established - as a religious sanctuary like the Catholic nunneries of earlier times and as an educational institution providing learning and skills to women who could afford to pay for them- need not be regarded as incompatible. Mary Astell claims that the kind of education that her 'monastery' will provide will be useful to a woman 'not only in the Conduct of her own Soul but in the management of her Family' (p. 129). In this management, she specially emphasises the 'Education of Children [which] is a most necessary Employment, perhaps the chief of those who have any; But it is as Difficult as it is Excellent when well perform'd; and I question not but that the mistakes which are made in it, are a principal Cause of that Folly and Vice, which is so much complain'd of and so little mended' (p.129). She also makes the claim that 'Knowledge' will not 'lie dead upon their hands who have no children to Instruct; the whole World is a single Ladys Family, her opportunities of doing good are not lessen'd but encreas'd by her being unconfin'd. Particular Obligations do not contract her Mind, but her Beneficence moves in the largest Sphere. And perhaps the Glory of Reforming this Prophane and Profligate Age is reserv'd for you Ladies, and that the natural and unprejudic'd Sentiments of your Minds being handsomly express'd, may carry a more strong conviction than the Elaborate Arguments of the Learned'. (p.130).

The role that Mary Astell envisages for her 'single Ladys' is essentially to spread new ideas in society and thus 'mend the present and improve the future' (p.14). They have, of course, to serve God though Astell herself forbids them to 'teach in the Church, or usurp Authority where it is not allow'd them'. (p.20). The service to God that Mary Astell has in mind for them is that they would 'by their good Example' 'so influence the rest of their Sex, that Women may no longer pass for those little useless and impertinent Animals, which the ill conduct of too many has caus'd 'em to be mistaken for'. (p.17).

There is no doubt that women's status in Mary Astell's age was very low and men did often treat them more or less as 'impertinent Animals'. It was natural in a situation where all that a young woman was taught was to 'value herself on nothing but her clothes, and to think she's very fine when well accoutred'. (p.11). Mary Astell recognises 'that if a woman is taught that 'tis Wisdom enough to know to dress her self', we cannot 'blame her if she lay out her Industry and Money on such Accomplishments'. (pp.11-12). She also recognises that such a woman can easily become man's slave. Her view is that 'till [we] are capable of Chusing [our own] Actions and directing them by some Principle, tho [we] Move and Speak and do many such like things, [we] live not the life of a Rational Creature but only of an Animal'. (p.62). The choosing our actions and directing them by some principle is possible only in the case of those whose rational faculty is highly developed. Mary Astell is, of course, clearly one of them. She is a rationalist and a true disciple of Descarte. She does not take even religion for granted. She believes that one should be 'a Christian by choice, not in conformity to those among whom she lives; and cleaves to Piety, because 'tis her Wisdom, her Interest, her Joy, not because she has been accustom'd to it; she who is not only eminently and unmovably good, but able to give a Reason *why* she is so'. (p.12. Italics Mary Astell's). But to achieve this level of rationality, a fairly rigorous educational training is the first requisite. And this was almost totally lacking in the case of most women in this period.

I

Even before Mary Astell came on the scene, some writers had already expressed their dissatisfaction with the state of things. Their complaint was that contemporary parents had spoiled their daughters by giving them foolish ideas about cultivation of manners, forgetting altogether that morals and cultivation of the mind are much more important in bringing up of children. Perhaps the complaint of Mrs. Bathsua Makin, who had opened a school of her own for girls and had issued a regular prospectus entitled *An Essay to Revive the Antient Education of Gentlewomen* (1673) was most pointed in this respect. She was indignant that instead of gaining 'useful knowledge' most young women 'trifle away so many precious minutes merely to polish their Hands and Feet, to curl their Locks, to dress and trim their Bodies; and in the meantime neglect their Souls' (p.22). She admitted that women should, of course, 'be brought up to a comely and decent carriage, to their Nedle, to Neatness, to understand all those things that particularly belong to their sex' but 'mearely to teach Gentlewomen to Frisk and Dance, to paint their Faces, to curl their Hair, put on a Whisk, to wear gay clothes, is not truly to adorn, but to adulterate their Bodies' (p.22). Her view is that as 'Men, by liberal Education, are much better'd, as to Intellectuals and Morals' (p.7), so also should women improve their intellectual and moral calibre through education.

However laudable Mrs. Makin's views, it is also a fact that her views were not acceptable to most people in the period. She sadly admitted:

> The Barbarous custom to breed Women low, is grown general amongst us, and hath prevailed so far, that it is veriably believed (especially amongst a sort of debauched Sots) that Women are not endued with such Reason, as Men, nor capable of improvement by Education, as they are. It is lookt upon as a monstrous thing, to pretend the contrary. A Learned Woman is thought to be a Comet, that bodes Mischief, when ever it appears. To offer to the World the liberal Education of Women is to deface the Image of God in Man, it will make Women so high, and men so low like Fire in the House-top, it will set the whole World in a flame'. (p.3).

The effect of such prejudice against women's education was so strong that parents were reluctant to send their daughters to school for fear that if they 'bring up their daughters to Learning, no Persons will adventure to marry them'. (p.30). This was a normal fear in the minds of parents who intended sending their daughters to school. Lady Damaris Mesham in 1694 said more or less what Mrs. Makin had said. She expressed the opinion that should 'daughters be perceived to understand any learned language or be conversant in books, they might be in danger of not finding husbands'.[3] Parents were, therefore, anxious that their daughters should not show off their knowledge. Indeed, the advice was that they should hide their knowledge or intelligence. Lady Mary Wortley Montague's advice to her daughter was to 'conceal whatever learning [her grand-daughter] attains, with as much solicitude as she would hide crookedness or lameness'.[4]

The reason for the distrust of educated women by men was their fear that education was likely to corrupt their sexual morals. Even women holding fairly advanced views about women's place in society shared this fear of men. Elizabeth Montague, for instance, expressed the view that 'wit in a women is apt to have bad consequences'. 'I am sorry to say', she added, 'the generality of women who have excelled in wit have failed in chastity'.[5] The fact is that men have always distrusted educated women. King James is reported to have said that 'to make a woman learned and foxes tame has the same effect: to make them more cunning'.[6] The general view about women was the one expressed by Martin Luther: 'Women should stay at home, sit still, keep home and bear and bring up children'.[7]

What angers Mary Astell is women's readiness to accept whatever role 'custom' has prescribed for them. The reason for such an attitude is simple. As she says: 'For custom has usurpt such an unaccountable Authority, that she who would endeavour to put a stop to its arbitrary sway, and reduce it to Reason, is in a fair way to render herself the Butt of all the Fops in Town to shoot their impertinent censures at. And tho' a wise woman will not value their censure, yet she cares not to be the subject of their Discourse'.[8] For Mary Astell, 'Reason' is the final arbiter of all actions and women should have the courage to face public censure, if necessary, and not give up this anchor. Hence she recommends a conduct different from the normal fashionable conduct for women in her society.

> For shame let's abandon that Old, and therefore one wou'd think, unfashionable employment of pursuing Butter-flies and Trifles! No longer drudge on in the dull beaten road of Vanity and Folly which so many have gone before us, but dare to break the enchanted Circle that custom has plac'd us in, and scorn the Vulgar way of imitating all the impertinencies of our Neighbours. Let us learn to pride ourselves in something more excellent than the invention of a Fashion, and not entertain such a degrading thought of our own worth, as to imagine that our Souls were given us only for the service of our Bodies, and that the best improvement we can make of these, is to attract the Eyes of Men. We value *them* too much, and our *selves* too little, if we place any part of our desert in their Opinion, and don't think our selves capable of Nobler Things than the pitiful Conquest of some worthless heart'. (pp. 3-4). (Italics Mary Astell's).

Realizing that perhaps her rebuke is too sharp, she says: 'My design in not to expose, but to rectifie your Failures'. In a conciliatory tone she declares that her 'earnest desire is, that you Ladies, would be as perfect and happy as 'tis possible to be in this imperfect State'. (p. 4).

Her main complaint, of course, is against men who deny women 'opportunities of improvement' (p. 5). She particularly resents the attitude of those men who have 'more Wit than Wisdom, and perhaps ... more malice than either', who claim that 'Women are naturally incapable of acting prudently, or that they are necessarily determined to folly' (p. 5). 'The Incapacity, if there be any', she claims, 'is acquired not natural' (p. 6). 'Neither God nor Nature', she asserts, 'have excluded them from being Ornaments to their Families and useful to their Generation; there is therefore no reason why they should be content to be Cyphers in the World, useless at the best, and in a little time a burden and nuisance to all about them' (p. 6). She accuses men of encouraging precisely those traits in women's character which later they find contemptible. How 'partial are Men', she laments, 'as to expect Brick where they afford no Straw' (p. 6). Her conclusion is that 'the Cause therefore of the defects we labour under is, if not wholly, yet at least in the first place, to be ascribed to the mistakes of our Education, which like an Error in the first concoction, spreads its ill influence through all our Lives' (p. 6). 'If our Nature is spoil'd', she adds, 'indeed of being improv'd, at first; if from our Infancy we are nursed up in Ignorance and Vanity; are taught to be Proud and Petulant, Delicate and Fantastick, Humorous and Inconsistant, 'tis not strange that the ill effects of this Conduct appear in all the future Actions of our Lives' (p. 7).

II

Even though an unmarried woman herself, Astell does not fully appreciate the difficulties of unmarried women in her age. This is largely because she can earn her living through writing and lead an independent and dignified life. In fact, for her education has become almost a substitute for marriage but that is both because she is a highly talented woman and also because there is a strong monastic trait in her character. It is, of course, true that like most writers of conduct-books in the period, Mary Astell also regarded men as sexual predators and warned women not to trust their professions as these were often inspired not by love but by 'brutish Appetite' (p.40). But her bitter condemnation of the male sex and almost wholesale distrust of the marriage institution can be understood only in terms of her dedication to religious life. If she were living in earlier times, she might have become a nun. Ruth Perry says, somewhat too emphatically: 'I am sure that Mary Astell never physically acted out a passion with any one of either sex'.[9]

But she was not writing for nuns. Indeed, she was writing for women who were likely to prefer a different way of life and expect to marry and have a home of their own. What a character in Thomas Wright's *The Female Virtuoso's* (1693) says reflects the mind of a normal seventeenth century girl: "When I reflect on Marriage, all I can see in it, is a dear Husband that will love me, pretty children that will play about me, and a House of my own to manage' (p.1). Such a marriage may not prove successful and the woman's expectations may not be fulfilled but that can happen in almost any age or society. But not many women would have accepted Mary Astell's prescription of an ideal life which is to be found only in renunciation of worldly pleasures. Nor could they accept education as a substitute for marriage. In any case this option could be accepted only as a last resort and then too only by exceptional women. If women wanted a husband - as in almost all cases they did - they had to try to catch the eyes of men and try to win some heart, however worthless that heart might look in the eyes of a woman like Astell.

Mary Astell perhaps does not fully realize that the most depressing feature of women's lives in this period was their poor bargaining position in the marriage market owing to the adverse sex ratio. In London, according to Gregory King's figures collected in 1694, there were ten men to every thirteen women. In other cities and market-towns, the sex ratio was eight men to every nine women.[10] Ruth Perry has estimated that in 1694-97 (the years when Astell's *A Serious Proposal* appeared), 'there were 77 males for every 100 females in London'. She rightly points out that 'there was no creditable social solution for those who stayed single'.[11] Indeed, in Perry's words, the conditions in late seventeenth century London, when Mary Astell was writing, 'were extremely unfavourable to the biological female'.[12] That the situation did not improve in the eighteenth century is evident from Harriet Byron's lament in Richardson's *Sir Charles Grandison* (1753-4) that 'there are more bachelors now in England, by many thousands, than there were a few years ago: and, probably, the numbers of them (and of single women, of course) will every year increase'. Ian Watt from whose *The Rise of the Novel* the quotation from Richardson is taken, adds:

> Miss Byron's alarm was probably well grounded. The proportion of bachelors among the literary men of the period is certainly very high: Pope, Swift, Issac Watts, James Thomson, Horace Walpole, Shenstone, Hume, Gray, and Cowper, for example, remained unmarried; and there seems in general to have been an unprecedented topicality in a burlesque poem of the period, *The Bachelor's Soliloquy* (1744), which began, 'to wed or not to wed, that is the question'.[13]

One effect of the disproportionate sex ratio in the age was the rise in the amount of dowry expected by boys's parents. Dowry was becoming a problem even in the Elizabethan and Jacobean periods but it is the Restoration period and the eighteenth century which are specially notorious in this respect. There is, of course, evidence to suggest that rise in the rate of dowries started hurting the nobility round about the middle of the sixteenth century. One reason for this may have been, as Lawrence Stone has pointed out, that 'with the abolition of nunneries .... the marriage market was flooded with girls who had hitherto been consigned to nunneries, but who now had to be married off, at considerable cost, to their social equals'.[14] This new turn of events also threatened the entire system of inheritance in England as it adversely affected the fortunes of the eldest son who was the chief inheritor of the ancestral property under the law of primogeniture. The portions found for younger sons and dowries for daughters often compelled the head of the family to mortgage his property and even to sell portions of it if he was entitled to do so, thus creating a real crisis for his successor.

Sir Josiah Child's belief in 1668 was that 'portions had increased over four times in 60 years'[15] - an estimate that has been found rather low by modern scholars. About one thing, of course, there is no disagreement: the somewhat sudden rise in the prosperity of the London merchants and the equally sudden fall in the fortunes of the aristocracy brought down the value of the daughters of the aristocracy considerably. Lawrence Stone makes a somewhat modest claim when he says that the value of a peer's daughter had decreased on average by more than half.[16] This was natural in a situation where merchants could pay huge dowries to their daughters whereas most members of the aristocracy found themselves utterly unable to do so. The situation is best seen through the eyes of a member of the aristocracy itself. Writing in 1661, Sir William Morrice said: 'There are many merchants' daughters that weigh so many thousands that ours are commodities lying on our hands, we can't set them off with so great weight'.[17]

Sedley in his comedy *Bellamira* (1687) reflects this aspect of contemporary reality. Merryman mentions the dangers of begetting daughters 'without I know where to get the portions for 'em'. What he further says echoes many a parent's anxiety: 'in this Age, [daughters] soure and grow stale on their Parents' hands'. (II.iii). Richard Steele becomes even more explicit in *The Tender Husband* (1705) when he makes one of his characters offer the sad comment: 'The war has fetched down the price of women; the whole nation is overrun with petticoats; our daughters lie upon our hands ...; girls are drugs, sir, mere drugs'. (I.ii).

III

George Wheler's description of the dilemma faced by single women in that age in his *A Protestant Monastery* (1698) seems quite disturbing:

> How many Families are there so burdened with Daughters, their Parents cannot, either for want of Beauty, or Money, dispose of

> in Marriage or in any other decent manner provide for? Yet are they obliged to maintain them according to their Quality; till usually at their Decease, they leave them without Habitation; and many times, scarce a quarter enough to keep them decently. Whereupon, it too often comes to pass, that they are forced to wander about from Lodging to Lodging, or to betake themselves to servile Employment; or, which is worse, are tempted to prostitute their Virtue to gain their Bread'. (p.17).[18]

It is for such unfortunate women that Mary Astell proposes to make provision in her Monastery which is a place for '*Religion Retirement* .... a Retreat from the world for those who are sick of its vanity .... and its impertinancies'. (p.40). Perhaps the first person to have thought of a seminary for 'unmarried and unmarriageable women' which should 'take over the role from the dissolved convents' was Lattice Carey, Lady Falkland.[19] She made this suggestion in the thirties of the 17th century but later on we hear more persons thinking on these lines. The not altogether serious reference of Wycherley's Hippolita in *The Gentleman-Dancing Master* (1673) to 'the new Protestant Nunnery they talk of' does at least show that some such thing was in the air. Gerald Weale thinks that Hippolita has in mind Edward Chamberlayne's brochure proposing the founding of *An Academy or College: Wherein Young Ladies and Gentlewomen May at a very moderate Expence be duly instructed in the true Protestant Religion* (1671). The academy, of course, never came into existence but the brochure clearly highlights one special feature of contemporary life when, apart from promising 'Virtuous Wives' from out of the academy to 'Persons of Honour and Worth', it makes 'Provision (whereof there is great want in England) .... for sober, pious, elder Virgins and Widdows, who desire to separate themselves from the vanities of the World, and yet employ their Talents for the benefit of the Public'.[20] Richard Allestree, probably the author of *The Ladies Calling* (1671), had in mind perhaps a similar desire of unmarried women 'to separate themselves from the vanities of the World' in order to escape humiliation when he recommended religion as a refuge. His advice to such women (whom he unkindly calls 'superannuated virgins') was 'to turn to their spiritual bridegroom'.[21]

It is easy to tell single women 'to turn to their spiritual bridegroom' but how many women - or men - possess this spirit of renunciation or strength of religious faith? An over-whelming majority - if not all - wish for a human spouse and a home of their own. When a society fails to meet these demands and it is flooded with unmarried women, it is likely to raise the problem of illegitimate children, specially in periods when no means of birth control are available. In eighteenth century England, authorities concerned with poor relief were worried about this problem which was assuming alarming proportions. As if in desperation some people suggested polygamy as a solution. Ian Watt tells us that 'Richardson's friend, Dr. Patrick Delany, wrote a treatise, *Reflections upon Polygamy*, whose somewhat hysterical tone suggests a deep alarm. He feared that although 'Polygamy is indeed at present abolished .... how long it may continue so, under the present increase of infidelity and licentiousness, is not easy to pronounce'. Watt adds: 'His book, which Richardson printed in 1737, probably supplied the material for the discussion of polygamy in the second part of *Pamela*, where Mr. B. appropriately makes use of the arguments of the licentious Deists, although his bride eventually makes him renounce 'that foolish topic'. Lovelace, however, continues in Mr.B's evil ways and proposes .... an Act of Parliament for annual marriages; such a practice, he argues, would stop polygamy being 'panted after'; it would end the prevalence of 'the spleen of vapours'; and it would ensure that there would no longer remain a single 'old maid in Great Britain and all its territories.'[22]

All this talk of polygamy and annual marriages is, of course, absurd and yet the problem remains. It was to haunt English women till almost the time that reliable modes of preventing pregnancy were invented. In the earlier period we hear shrill cries of women whom society despises for no fault of theirs. That the problem of single women troubled women's minds even in the nineteenth century is evident from what Caroline in Charlotte Bronte's novel *Shirley* (1849) says about their deplorable situation. She believes that "God surely did not create us, and cause us to live, with the sole end of wishing always to die. I believe, in my heart, we were intended to prize life and enjoy it, so long as we retain it. Existence never was originally meant to be that useless, blank, pale, slow-trailing thing it often becomes to many, and is becoming to me, among the rest."[23] But God's purpose seems to have been defeated in the way that old maids live in England.

She then describes the hard life that single women have to lead:

> I believe single women should have more to do - better chances of interesting and profitable occupation than they possess now. .... Look at the numerous families of girls in this neighbourhood: the Armitages, the Birtwhistles, the Sykes. The brothers of these girls are every one is business or in professions; they have something to do; their sisters have no earthly employment, but household work and sewing; no earthly pleasure, but an unprofitable visiting; and no hope in all their life to come, of anything better. This stagnant state of things makes them decline in health; they are never well; and their minds and views shrink to wondrous narrowness.[24]

The degradation to which they are reduced is obvious in what she further says:

> The great wish - the sole aim of every one of them is to be married, but the majority will never marry; they will die as they now live. They scheme, they plot, they dress to ensnare husbands. The gentlemen turn them into ridicule; they don't want them; they hold them very cheap; they say - I have heard them say it with sneering laughs many a time - the matrimonial market is overstocked. Fathers say so likewise, and are angry with their daughters when they observe their manoeuvres; they order them to stay at home. What do they except them to do at home? If you ask, - they would answer, sew and cook ....[25]

She then appeals to men - specially the girls' parents - to provide proper education to their daughters so that they can acquire some skill or some useful occupation and spend their life cheerfully:

> Men of England! look at your poor girls, many of them fading around you, dropping off in consumption or decline; or what is worse, degenerating to sour old maids - envious, backbiting, wretched, because life is a desert to them; or, what is worst of all, reduced to strive, by scarce modest coquetry and debasing artifice, to gain that position and consideration by marriage, which to celibacy is denied. Fathers! cannot you alter these things? Perhaps not all at once; but consider the matter well when it is brought before you, receive it as a theme worthy of thought; do not dismiss it with an idle jest or an unmanly insult. You would wish to be proud of your daughters and not to blush for them - then seek for them an interest and an occupation which shall raise them above the flirt, the manoeuvrer, the mischief-making tale-bearer. Keep your girls' minds narrow and fettered - they will still be a plague and a care, sometimes a disgrace to you; cultivate them - give them scope and work - they will be your gayest companions in health; your tenderest nurses in sickness; your most faithful prop in age.[26]

IV

In the situation prevailing in the times of Mary Astell, it would be highly unusual if a woman were not to regard marriage as 'her only Preferment, the Sum-Total of her Endeavours, the Completion of all her Hopes'. (*Some Reflections*, pp. 57-58). Indeed it would be quite difficult for her to distrust the professions of love made to her by a young man as she could hardly imagine that he would have 'any other Design or Desire than to please her'. Moreover, it is natural for all women to be 'dazled with all the Glitter and Pomp of a Wedding' and 'transported with the Pleasure of being out of Pupillage and Mistress not only of her self, but of a family too'. (Ibid., p. 58). This is how young women throughout the world behave. But Mary Astell is so sceptical of man's conduct that she is convinced that the woman 'will find a terrible Disappointment when the Hurry is over, and when she comes calmly to consider her Condition, and views it no more under a false Appearance, but as it truly is'. (p.58). What Mary Astell says may actually happen but there is a chance that it may not. Marriage is a gamble and not all offers of marriage can be looked at with suspicion. Many marriages in the seventeenth century ended in misery for the women but that can happen in all ages in the case of any woman.

But Mary Astell is perfectly justified in suggesting that women should be so trained through education that they can face all eventualities. But when no professions are available for women to earn their living in an honourable way, what should even an educated woman do? Education, however, has a *value* of its own which Mary Astell rightly emphasises in her pathetic picture of a woman who spends her entire youth in ignorance and neglects cultivation of her intellect:

> For the poor Lady having past the prime of her Years in Gaity and Company, in running the Circle of all the Vanities of the Town, having spread all her Nets and us'd all her Arts for Conquest, and finding that the Bait fails where she wou'd have it take; and having all this while been so over-careful of her Body, that she had no time *to improve her Mind, which therefore affords her no safe retreat*, (Italics mine) now she meets with Disappointments abroad, and growing every day more and more sensible that the respect which us'd to be paid her, decays as fast as her Beauty; quite terrified with dreadful Name of *Old Maid*, which yet none but Fools will reproach her with, nor any wise Woman be afraid of; to avoid this terrible *Mormo*, and the scoffs that are thrown on superannuated Virgins, she flies to some dishonourable Match as her last, tho' much mistaken Refuge, to the disgrace of her Family, and her own irreparable Ruin. (*A Serious Proposal*, pp.39- 40).

Mary Astell is, of course, justified to ask 'any Person of Honour' to tell her 'if it were not richly worth some thousand

Pounds, to prevent all this mischief' (p.40) by sending their daughters to the institution that she intends establishing - or any other such institution. Mary Astell has in mind only a subscription of 500 or 600 pounds to her institution, (p.39). She rightly claims that she cannot 'think of an expedient so useful as this to Persons of Quality' to 'honourably dispose of [their daughters] without impairing their Estates'. If parents cannot 'maintain them in that *Port* which Custom makes almost necessary, nor procure them an equal Match, those of their own Rank ... chusing rather to fill their Coffers than to preserve the purity of their Blood'(p.39), the minimum that they can do is provide a proper education to them. In the earlier period, parents sent their daughters to nunneries and paid handsome sums to those institutions. But since that arrangement for English girls did not exist, Mary Astell's proposal is perfectly feasible. Indeed, not one but quite a large number of such institutions were needed to save girls from such families the unnecessary harassment and humiliation.

The emphasis in the institution that Mary Astell is proposing to start would mainly be on religious instruction and it would be provided by 'persons of irreproachable Lives, of a consummate Prudence, sincere Piety and unaffected Gravity' - indeed by such women as 'have spent the greatest part of their lives in the study and practice of Christianity'.(p.24). But it would be altogether different from Catholic nunneries of earlier times as in her institution there would be 'no Vows or irrevocable Obligations, not so much as the fear of Reproach to keep our Ladies here any longer than they desire'.(p.25). Of course, in this 'Religious Retirement'(p.14), there would be 'No impertinent Visits, no foolish Amours, no idle Amusements' to 'distract'(p.25) the thoughts of the young ladies who would compulsorily 'spend part of their time .... in adorning their minds with useful knowledge'(p.20). This would, moreover, be an excellent sanctuary for 'Heiresses and Persons of fortune' as they 'would be kept secure from the rude attempts of designing Men'. She reminds women that quite often a woman 'who has more Money than Discretion', has to 'curse her Stars for being expos'd a prey to bold, importunate and rapacious Vultures'. In her institution, 'she will not .... be inveigled and imposed on, neither be bought nor sold, nor be forc'd to marry for her own quiet, when she has no inclination to it'. She further adds: 'Or if she is dispos'd to marry, here she may remain in safety till a convenient Match be offer'd by her Friends, and be freed from the danger of a dishonourable one'. (p.35). Clearly she is offering a very attractive alternative to the daughters of well-to-do parents - and all for just 500 or 600 (or at best a thousand) pounds! In addition, of course, she is going to provide to the young ladies religious instruction and secular education of a high order. Her institution may be compared with residential Colleges for Women run by some religious organizations in earlier times.

As we have seen, some tentative proposals had been made by well-meaning individuals to relieve the distress of old maids in the seventeenth century but no one had dealt with the subject with the seriousness that we find in Mary Astell's *A Serious Proposal*. Ruth Perry rightly says that 'her overriding concern was to teach other women how to think vigorously, so as to give them the wherewithal to make the important choices of their lives'.[27] Mary Astell's preference is clearly for a religious life for women so that they are not attracted by the shallow pleasures of the world. Knowing the hardships that they had to face in life - whether married or unmarried - Mary Astell was keen that they should learn how to 'withdraw' their 'Minds from the World, from adhering to the Senses, from the Love of Material Beings, of Pomps and Gaieties; for 'tis these that usually Steal away the Heart, that seduce the Mind to such unaccountable Wanderings, and so fill up its capacity that they leave no room for Truth'. (*A Serious Proposal*, pp. 106-7).

V

The capacity to withdraw the mind from the world is an admirable quality and all human beings need to cultivate it in a smaller or a larger measure. But it is not a practical answer to the problems that women face in marriage. This answer is to be found in Mary Astell's *Some Reflections Upon Marriage*. It was prompted by the unhappy account of the marriage of the Duchess of Mazarin. Fearing that her *A Serious Proposal* might have given her readers a somewhat wrong impression about her views on marriage, in *Some Reflections* Mary Astell declared: 'I am far from designing a Satire upon Marriage, as some pretend, either unkindly or ignorantly'.[28] Indeed, she claimed that 'Marriage in general is too sacred to be treated with Disrespect, too venerable to be the Subject of Raillery and Buffoonery'. She called it 'a Divine Institution' and said that she cannot imagine 'a better Way for Society and Posterity'.(p.16). So it should be clearly understood that when Mary Astell attacks marriage, she does not attack the institution but the 'ill choice, or foolish conduct' (p.16) of the partners. She concedes that 'there are and may be, happy marriages' but this can happen only if 'we act reasonably in our Choice and Conduct' (p.17).

Women were not free to choose their partners in that age. Mary Astell complained that 'A Woman, indeed, can't properly be said to Choose; All that is allow'd her, is to Refuse or Accept what is offer'd (p.29). Men, on the other hand, had much greater freedom in this matter. But the motives that often guided men in their choice were quite mercenary. Mary Astell bluntly asks:

> For pray, what do Men propose to themselves in Marriage? What Qualifications do they look after in a Spouse? What will she bring? is the first Enquiry: How Many Acres? Or how much ready Coin? (p.20).

Dowry was a ruinous custom and most marriages in the period were unhappy on account of the evil effects of this custom. Mary Astell does not regard it as 'altogether an unnecessary Question, for Marriage without a Competency, that is, not only a bare Subsistence, but even a handsome and plentiful Provision, according to the Quality and Circumstances of the Parties, is not very comfortable Condition' (p.20). But why should it be the responsibility of a daughter's parents to make 'this handsome and plentiful provision'? It is a pity that Mary Astell approves this custom which, among other things, damages the woman's self-respect. She is clearly thinking only of girls from upper class families amongst whom this custom was prevalent. Such families normally made provision for the daughters' portion though it meant great strain on the financial situation of the family. Mary Astell perhaps recognises that dowry as an institution can do much harm to married life. She says that dowry 'should not be the *Main*, much less the only Consideration; for Happiness does not depend on Wealth' (p.20). She also warns that a person who 'marries himself to a Fortune only, must expect no other Satisfaction than that can bring him'. (p.20).

The contemporary social and economic changes were perhaps responsible for the importance that people had come to attach to dowry. It has been claimed by social historians that in this period the surest way to become rich was through dowry and the members of the aristocracy were keen to repair the fortunes of their families which had been greatly impoverished owing to the upheavals in the seventeenth century. Mary Astell notes that they chose brides 'rather to fill their coffers than to preserve the purity of their Blood, and therefore think of a weighty Bag the best Gentility, preferring a wealthy Upstart before the best Descended and best Qualified Lady; their own extravagancies perhaps having made it necessary, that they will keep up an empty shadow of Greatness, which is all that remains to show what their Ancestors have been'. (*A Serious Proposal to the Ladies*, p.39).

Mary Astell recognises that the men who are attracted only by the fortune that the bride was likely to bring to them are bound to prove bad husbands. Since they were attracted by fortune and not by the person whom they were marrying, they soon stop showing even normal consideration to them. Mary Astell laments that 'Few men have so much Goodness as to bring themselves to a Liking of what they loath'd, merely because it is their Duty to like' (*Some Reflections*, p.21). The more 'Kindness and Complaisance' the woman shows, the greater the man's 'Aversion' towards her. (p.21). The man's excuse is that he gets no pleasure in her company. Hence finding no satisfaction at home, he seeks it elsewhere 'and the Furtune so unjustly got, is as carelessly squander'd'. (p.21). 'Man takes a Loose', Mary Astell complains, and society can do nothing in the matter. She says that 'Custom' which prevents women from taking liberties with their marriage oath, 'has almost taken off that small Restraint Reputation us'd to lay' (p.21) in the case of men.

All the money that the woman brought with her by way of dowry has gone into the man's 'Possession' and she 'must make Court to him for a little sorry Alimony out of her own Estate' (p.22) for her survival. Often she would hesitate to ask for money which she may badly need and quietly submit to her lot. Indeed, she would go so far as not to lay 'a Load upon her Husband to ease herself, but would, if it were possible, conceal his Crimes, though her Prudence and Virtue give him a thousand Reproaches without her Intention and Knowledge' (p.22).

Should a woman not retaliate? Must she quietly submit? Mary Astell asks this question and also gives a reply: 'But shall a Wife retaliate? God forbid! no Provocation, though ever so great, can excuse the Sin, or lessen the Folly: It were indeed a revenging the Injury upon herself in the most terrible Manner' (p.8). She is emphatic in her opinion that 'Devotion is the proper Remedy, and the only infallible Relief in all Distresses'. (p.8.). But many women find this attitude unacceptable. The Duchess of Mazarin whose case inspired Mary Astell's *Reflections* may have had the gravest provocation to reject this view but Mary Astell warns other women not to follow her perilous path:

> A woman who seeks Consolation under Domestick Troubles from the Gaieties of a Court, from Gallantry, Gaming, rambling in Search of odd Adventure, childish, ridiculous and ill- natur'd Amusements, such as we find in the unhappy Madam M——'s *Memoirs*, the common Methods of getting rid of Time, that is, of our very Being, and keeping as much as we can at a Distance from ourselves, will find these are very insignificant Applications; they hardly skin the Wound, and can never heal it, they even hurt, they make it fester, and render it almost incurable. (pp.8- 9).

If the Duchess of Mazarin had received proper education,

Mary Astell believes, she would not have behaved so disgracefully. In that case, she would have depended on herself and behaved with dignity - with 'Patience and Fortitude'. (p.9). In fact, according to Mary Astell, the 'Husband' Vices may become an Occasion of the Wife's Vertues, and his Neglect do a more real Good than his kindness could'. (p.24). Education - and specially religious education - is woman's real defence. It gives her inner resources which most women lack and in moments of distress she will fall back on these inner resources rather than find solace in life's trivialities.

Moreover, an educated woman has a much better chance of achieving a successful marriage than an uneducated one. Through education a woman acquires the skill to 'reclaim evil men' (p.38) - and most husbands in late seventeenth century clearly needed such reclamation. A 'good and prudent Wife wou'd wonderfully work on ill men; he must be a Brute indeed, who cou'd hold out against all those innocent Arts, those gentle persuasives and obliging methods she wou'd use to reclaim him'. (p.38). Moreover, her 'ingenious Conversation will make his life comfortable, and he who can be so well entertain'd at home, needs not run into Temptations in search of Diversions abroad' (p.38). There are, of course, some real difficulties in such a marriage if the wife is 'more knowing than the Husband' (p.38). Mary Astell says that in that case the man will acquire 'a wise Woman to govern him' but which man wants such a wife even though her 'prudence' may conceal his ignorance 'from publick Observation', and at once both 'cover and supply his defects'? (p.38).

VI

Unfortunately most marriages in Mary Astell's time were mercenary and rarely was the relationship between wife and husband wholly satisfactory. Indeed what William Stout said in 1699 can easily serve as an epitaph on most seventeenth century marriages: 'They lived very disagreeably but had many children'.[29] Mary Astell has the following comment to make on such loveless marriages:

> They only who have felt it, know the Misery of being forc'd to marry where they do not love; of being yok'd for Life to a disagreeable Person and imperious Temper, where Ignorance and Folly (the Ingredients of a Coxcomb, who is the most unsufferable Fool) tyrannizes over Wit and Sense. To be perpetually contradicted for Contradiction-sake, and bore down by Authority, not by Argument; to be denied one's most innocent Desires, for no other Reason but the absolute Will and Pleasure of a Lord and Master, whose Follies a Wife, with all her Prudence, cannot hide, and whose commands she cannot but despise at the same Time that she obeys them. (p. 7).

But Mary Astell has no faith in a marriage inspired by love either which, in her opinion, can be as unsatisfactory as one prompted by greed. As she says:

> Or, suppose on the other Hand, she has married the Man she loves, heap'd upon him the highest Obligations, by putting into his Power the Fortune he coveted, the Beauty he profess'd to adore; how soon are the Tables turn'd? It is her Part now to court and fawn; his real or pretended Passion soon cools into Indifference, Neglect or perhaps Aversion. 'Tis well if he preserves a decent Civility, takes a little care of Appearances, and is willing to conceal his Breach of Faith. (pp.7-8).

According to Mary Astell, there is no difference between a marriage where a man is attracted by the woman's wealth or by her beauty. 'There's no great Odds', she says, 'between his marrying for the Love of Money, or for the Love of Beauty; the Man does not act according to Reason in either Case, but is govern'd by irregular Appetites' (p.25). There is a third kind of marriage where a man is attracted neither by the woman's money nor by her beauty but by her wit. But Mary Astell is not greatly impressed by these pretenders to wit either. Only superficially, their claim may sound somewhat superior to the claims of those who are merely concerned with money or beauty. Mary Astell says that the man loves the woman's wit and feels that he is superior to people who are just mercenary. He also claims that his love is 'more Spiritual, more Refin'd'. But Mary Astell says that this claim is found hollow if 'you examine it to the Bottom' (p.25). She has a low opinion of the contemporary fashionable notion of wit. What passes for Wit in fashionable circles, she says, 'is a bitter and ill-natur'd Raillery, a pert Repartee, or a confident talking at all' whereas in reality genuine wit consists of 'Sprightliness of Imagination', and 'a Reach and Turn of Thought, so properly express'd, as strikes and pleases a judicious Taste' (pp.25-26). She recognises that 'Wit is indeed distinct from Judgment, but it is not contrary to it; 'tis rather its Handmaid'. (p.26).

This latter quality the 'Witty-Men', according to Mary Astell, lacked and they were notorious for the 'Liberty' that they took with 'Religion, good Manners, or their Neighbours Reputation'. (p.27). Surely if these men were to be models for the women of wit, there was not much hope for them. To win Mary Astell's approval, it was not enough for a woman to be 'eminent in Wit and Beauty'. She had also to possess 'what is more valuable and lasting, solid Sense and real Virtue' (p.6). Since contemporary women often lacked these solid qualities, Mary Astell is compelled to come to the conclusion that, broadly speaking, 'whether it is Wit or Beauty that a Man's in Love with, there are no great Hopes of lasting Happiness' (p.27) in such a marriage.

But surely there must be some marriages which can give both men and women lasting happiness. Mary Astell does not deny that happiness in marriage is possible, but not when men 'marry without any Thought at all, further than it is the Custom of the World, what others have done before them, that the Family must be kept up, the antient Race preserv'd, and therefore their kind Parents and Guardians choose as they think convenient, without ever consulting the Young one's Inclinations, who must be satisfied, or pretend so at least, upon Pain of Displeasure, and that heavy Consequence of it, Forfeiture of their Estate'. (pp.28-29). To obtain real happiness in marriage, the man has to be guided in his choice 'by Reason, and not by Humour and Brutish Passion'. Mary Astell is fact lays down a general formula for happiness in marriage when she says:

> He who does not make Friendship the chief Inducement to his Choice, and prefer it before any other Consideration, does not deserve a good Wife, and therefore should not complain if he goes without one.(p.18).

VII

Her complaint against the three kinds of marriages mentioned by her did not give lasting happiness to man because sooner or later his 'Love of Variety' (p.19) wrecked the marriage. But if friendship was to form the chief ingredient of man's relationship with the woman he marries, this need not happen. This, in fact, is the Christian notion of marriage and hence, according to Mary Astell, it 'provides the best that may be for Domestic Quiet and Content, and for the Education of Children'. (p.18).

It may be noticed that Mary Astell is not saying anything very original here, but only repeating what the Christian Fathers had always said in defence of monogamy. What Daniel Rogers says in a famous passage in *Matrimoniall Honour* (1642) deserves to be cited here:

> Husbands and wives should be as two sweet friends, bred under one constellation, tempered by an influence from heaven, whereof neither can give any great reason, save that mercy and providence first made them so, and then made their match: saying, see God hath determined us, out of this vast world, each for other; perhaps many may deserve as well, but yet to me, and for my turne, thou excellest them all, and God hath made me to thinke so (not for formality sake to say) but because it is so.[30]

It is not an accident that, as Jean H. Hagstrum has said, this 'ideal of heterosexual friendship in marriage' is so powerfully and beautifully expressed by Milton, the greatest exponent of the 'Art of Puritan Love'.[31] Hagstrum reminds us that Shakespeare too was not unfamiliar with this ideal. As Romeo descends from Juliet's Balcony to leave for his Mantuan exile, she says, "Art thou gone so? Love, lord, ay, husband, friend!" (III.5). But Juliet and Romeo have not known each other for long nor is their understanding of life mature enough. It is almost a general principle in Shakespeare that his women do not rush into marriage without exploring the personalities of the men they marry. They recognise that if marriage is not to amount to 'wooing wedding and repenting' (*Much Ado About Nothing*, II.L.62), if the relationship is to be a permanent and stable one, then there must be mutual understanding and more than mere sexual attraction.

It is interesting to notice that at a time when Restoration Comedy was presenting a somewhat distorted version of man-woman relationship, Wycherley, in his most notorious play, *The Country Wife* (1675), declared that 'love proceeds from esteem' (II.i). The same year came Hannah Wooley's *The Gentlewoman's Companion* (1675) where she described a happy marriage as 'a fellowship not of hot distempered love, but endeared affection' (p.156). There is perhaps no evidence that Mary Wollstencraft ever read Mary Astell's writings - or had ever heard of her - but she clearly repeats Mary Astell: 'Love, from its very nature, must be transitory .... The most holy bond of society is friendship'.[32]

VIII

Unless a wife is regarded as a friend and an equal partner in marriage, she cannot adequately carry out the burdens that marriage places on her. Mary Astell describes her responsibilities as a wife and her husband's expectations from her in a well-known passage:

> He wants one to manage his Family, an House-keeper, one whose Interest it will be not to wrong him, and in whom therefore he can put greater Confidence than in any he can hire for Money. One who may breed his Children, taking all the Care and Trouble of their Education, to preserve his Name and Family. One whose Beauty, Wit, or good Humour and agree-

> able Conversation, will entertain him at Home when he has been contradicted and disappointed Abroad, who will do him that Justice the ill-natur'd World denies him; that is, in any one's Language but his own, sooth his Pride and flatter his Vanity, by having always so much good Sense as to be on his Side, to conclude him in the Right, when others are so ignorant, or so rude, as to deny it. Who will not be blind to his Merit nor contradict his Will and Pleasure, but make it her Business, her very Ambition to content him, whose Softness and gentle Compliance will calm his Passions, to whom he may safely disclose his troublesome Thoughts, and in her Breast discharge his Cares; whose Duty, Submission and Observance, will heal those Wounds other Peoples Opposition or Neglect have given him. In a word, one whom he can intirely Govern, and consequently may form her to his Will and Liking, who must be his for Life, and therefore cannot quit his Service, let him treat her how he will. (pp.41-42).

Mary Astell is not exaggerating though she may seem to be doing so. Her tone is somewhat strident but otherwise a wife is expected to perform most of the tasks mentioned by her. But can a wife who has been denied education perform all these tasks very effectively? So Mary Astell advises men 'for their own Sakes to do what in them lies to make Women Wise and Good' (p.33). Then alone will the women be capable of becoming suitable companions of men.

But it must be admitted that however wise and good women may be, they are always at a disadvantage. Mary Astell pleads with men to appreciate their difficulties even in the best of situations:

> Let the Business be carried as prudently as it can be on the Woman's Side, a reasonable Man can't deny that she has by much the harder Bargain: because she puts herself entirely into her Husband's Power, and if the Matrimonial Yoke be grievous, neither Law nor Custom afford her that Redress which a Man obtains.(p.34).

Even the best of husbands can treat his wife as 'nothing better than a Domestic Devil, an Evil he must tolerate for his own Conveniency'. (p.16). Also women in general are so vulnerable that any 'Gallant' possessing 'the cunning of the Fox, and the Audacity of the Tiger' could easily defame and complete 'the Destruction of his unhappy Prey' (p. 15). The times have, of course, changed but have they really changed in a meaningful way in the case of women who still lack education?

If the situation becomes wholly intolerable, the woman could perhaps ask for divorce. But it was so only in theory in Mary Astell's times. As she says: 'There are some Reasons, (for the Laws of God and Man allow Divorces in certain Cases) though not many, that authorize, a Wife's leaving her Husband', but if a wife, out of 'absolute Necessity', decides to break these 'sacred and strongest Bonds', she is exposed to 'Temptations and Injuries, Contempt and the just Censure of the World' (p. 10). Even if a woman were prepared to face the contempt and the censure of the world, it was not easy in England to get a divorce with the right to remarry in Mary Astell's period. Provision for such a divorce had, of course, been made in 1697 when it was decided by Parliament that a marriage could be dissolved and partners allowed to marry 'as a result of a petition and bill presented to the House of Lords'.[33] But it involved a very cumbersome and humiliating procedure. We can well imagine how awkward would be the situation of a woman if her private life became a subject of discussion in the House of Lords! Moreover, the procedure was so long and so costly that few persons benefited from it. Keith Thomas has calculated that 'there were only a little over 200 such divorces granted in the whole period up to 1857' and 'of these only about half a dozen were granted at the suit of a woman'.[34] And these women all belonged to the aristocracy. It may also be mentioned that the Act of Parliament which made provision for divorce insisted on adultery as one of the grounds for divorce. It was never easy to establish adultery for the satisfaction of law. And moreover, there can be cruelties which are even more oppressive than adultery.

Lawrence Stone has described in some detail the legal disabilities of married women in England in that period:

> By law the children belonged solely to the husband, and even after his death the widow had no rights over them, unless she was made their guardian in his will. If she should desert him, however severe the provocation, she could take nothing with her, neither her children nor her property. Her husband could, if he chose, compel her to return. Or he could at any time seize any income she might earn, or any means of support given to her by others. Only a legal separation, the cost of which put it beyond the reach of the majority, gave any protection to the deserting or deserted wife, and even then, before a change in the law in 1839, she had no claim upon her children unless her husband wanted to get rid of them. Moreover, in other ways the wife remained in a legally inferior status. A man convicted of murdering his wife would be hanged, but a woman convicted of mudering her husband would by law be burned alive. This barbarous penalty was in practice disappearing in the eighteenth century, but a woman was burned alive at Tyburn, for this crime as late as 1725.[35]

A logical consequence of such disabilities was that women were warned that they had to be very careful in the choice of a spouse. If a woman made a mistake and chose the wrong person, her situation could be very difficult. Mary Astell reminds women that this is one area where a mistake can be fatal:

> She who elects a Monarch for Life, who gives him an Authority, she cannot recall, however he misapply it, who puts her Fortune and Person entirely in his Power, nay, even the very Desires of her Heart, according to some learned Casuists, so as that it is not lawful to Will or Desire any Thing but what he approves and allows, had need be very sure that she does not make a Fool her Head, nor a Vicious Man her Guide and Pattern. (pp. 37-8).

Hence a woman should not take this most important decision in her life without serious thought and in this she should not act under pressure. Mary Astell's advice is that she should wait

> till she can meet with one who has the Government of his own Passions, and has duly regulated his own Desires, since he is to have such an absolute Power over hers. But he who doats on a Face, he who makes Money his idol, he who is charm'd with vain and empty Wit, gives no such Evidence, either of Wisdom or Goodness, that a Woman of any tolerable Sense shou'd care to venture her self to his Conduct. (pp. 37-8).

But how can she wait when 'alas! what poor Woman is taught that she should have a higher Design than to get her a Husband?' (p.66). 'A Husband indeed is thought by both Sexes so very valuable', Mary Astell says regretfully, 'that scarce a Man who can keep himself clean and make a Bow, but thinks he is good enough to pretend to any Woman, no matter for the Difference of Birth or Fortune, a Husband is such a Wonder-bearing Name as to make an Equality, or something more, wherever it is obtained'. (p.66). Unless women can resist the temptation to fall for the first person who proposes to them, they can hardly be described as competent to make the right choice.

IX

What qualities should a woman seek in a man so that her marriage can be reasonably happy? Mary Astell, a devout Christian, is categorical that 'the Soul be principally consider'd'. But soul is too abstract a term and in any case it is not easy to judge any body on that basis unless the idea is translated into some concrete attributes. These attributes, in Mary Astell's words, are 'a good Understanding, a Virtuous Mind; and in all other respects .... as much *Equality* (Italics mine) as may be'. (pp. 45- 46). If these conditions are met and they 'are good Christians and of suitable Tempers all will be well; but I should be shrewdly tempted to suspect their Christianity who marry after any of those Ways we have been speaking of'. (p.46). Mary Astell's mention of 'as much Equality as may be' is an important attribute of a happy marriage and she defines this concept of equality in very meaningful terms when she says that 'Love, Honour, and Worship, by which certainly Civility and Respect at least are meant, are as much the Woman's Due, as Love, Honour and Obedience are the Man's'. (p.47). Some people object to the word 'Obedience' but Mary Astell states the bitter truth that the woman 'who Marries, ought to lay it down for an indisputable Maxim, that her Husband must govern absolutely and intirely, and that she has nothing else to do but to Please and Obey'. (p.60). She bluntly adds: 'She who can't do this is no way fit to be a Wife' (p.61). Hence it is much more necessary that the man of her choice is such that 'the Goodness of his Temper, and Reasonableness of all his Commands, ... make it a Woman's interest as well as Duty to be observant and obedient in all Things'. (p.48).

Mary Astell makes an important point when she mentions 'as much Equality as may be' as the basis of happiness in marriage. She does not, of course, insist on absolute equality. She believes that 'A peaceable Woman, indeed, will neither question her Husband's Right, nor his Fitness to Govern, but how? Not as an absolute Lord and Master, with an arbitrary and tyrannical Sway, but as Reason governs and conducts a Man, by proposing what is just and fit'. (p.91). This is the surest way to ensure that 'the Man's Prerogative is not infringed, whilst the Woman's Privileges are secured'. (p.91). Mary Astell advises men 'for [their] own sake' to 'treat Women with a little more Humanity and Regard than is usually paid them' (p.54). This is another way of saying that they must respect women's 'Privileges' if they want to exercise their 'Prerogatives'.

Mary Astell raises a larger question when she asks: 'But how can a Man respect his Wife when he has a contemptible Opinion of her and her Sex? When from his own Elevation he looks down on them as void of Understanding, full of Ignorance and Passion, so that Folly and a Woman are equivalent Terms with him?' (p.52). This question troubled many women in seventeenth century England and they all believed that education alone could raise their status in men's eyes. In her *Introduction to the Gentlewoman's Companion* (1675), Hannah Wolley indeed rebuked men for their contempt for women:

> Vain man is apt to think we were merely intended for the world's propagation and to keep its inhabitants sweet and clean; but, by their leave, had we the same Literature, he would find our brains as fruitful as our bodies. Hence I am induced to believe that we are debarred from the Knowledge of humane Learning lest our pregnant wits should rival the to[w]ring Lords and Masters.

The Duchess of Newcastle was regarded as some kind of a figure of fun by her contemporaries. But however pretentious her claims and however bizarre her deportment, she did raise the question of women's education very powerfully. Men regard 'Books', she says, 'as their Crowne .... by which they rule and govern'.[36] But women, the Duchess says, are denied access to books and are treated 'like Children, Fools, or Subjects, that is, to flatter us to obey, and .... not let us divide the World equally with them'. The effect of this situation has been that women have become 'stupid .... whereas in Nature we have as clear understanding as Men, if we were bred in Schools to mature our Brains, and to manure our Understandings, that we might bring forth the Fruits of knowledge'.[37] The Duchess accuses men of 'endeavour[ing] to bar us of all sorts of Liberty, and would fain bury us in their houses or Beds, as in a Grave. The truth is we live like Bats, or Owls, labour like Beasts, and dye like Worms'.[38] In spite of this, however, as the Duchess claims, some women are able to make their mark. 'Thoughts are free', she says, 'those can never be enslaved, for we are not hindered from studying .... but may as well read in our Closets, as man in their Colleges .... and though most of our sex are bred up to the Needle and Spindle, yet some are bred up in the Public Theaters of the world'.[39]

Education may not give women absolute equality with men -

and Mary Astell in any case did not insist on *absolute* equality - it can certainly raise their status both in the family and in society. That it is in men's own interest that they should acquire knowledge and culture was Mary Astell's appeal to men. And she was not alone in making such an appeal. In the same year that her *Some Reflections Upon Marriage* appeared, a pamphlet entitled *The Female Advocate* (1700) also appeared. This author called herself "Eugenia" which seems to be a pseudonym. She says more or less what Mary Astell says on the question of a companionate marriage though in a somewhat subdued language:

> Now I own 'tis true that woman was made for the comfort and benefit of man; but I think it a much nobler comfort to have a companion, a person in whom a man can confide, to whom he can communicate his very soul, and open his breast and most inward thoughts, than to have a slave sitting at his footstool, trembling at every word that comes like thunder and lightning from the mouth of the domestic Pharoah. (p.20).

On the other hand, Swift gave a warning to women that unless their minds were well developed, they did not have much chance of making a good wife. In his *A Letter to a Young Lady* (1723), he told the lady that her parents had 'failed, as it is generally the Case, in too much neglecting to cultivate your Mind; without which it is impossible to acquire or preserve the Friendship and Esteem of a Wise Man, who soon grows weary of acting the Lover and treating his Wife like a Mistress, but wants a reasonable Companion, and a true Friend through every Stage of his Life'.[40]

It is, of course, difficult to estimate the influence of Mary Astell's ideas on her age. But there is no doubt that most of her ideas, specially about marriage, acquired common currency in the coming years. They came to be reflected not only in the writings on women's education by some of the eighteenth century women writers, but also in contemporary fiction. In any case, she must be regarded as a pioneer in various areas concerning women's rights and true status in society. Some of the modern feminists do not find her radical enough but to say what she did in the nineties of the seventeenth century showed remarkable perceptiveness and courage. Modern feminists should not forget that their favourite feminist, Mary Wollstonecraft, came on the scene almost hundred years later by which time, among other things, even the French Revolution, had taken place.

NOTES

1. All citations are taken from the last (4th) edition (1730) as reproduced by the Source Book Press, New York, 1970.
2. All citations are taken from the 4th edition (1701) of *A Serious Proposal* which contains the text of both the parts in one volume. I have used the text reproduced by Source Book Press, New York, 1970.
3. Cited by Myra Reynold, *The Learned Lady in England 1650-1760* (1964), p.102.
4. Cited by M. Phillips and W.S. Tomkinson, *English Women in Life and Letters* (Oxford, 1927), p.184.
5. Cited by Roy Porter, *English Society in the Eighteenth Century* (Penguin Books, 1990 (rev. ed.), p.23.
6. Antonia Fraser, *The Weaker Vessel: Women's Lot in Seventeenth Century England* (London, 1984), p.122.
7. *Ibid.*, p.122.
8. *A Serious Proposal*, p.75.
9. Ruth Perry, *The Celebrated Mary Astell: An Early English Feminist* (Chicago, 1986), p.141.
10. See Roger Thompson, *Women in Stuart England and America: A Comparative Study* (London, 1974), p. 31.
11. Ruth Perry, p. 105.
12. *Ibid.*, p. 143.
13. See Ian Watt, *The Rise of the Novel: Studies in Defoe, Richardson and Fielding* (Penguin Books, 1957), pp. 165-6.
14. *The Family, Sex and Marriage in England 1500-1800* (abridged edition, London, 1977), p.41.
15. Cited by J.P. Cooper, "Patterns of inheritance and settlement by great landowners from fifteenth to eighteenth century", *Family and Inheritance: Rural Society in Western Europe*, ed. Jack Goody, Joan Thirsk and E.P. Thompson (Cambridge, 1976), p.223.
16. *The Crisis of the Aristocracy* (Oxford, 1965), p.537.
17. Cited by Roger Thompson, p.48.
18. Cited by Ruth Perry, p.133.
19. See Roger Thompson, p.40.

20. See *The Complete Plays of William Wycherley*, ed. Gerald Weale (New York, 1966), p.239.
21. See Roger Thompson, p.45.
22. See Ian Watt, *The Rise of the Novel: Studies in Defoe, Richardson and Fielding* (Penguin Books, 1957), pp. 161-2, 166-7.
23. The quotation is from the edition of the novel in Penguin Classics (1987), p. 376.
24. *Ibid.*, pp. 367-7.
25. *Ibid.*, p. 377.
26. *Ibid.*, pp. 378-9.
27. *Op. cit.*, p. 86.
28. *Some Reflections Upon Marriage*, p.5.
29. Cited by Lawrence Stone, *The Family* (abridged), p. 81.
30. Cited by William and Malleville Haller, "The Puritan Art of Love", *Huntington Library Quarterley* (1942), p.269.
31. *Sex and Sensibility: Ideal and Erotic Love from Milton to Mozart* (Chicago, 1980), p.49.
32. *Vindication of the Rights of Women* (1792), ed. Miriam Brody Kramnick (Penguin Books, 1982), p.113.
33. Keith Thomas, "The Double Standard", *Journal of the History of Ideas* (1959), p. 201.
34. *Ibid*, p.201.
35. *The Family* (abridged), p.222.
36. "To All Noble, and Worthy Ladies", *Poems and Fancies* (1653), cited by Hilda Smith, *Reason's Disciples: Seventeenth-Century English Feminists*, p.78.
37. "Preface to the Reader," *World Olio* (1655), Ibid., p.80.
38. "Female Orations", *Orations of Diverse Sorts* (1668), Ibid., p.82.
39. "Preface to the Reader", *World Olio* (1655), Ibid., p.110.
40. *Satires and Personal Writings*, ed. William Alfred Eddy (Oxford, 1932), p.61.

Chapter II

Defoe's Views on Marriage

From Defoe's *An Academy For Women* it is easy to draw the inference that it was prompted by Mary Astell, the 'Ingenious Lady' who wrote 'a little Book called *Advice to the Ladies*', though Defoe claims that the views in women's '*Academy*' are his own and indeed less 'impracticable'[1] than Mary Astell's. The very first sentences of the *Academy*, however, echo Mary Astell's sentiments:

> I have often thought of it as one of the most barbarous Customs in the world, considering us a Civilized and a Christian countrey, that we deny the advantages of Learning to Women. We reproach the Sex every day with Folly and Impertinence, while I am confident, had they the advantages of Education equal to us, they wou'd be guilty of less than ourselves.[2]

Defoe also says that '*Men [should] take Women for Companions, and Educate them to be fit for it*'[3] (Italics Defoe's), a view that Mary Astell had expressed even more strongly.

It is, of course, not easy to say whether his verse pamphlet entitled *Good Advice to Ladies: Shewing that as the World goes, and is like to go, the best way for them is to keep Unmarried* (1702) is also influenced by Mary Astell. Perhaps it is a Puritan's protest against the immoral tone of the Restoration aristocratic society, and more particularly against the dissolute culture of the Restoration rakes, which had made a dignified marriage almost unviable. As he says in the Preface to *Good Advice*, the reason for his extreme view is the moral degeneration in 'the Lives and Manners of Men' 'who proclaim that they have too much Wit to have either Morality, or Religion, and by consequence either Honour or Conscience'. The status of married women had specially suffered at the hands of these men in this period. Lawrence Stone claims that 'in the early sixteenth century open maintenance of a mistress - usually of lower-class origin - was perfectly compatible with a respected social position and a stable marriage. Peers clearly saw nothing shameful in these liaisons and up to about 1560 they are often to be found leaving bequests to bastard children in their wills. In practice, if not in theory, the early sixteenth-century nobility was a polygamous society, and some continued to live with a succession of women despite the official prohibition on divorce'.[4]

The institution of keeping mistresses flourished till the middle of the eighteenth century though it was not openly done as in the earlier period. In Charles II's reign especially, courtiers treated debauchery almost as a proof of their loyalty to the King. Sir Keith Thomas has mentioned the case of Francis North, Lord Guilford, who was seriously advised to 'keep a whore' as 'he was ill looked upon for want of doing so'.[5] Keeping a mistress had clearly become a status symbol amongst the aristocracy and Petulant's ploy in *The Way of the World* (1700) to give 'coach-hire, and something more, by the week,' to some women of easy virtue to 'call him once a-day at public places' (I.ii), merely refers to the craze of the contemporary gentlemen to be seen possessing a mistress or two. Petulant, of course, is not a gentleman and he is merely trying to ape high life. Ranger, the hero of Thomas Durfey's *A Fond Husband* (1677), is a more authentic witness of this fashionable tendency:

> 'Tis a damn'd thing, this wenching, if a man considers seriously on it: and yet 'tis such a damnable age we live in, that, Gad, he that does not follow it is either accounted sordidly unnatural, or ridiculously impotent. (V.v.).

Such views were perhaps natural in a circle where the King himself set an example in having innumerable mistresses. The King did even greater damage to contemporary morals by 'forcing on his Queen the shameful humiliation of honouring one of his mistresses in her own household'.[6]

Restoration Comedy is full of protests against this practice but the wailings of wives are in vain. Their economic dependence on their husbands is so complete that they are helpless. Even though they may have brought very handsome dowries at the time of their marriage, married women in England were *legally prohibited* from owning any property. Hence they were completely at the mercy of their husbands.

In Cibber's *The Careless Husband* (1704) in the writing of which Defoe is suspected of having had some hand,[7] we see how helpless Lady Easy feels on discovering that her husband is carrying on with her own maidservant:

> Was ever Woman's Spirit, by an injurious Husband, broke like mine? A vile, licentious Man! must he bring home his follies too? Wrong me with my own Servant! O! how tedious a Relief is patience! and yet in my Condition 'tis the only Remedy: For to reproach him with my Wrongs, is taking on my self the Means of Redress, bidding Defiance to his Falsehood, and naturally but provokes him to undo me. (I.i).

Only two years before Cibber's Comedy, Defoe had condemned this practice in his *Advice to Women*:

> Some Kitchen Wench, or filthy thing that's grown
> The Common Talk and Scandal of the Town;
> This loathsome Creature shall outdo thy Charms,
> And tear thy wretched Husband from thy Arms:
> Under thy Nose, he'll keep the Baggage fine,
> And whatso'ere is Dear, and should be thine,
> She shall possess; and if you speak a word,
> O! then his Wife is not to be indur'd,
> A jealous peevish thing. Diseas'd or Mad,
> Not fit for Commerce, nor the Marriage-bed. (p.20)

Elsewhere he describes another husband in the following words:

Oft have I seen a Bully reeling home,
Drench'd in the Rogueries of the Town;
Altho' 'tis by his Wife that he's grown Rich. (p.3)

A 'truly Good and Wise' (p.15) man would, of course, not be 'Unjust' to his wife nor would he 'Tyrannise' (p.15) over her but in these degenerate times, such men are hardly to be found anywhere:

A true Wise man's like a Prodigious Birth,
A Rarity, and scarcely found on Earth,
The Infant World might boast of such a Race;
And tell us Men had Honesty and Grace;
But in this Iron age, Time downward rouls,
And gives harden'd Bruits and rusty Souls. (P.15)

On page 11, he says:

Fly then, Dear *Lesbia*, shun the Crocodile,
Fierce to Devour, and subtile to beguile;
Keep, dearest Saint, your Freedom while you may,
Nor, for a triffle, sell your joys away:
Just like fall'n Spirits, to whom they'r near a kin,
They will tempt, and they'll plague you for the Sin.
This Legion shall continue to run you down,
And make you guilty, tho' the crime is their own.

He sums up his advice' in the last two lines:

Then, *Lesbia*, be as wise as you are Fair,
Despite Mankind, and keep you as you are. (p.16)

In the Preface, Defoe recognises that it may be regarded as 'a great fault to persuade People against Marriage'. This is how he justifies the extreme view that he has taken:

> "I answer, That to the utmost of my Power I will ever Expose those Impious, Impertinent, Cowardly, Censorious, Sauntring, Idle Wretches called Wits and Beus, the Plague of the Nation, and the Scandal of Mankind. But if *Lesbia* is sure she hath found a Man of Honour, Religion and Vertue, I will never forbid the Banes: let her love him as much as she pleases, and value him as an Angel, and be Married tomorrow if she will".

But in an age of Wits and Beus, he implies, marriage is a hazardous undertaking which exposes the woman to 'The False-hood and the Cruelties of Man'. (p.1).

I

It is clear that Defoe is *not* against marriage as an institution but against its degeneration. The degeneration had started in the Restoration period when one of Shadwell's characters described it as "the worst of prisons", indeed as an "Ecclesiastical Mouse-Trap". (Thomas Shadwell), *Epsom Wells*). The Restoration aristocracy was largely responsible for this degeneration and Defoe, as the spokesman of the middle classes, showed how the sacred relationship between husband and wife had been defiled in his times.

Lawrence Stone has made the claim that 'in the period between about 1680 and 1710, the country, both high and low, seems to have lost its moral moorings.' He finds enough 'evidence of an abnormally cynical, mercenary, and predatory ruthlessness about human relationships, which is deeply offensive to modern sensibilities'. This 'moral decay [is] displayed in the popular literature of the age, especially in Mary de la Rivière Manley's *New Atlantis* of 1714-20, and Mrs. Haywood's *Memoirs of a Certain Island* of 1725-6, both of which were bestsellers.' The first, Lawrence claims,

> 'was a veiled attack on the Whigs as the prime exponents of

male aristocratic debauchery, based on a philosophy of atheism or epicureanism, and an obsession with money, lust, and personal advancement. Virtue is made to lament that

> Innocence is banished by the first dawn of early knowledge. Sensual corruptions and hasty enjoyments affright me from their habitation.... By a diabolical way of argument they prove the body is only necessary to the pleasures of enjoyment; that love lies not in the heart but in the face.... Hymen no longer officiates at their marriages.... Interest is deputed in his room, he presides over the feast, he joins their hands.

Virtue goes on to lament that 'avarice, contemptible covetousness, sordid desire for gain .... have quite extinguished the very glimmerings of [love]'.[8]

In his *Conjugal Lewdness: or Matrimonial Whoredom: A Treatise concerning the Use and Abuse of the Marriage Bed* (1727), Defoe offers the following comments on the general deterioration of the married state in his period:

> I know not by what degeneracy in our Manners, or corruption of Principles, it is come to pass, but 'tis too general in practice, that Matrimony is now looked upon only as a politick Opportunity to gratify a vitious Appetite: The Form, how sacred soever graver Heads may pretend it is in its Institution, is now become our Jest, and not only ridiculed and bantered in our Discourse, for that might be born with, but 'tis become a Jest in practice; all the solemn Part is dropt out of our Thoughts, the Money and the Maidenhead is the Subject of our Meditations.[9]

In such a situation, even

> the best of Women are betrayed .... into the hands of the vilest of Men, and in the grossest manner abus'd; nay, which is still worse, this is done with a Banter and a Jest, all the sacred

> Obligations, the indissolvable Bands of Religion and Virtue, are trampled under foot; the modest and most virtuous Lady is impudently defloured, and the Night's Enjoyment boasted of the next Day in the Arms of a Strumpet. (p.33).

For Defoe marriage is a sacred institution, indeed "*God's holy Ordinance*". (p.25) (Italics Defoe's). Originally man and woman "were single and separate but God made them associate together *he brought the Woman to him .... God married them*". (p.25). (Italics Defoe's). For him, women are not meant to satisfy man's 'brutal Appetite'. (p.33). According to him,

> the Matrimonial Duty is all reciprocal: 'tis founded in love, 'tis performed in the height of Affection; its most perfect Accomplishment consists *not in the Union of Sexes, but in the Union of the Souls*; uniting their Desires, their Ends, and consequently their Endeavours, for completing their Felicity. (p.27) (Italics mine).

At a time when the status of women was very low in society and the family, Defoe categorically states that the wife is not

> to be us'd only as the upper Servant in the House. The great Duty between the Man and his Wife, I take to consist in that of Love, in the Government of Affection, and the Obedience of a complaisant, kind, obliging Temper; the Obligation is reciprocal, 'tis drawing in an equal Yoke; Love knows no superior or inferior, no imperious Command on one hand, no reluctant Subjection on the other; the End of both should be the well-ordering their Family, the good-guiding their Household and Children, educating, instructing and managing them with a mutual Endeavour, and giving respectively good Examples to them. (p.26).

Most marriages in the period, however, were mercenary marriages and Defoe was unhappy that 'Not one in five hundred of those that now marry, really understand what they marry for'. (p.27).

> Ask the Ladies why they marry, they tell you 'tis for a good Settlement; tho' they had their own Fortunes to settle on themselves before. Ask the Men why they marry, it is for the Money. How few Matches have any other Motive .... How little is regarded of that one essential and absolutely necessary Part of the Composition, called Love, without which the matrimonial State is, I think, hardly lawful, I am sure is not rational, and I think, can never be happy.
>
> Hence it follows, that we have such few happy and successful Matches. How much Matrimony, how little Love, how many Coupled, how few Join'd; in a word, how much Marriage, how little Friendship. O Friendship! thou exalted Felicity of Life, thou glorious Incorporation of Souls. (pp.27-28).

Like Mary Astell, he regards *friendship* as the most essential feature of marriage, indeed more essential than any other aspect whatsoever:

> Where does the kind expecting Husband find a sincere Friend in his Bosom? How seldom does the tender affectionate Wife take a Friend into her Arms, even though she does take the Person, she takes the Man without the Husband, and the Husband without the Friend? Not Virtue, not Fidelity to the Marriage Bed, not Conscience of the Conjugal Duty, not Religion, will do it; *no not RELIGION*! How many Husbands and Wives will go to Heaven from the Arms of the Wives nd Husbands they had no Friendship for? (p.28) (Italics Defoe's).

In practical terms, for Defoe the ideal marriage is

> a chast and modest Scheme of Living; 'tis a State, not a Circumstance of Life; the End and Meaning of it is the raising Families, procreating Children, to be brought up religiously; 'tis an Establishment contracted, or at least ought to be so, as an

> Appointment of Heaven; and for solid and substantial Enjoyments; it is durable as Life, and bounded only by the Duration of Life. (p.343).

Elsewhere he calls marriage a 'Partnership', a 'Partnership in Life; a Partnership of Souls, they [husband and wife] are embarked in the same Ship, they go the same Voyage, and .... they swim, they sink, they are happy, they are miserable, they are poor, they are rich .... have but one Fate. (p.25).

A successful 'partnership' presupposes that the man should do 'justice' to his wife. Defoe elaborates his conception of justice in the following words:

> Justice is another of the Particulars which Decency still requires between a Man and his Wife; he is far from acting decently with a Wife that will not on all Occasions do her Justice: To be injurious to a Wife destroys all Family-Peace between them; and whether this Injustice be occasioned by and relating to Matters of Property, or Matters of Duty, 'tis all the same; there is no Decency can be preserved where Justice is not done; if the Wife be oppressed, if her Right and Allowances expressly capitulated or are unjustly detained from her, or if she be any way stript, either of her Ornaments, or of her Settlements, these are injurious things which destroy Affection, and the destroying of Affection ruins the peace of the Family. (p.77).

But 'Justice' is possible only if the man respects his wife. So Defoe insists that there should not only be love between husband and wife but also mutual respect. 'A Man', be says,

> can never pretend to love his Wife and have no Respect for her at the same time; that would be to love her, and not to love her altogether, which is incongruous in its nature. (p.75).

Defoe insists that this respect for the wife should not only be reflected in the man's actions but also in his conversation, especially in company. Often men tend to neglect their wives without realizing that it might lower them in the eyes of other women. This can hurt the wife so much that she might start hating her husband. This can lead to female adultery. But would the fault in that case be entirely that of the woman?

This question had first been raised by the Restoration Comedy. A character in Vanbrugh's *The Provok'd Wife* (1697) thus states the woman's point of view:

> A man of real worth scarce ever is a cuckold, but by his own fault. Women are not naturally lewd; there must be something to urge 'em to it. They 'll cuckold a Churl, out of Revenge; a Fool, because they despise him; a Beast, because they loathe him. But when they make bold with a Man they once had a well-grounded Value for, 'tis because they first see them neglected by him. (V.iv.).

Defoe is clearly of the opinion that it is

> a wise Man's Business after Matrimony, by all means possible to preserve the Affection of his wife entire, to engross her to him, and to make and keep himself the single and entire Object of her best Thoughts. If she is once brought to hate him, to have an aversion to him, to loath and abhor him, she must have an uncommon Stock of Virtue, and be more a Christian than he ought to expect of her, if she does not single out some other Object of her Affection; and can a Man think his Wife, who is thus every Day disobliged, in the grossest manner ill used, and, in spite of her Resentments, exposed to be laught at by him, will long preserve an inviolable Affection to him? (p.79).

Defoe concludes his views on marriage with the following emphatic statement:

> Marriage without Love, is the completest Misery in Life. Besides, I must say, it is to me utterly unlawful, and entails a Curse upon the persons, as being wilfully perjured, invoking the name of God to a Falsehood, which is one of the most provoking Crimes that Mankind can commit. He or She who, with that slight and superficial Affection, Ventures into the Matrimonial Vow, are to me little more than legal Prostitutes. (pp.102-3).

II

Defoe condemns the violation of 'Matrimonial Vows' so violently in *Conjugal Lewdness* precisely for the reason that they were so frequently violated in real life in his times. Indeed, marriage had lost all sanctity and, as Lawrence Stone has pointed out,

> 'the period 1680 to 1710 was one of acute crisis in many propertied families, from the lowest to the highest. The clash between the conflicting ideals of patriarchy and individualism in the choice of a spouse reached an acute stage at this time, just as the rival motives of affection or interest also came into serious conflict. To make matters worse, this was the period when fortune-hunting male, and occasionally female, predators and impostors were both peculiarly common and peculiarly ruthless in their tactics'.[10]

Marriage licenses were freely available and so were clergymen. Indeed, there were professional marriage shops in London and the country-side was flooded with half starved curates and penniless clergymen who were willing to commit any kind of irregularity or impropriety to meet the 'insatiable public demands for secret weddings'.[11] It was the Hardwicke Marriage Act of 1753 which ended this confusion and defined the *legally binding* marriage though it is difficult to claim in a matter like marriage that an Act of Parliament can set everything right. Lawrence Stone says that 'the root cause of the trouble was that there was no consensus within the society at large about how a legally binding marriage should be carried out. Popular custom took one position, the church another, and the state and the propertied laity a third'.[12] Surprisingly, this confusion is fully reflected in *Moll Flanders*.

Moll Flanders marries five times and has various love affairs. Obviously, this makes nonsense of what Defoe had said about the sanctity of the marriage relationship in *Conjugal Lewdness*. But it is not easy to clearly define Defoe's attitude to Moll. The title of the novel is somewhat sensational but it contains no moral judgement: its purpose may simply be to improve the book's saleability: "The Fortunes and Misfortunes of the Famous Moll Flanders etc.: Who was Born in *Newgate*, and during a Life of Continu'd Variety for Three-score Years, besides her Childhood, was Twelve Years a *Whore*, five times a *Wife* (whereof once to her own Brother), Twelve Years a *Thief*, Eight Years a Transported *Felon in Virginia*, at last grew *Rich*, liv'd *Honest*, and died a *Penitent*". But can we say with any assurance that he condemns her or that he approves of her conduct? As Juliet Michell says, this 'juxtaposition of contradictory moral elements' is the 'major theme' of the novel: 'Moll is heroine and villain, fair and foul, business woman and thief, wife and prostitute'.[13] She cites Arnold Kettle's emphatic comment:

> Moll speaks as though she were not implicated in the common lot of criminals. She doesn't think of herself as a criminal. When she learns what the other criminals in Newgate think of her she is morally outraged. Occasionally, for a moment, like Joyce Cary's Sara, she catches sight of herself in some mirror and sees herself, surprised. And she does think of herself as .... a gentlewoman ....
>
> The underlying tension which gives *Moll Flanders* its vitality as a work of art can be expressed by a contradiction which is at once simple and complicated. Moll is immoral, shallow, hypocritical, heartless, a bad woman: yet Moll is marvellous. Defoe might almost (though he wouldn't have dreamed of it) have subtitled his book 'A Pure Woman'.
>
> Moll's splendour - her resilience and courage and generos-

ity - is inseparable from her badness. The fair and the foul are not isolable qualities to be abstracted and totted up in a reckoning, balancing one against the other. The relationship is far more interesting.[14]

Even an older critic who is not given to hyperbolic language, Ernest Baker, says:

From the artistic point of view, Moll Flanders may be regarded as the female counterpart of Robinson Crusoe. His history was a great realistic epic of human courage and energy fighting a lonely battle in the most desparate circumstances. She is the lonely woman cast upon her own resources, fighting a world that has done its worst to destroy her, body and soul. Born in shame, outcast from the cradle, damned by her very nativity to more than her portion of original sin, the weaker nature of a woman rendering her a more inevitable victim of the bad blood she has inherited, Moll is cruelly betrayed, meets with the blackest misfortune, and falls into vice and crime, all through the force of circumstances and the defective ordering of society. But she keeps the reader's sympathy, because her weaknesses are human, and even his esteem, because of her courage, her self-reliance, and a certain good-nature that no external ills can utterly stifle.[15]

James Sutherland's response to Moll Flanders is equally warm:

What delights most readers of *Moll Flanders* is partly Moll's irrepressible vitality, the determination to survive which she shares with Crusoe and with other of Defoe's heroes and heroines. But she has not merely the will to live; she gets, being Moll, a great deal of pleasure out of life, she is gay and good-humored and lively. We are given one especially memorable glimpse of Moll having fun when her gentleman-draper husband takes her to Oxford in a magnificent hired equipage, and passes himself off as a lord and Moll as his countess. "Give him his due," Moll remarks humorously, "not a beggar alive knew better how to be a lord than my husband." But the fun was only beginning:

> 'We saw all the rarities at Oxford, talk'd with two or three fellows of colleges about putting a nephew that was left to his lordship's care to the University, and of their being his tutors; we diverted our selves with bantering several other poor scholars with the hope of being at least his lordship's chaplain and putting on a scarf; and thus having liv'd like quality indeed as to expence, we went away for Northampton, and in a word, in about twelve days' ramble came home again, to the tune of about $93 expence.'

Moll was still a young woman when this escapade occurred, but she never lost her *joie de vivre*.'[16]

III

Let us now turn to Moll's career. Born in Newgate to a mother who escaped hanging only because of the expected birth of her child - that child being Moll herself - she begins life one does not know exactly where. In a vague sort of way, she tells us that perhaps she spent some time with her mother's relations, some time with some gypsies and then with a poor woman where she was sent by the parish authorities. Luckily for her, this woman who kept a little school, became very fond of the little girl. The other girls in her school also liked her. It was perhaps here that she developed 'the love of fine clothes, a dislike of hard work, and a desire to be regarded as a gentlewoman'.[17]

That she will have to pay a very heavy price for such aptitudes and tastes does not become clear to us till we see her seduction by the elder brother. She is between 17 and 18 years old and wants to be married like other middle-class girls. The elder brother promises love and marriage and the girl is dazzled. This is how he proceeds:

> he held me fast, and still Kiss'd me, till he was almost out of Breath, and then sitting down, says, dear Betty I am in Love with you.
>
> His Words I must confess fir'd my Blood; all my Spirits flew about my Heart, and put me into Disorder enough, which he might easily have seen in my Face: He repeated it afterwards several times that he was in Love with me, and my Heart spoke as plain as a Voice, that I lik'd it; nay, when ever he said, I am in Love with you, my Blushes plainly reply'd, wou'd you were Sir. (p.60).[18]

What Moll does not know - but what Defoe not only knows but emphasises here and elsewhere - is that there is no natural relationship between love and marriage in this society. Whatever her merits, it is not easy for Moll to secure a husband as she is only a domestic servant with no money or family connections. Moll, of course, has 'the common Vanity of [her] Sex' (p.56) and, perhaps, it was natural in her case, as people had started describing her as 'the Handsomest young Woman in *Colchester*. (p.58). She is also vain enough to claim:

> I had the Advantage of my Ladies, tho' they were my Superiors; but they were all the Gifts of Nature, and which all their Fortunes could not furnish. First, I was apparently Handsomer than any of them. Secondly, I was better shap'd, and Thirdly, I Sung better, by which I mean, I had a better Voice'. (p.56).

But all her superiority cannot help her in the contemporary marriage market. As the Mayoress' daughter says to her elder brother, the 'Market is against our Sex just now':

> if a young Woman have Beauty, Birth, Breeding, Wit, Sense, Manners, Modesty, and all these to an Extream; yet if she have not Money, she's no Body, she had as good want them all, for nothing but Money now recommends a Woman, the Men play the Game all into their own Hands. (p.58).

She, however, becomes the mistress of the elder brother believing his oral promise that he would marry her. When the time for decision comes, he tells her that he is not in a position to marry her though he would continue to support her. Moll is indignant at this and upbraids him:

> *I told him* .... that he had Engag'd himself to Marry me, and that my Consent was at the same time Engag'd to him; that he had all along told me I was his Wife, and I look'd upon my self as effectually so, as if the Ceremony had pass'd; and that it was from his own Mouth that I did so, he having all along persuaded me to call myself his Wife. (p.75).

Professor Novak, after quoting the above passage from the novel, says:

> Her arguments are impeccable by the standard of divine and natural law, but they have no effect on her lover, who may be a knave but is certainly no fool. When he threatens to expose their relationship and cast her out of the house, Moll had no choice but to accept the inevitable. Her lover slips out of the contract with Moll's reluctant consent, and thus her first 'natural' marriage ends.[19]

Moll finds herself in a situation where she has no option but to marry the younger brother, as suggested by the elder brother. But she has learnt the lesson that a woman should never accept a man's verbal promise of marriage but insist on a legal binding contract. The elder brother's conduct has also taught her that when one's self-interest is involved men 'banish all manner of Affection' and 'give up Honour and Justice, Humanity, and even Christianity, to serve themselves'. (p.101). Ian Watt's statement is applicable to this new Moll Flanders:

> 'Moll Flanders, like Rastignac and Julien Sorel, is a characteristic product of modern individualism in assuming that she

> owes it to herself to achieve the highest economic and social rewards, and in using every available method to carry out her resolve.[20]

The marriage with the younger brother lasted five years as he died at the end of this period. Moll confesses that she was not 'suitably affected with the loss of my Husband; nor indeed can I say that I even Lov'd him as I ought to have done'. (p.102). She also says:

> He had been really a very good Husband to me, and we liv'd very agreeably together; But as he had not receiv'd much from them, and had in the little time he liv'd acquir'd no great Matters, so my Circumstances were not great; nor was I much mended by the Match: Indeed I had preserv'd the elder Brother's Bonds to me, to pay me 500 l. which he offer'd me for my Consent to Marry his Brother; and this, with what I had saved of the Money he formerly gave me, and about as much more by my Husband, left me a Widow with about 1200 l. in my Pocket. (p.102).

Dorothy Van Ghent's comments on this passage are worth quoting:

> We know in some degree from this context, and with added conviction from other similar contexts, what Moll means by "very good husband" and by saying that they lived "very agreeably": the man had enough money to keep Moll from want, he spent money freely enough to maintain her in comfort and in that kind of social respectability which the spending of money guarantees - therefore he was "good" and their life was "agreeable". Any other characterization of this husband or of their marital life we should not be able to guess at; for Moll, simply by their exclusion of any other kind of perception from her story, stringently limits our own imagination of character; and we must judge that Moll has no other perception of character.[21]

From this, she concludes that 'Moll's world assumes a shape astonishingly without spiritual dimension'.[22]

But Moll had married the man under compulsion. Indeed, as she says, 'I never was in Bed with my Husband, but I wish'd my self in the Arms of his Brother: .... In short, I committed Adultery and Incest with him every Day in my Desires, which without doubt, was as effectually Criminal in the Nature of the Guilt, as if I had actually done it'. (p.102). This clearly was not the kind of marriage which could be described as one based on mutual love and affection - as also mutual esteem - which Defoe had so vehemently preached in his didactic writings. Hence it would be futile to search for any 'spiritual dimension' in this marriage.

After her husband's death she was 'left loose to the World', and she had to look to her future. She was still 'Young and Handsome' and it was not difficult for her to attract male attention. But she tells us that now she is no more the innocent girl who could be easily cheated by men:

> The Case was alter'd with me, I had Money in my Pocket, and had nothing to say to them: I had been trick'd once by that Cheat call'd *LOVE*, but the Game was over; I was resolv'd now to be Married or Nothing, and to be well Married or not at all. (p.103).

IV

Moll had, however, become too fond of the 'Company .... of Men of Mirth and Wit, Men of Gallantry and Figure' and she 'was often entertain'd with such .... [but] the brightest Men came for the dullest Errand, *that is to say*, the Dullest as to what I aim'd at; on the other Hand, those who came with the best Proposals were the Dullest and the most disagreeable Part of the World' (p.104). She had lived for five years as the wife of a gentleman and she was reluctant to accept proposals from tradesmen. Indeed, like women from the nobility, she regarded them as unworthy of her. This was, of course, foolish. Defoe as the spokesman of the middle classes often reproved women from good families whose fortunes were limited and who refused to marry tradesmen owing to class pride. He indeed believed that the future of England belonged to the trading classes and not the landed nobility. *In Conjugal Lewdness* he says that 'The Nobility are become poor, or at least poorer; be it by Sloth and Luxury, I do not determine' (p.257). As against this, 'The Commons have grown rich by Industry and Commerce' (p.256). About not marrying in the trading class, one of his Lords in *Conjugal Lewdness* tells his wife that if they can't marry their daughters to tradesmen,

> then you must let the Tradesmen keep their Money too, as well as keep their Daughters; and we shall continue to decline and become poor, by our riotous and extravagant Living; and so, in a few Ages more, the Wealth of the Nation may be almost all in the Hands of the trading Part of the People; and the decayed Nobility may be as Despicable as they may be Poor. Pray, added he, what would all our noble Blood do for us without our Estates? And pray, Madam, says he, be pleased to look into Things, and see how many noble Families are, at this time, the Offspring of Trade; we do not find, that their Posterity are less valued among the Nobility, or less deserve it. Two Dukes, adds his Lordship, are at this time, the Grandsons, and one Nobleman, the Son of Sir Josiah Child, who was but a Tradesman'. (p.258).

As if as a punishment for her snobbery, Moll is 'hurried on (by my Fancy to a Gentleman) to Ruin myself in the grossest Manner' (p.105) and marries '*a Gentleman - Tradesman*' (p.104). He was a tradesman with all the vices of a gentleman but none of the virtues of a tradesman. He was a 'Rake, Gentleman, Shop-keeper, and Beggar, all together' (p.104) and 'coming to a lump of Money at once, fell into such a profusion of Expence, that all that I had, and all he had before, if he had any thing worth mentioning, would not have held it out above one Year' (p.105). In about 'two Years and a Quarter he Broke' and was 'Arrested in an Action too heavy for him to give Bail to' (p.106). He, however, 'found means to break out of the Bailiff's House .... and got over into *France*' (p.107).

Thus ended her second marriage and her situation now became desperate. She was afraid that 'if the Commissioners were .... inform'd where I was, I should have been fetch'd up and examin'd upon Oath, and all I had saved be taken away from me' (p.108). So she changed her lodging and went into the *Mint* which was a sanctuary for insolvent debtors, 'took Lodgings in a very private Place, drest me up in the Habit of a Widow, and call'd myself *Mrs. Flanders*' (p.108). She 'had a Husband, and no Husband' as she knew well enough that he would never return to England even if he lived fifty years. Moll recognises that now she is not even in a position to marry again as it would be a bigamous marriage 'and I had not one Friend to advise with, in the Condition I was in, at least not one I durst Trust the Secret of my Circumstances to' (p.108).

Moll realized that whatever little she still owned was likely to be wasted soon and then she would have to face 'Misery and Starving' (p.110). So on the advice of an acquaintance she shifted to another part of London in the hope that 'some Captain of a Ship might take a Fancy to me, and Court me' (p.111). But she soon discovered that 'Marriages were here the Consequences of politick Schemes for forming Interest, and carrying on Business, and that Love had no Share, or but very little in the Matter' (p.112). It was clear to her that she could take a lover but not a husband - a role that she abhored at this stage of her life. She was still 'Handsome, Well-shaped' and had a 'good Mein and a graceful Behaviour' but these merits were needed in a 'Mistress', not a wife - 'for a Wife, no Deformity would shock the Fancy, no ill Qualities, the Judgement; the Money was the thing, the Portion was neither crooked or Monstrous, but the Money was always agreeable, whatever the Wife was'. (p.112). And money Moll did not possess. She rightly says: 'The Circumstances I was in, made the offer of a good Husband the most necessary Thing in the World to me' (p.122).

She was at last able to secure a man who claimed that a 'great part of his Estate consisted of Three Plantations .... in Virginia' (p.128). She did not deceive him about her fortune but even when she told him that she had no fortune, he pressed his proposal.

At last they were married and, as Moll says,

> very happily married on my side I assure you, *as to the Man*; for he was the best humour'd Man that ever Women had, but his Circumstances were not so good as I imagined, as on the other hand he had not bettered himself by marrying so much as he expected. (p.129).

This was her third marriage and clearly a bigamous marriage though she firmly believed that her Tradesman husband would never return to England to claim her. She went with her husband to Virginia and she found her husband's mother there who lived with him and who was very kind to her. Her husband also continued as affectionate as ever and Moll says:

> I thought my self the happiest Creature alive; when an odd and surprizing Even put an end to all that Felicity in a moment, and rendered my Condition the most uncomfortable, if not the most miserable, in the World. (p.133).

The odd event was that in conversation with her mother-in-law she discovered that she was her *own* mother. Further enquiries confirmed it. It was clear to Moll that she had lived in 'open avowed Incest and Whoredom, and all under the appearance of an honest Wife'. (p. 137). To add to her misery, she had had two children and 'was big with another'. (p.136). If this came to be known to other people, apart from the disgrace, she could be legally punished and the punishment could be very severe. She first told her mother whose reaction was sharp:

> *Unhappy Child*! says she, what miserable chance could bring thee hither? And in the Arms of my own Son too! *Dreadful Girl!* says she, *why we are all undone*! Married to thy own Brother! Three Children, and two alive, all of the same Flesh and Blood!

> My Son and my Daughter lying together as Husband and Wife! All Confusion and Distraction for ever! *miserable Family*! (pp.144-5).

Her own reaction is seen in the following:

> indeed I mortally hated him as a Husband, and it was impossible to remove that riveted Aversion I had to him; at the same time it being an unlawful incestuous living added to that Aversion; and tho' I had not great concern about it in point of Conscience, yet every thing added to make Cohabiting with him the most nauseous thing to me in the World; and I think verily it was come to such a height, that I could almost as willingly have embrac'd a Dog, as have let him offer any thing of that kind to me, for which Reason I could not bear the thoughts of coming between the Sheets with him. (pp.147-8).

She resolved to leave Virginia and though most reluctantly, her husband/brother helped her to return to England.

V

On her return to England, 'a new Scene of Misfortunes attended [her]' (p.155). At Bath she met some one who was very friendly and wanted her to be his mistress. But she resisted his offer and claimed that she was 'not wicked enough to come into the Crime for meer Vice of it' (p.157). After some time, however, she 'exchang'd the Place of Friend for that unmusical harsh sounding Title of Whore'. (p.168). Moll says in her defence: 'as Poverty brought me into it, so fear of poverty kept me in it'. (p.172). But she is not happy to be a mistress: she wants to be a wife. As she says:

> And now I was indeed in the height of what I might call my Prosperity, and I wanted nothing but to be a Wife, which however could not be in this Case, there was no room for it; and therefore on all Occasions I study'd to save what I could, as I

> have said above, against a time of scarcity; knowing well enough that such things as these do not always continue, that Men that keep Mistresses often change them, grow weary of them, or Jealous of them, or something or other happens to make them withdraw their Bounty. (pp.170-1).

And in her case this is exactly what happened. She remained the man's mistress for six years during which period she 'brought him Three Children' though only one of them survived. At last she received a letter from him in which he told her that he had been very seriously ill and on recovery he repented the kind of life that he had lived. He promised to take care of the child and sent her some money.

Moll was now a 'single Person .... loos'd from all the obligations either of Wedlock or Mistresship in the World, except my Husband the Linnen Draper' from whom she had not heard for 'almost Fifteen Years'. (p.180). As she says, she was now

> a loose unguided Creature, and had no Help, no Assistance, no Guide for my Conduct: I knew what I aim'd at, and what I wanted, but knew nothing how to pursue the End by direct means; I wanted to be plac'd in a settled State of Living, and had I happen'd to meet with a sober good Husband, I should have been as faithful and true a Wife to him as Virtue it self could have form'd: If I had been otherwise, the Vice came in always at the Door of Necessity, not at the Door of Inclination; and I understand too well, by the want of it, what the value of a settl'd Life was, to do any thing to forfeit the felicity of it; nay, I should have made the better Wife for all the Difficulties I had pass'd thro', by a great deal; nor did I in any of the Time that I had been a Wife, give my Husbands the least uneasiness on account of my Behaviour. (p.182).

But it was her misfortune that even when she obtained a sober good husband, he did not live long. Or she had to leave him because he was her own brother. As things are, she is keen to find a man who can offer marriage to her. She employs a somewhat new strategy to secure a husband now. She pretends that she is woman of fortune and thus tricks a man into formal marriage. However, she is deceived as he is just a fortune hunter with no money at all though he too pretends to be a man of vast fortune. He had, says Moll, 'the Appearance of an extraordinary fine Gentleman; he was Tall, well Shap'd, and had an extraordinary Address; talk'd as naturally of his Park and his Stables, and his Horses, his Game-Keepers, his Woods, his Tenants, and his Servants, as if we had been in the Mansion-House, and I had seen all of them'. (pp.198-9). Moll was so impressed by all this that she consented to marry. The marriage was conducted by a 'Romish Clergyman, which I was assur'd would marry us as effectually as a Church of *England* Parson'. (p.199).

After their marriage, they discovered that it was a 'double Fraud' (p.204) as neither of them had any fortune. But he had shown so much 'Affection' and 'Tenderness' (p.204) that Moll was ready to 'do anything that became me on my part, and that I would live as close and as narrow as he cou'd desire' (p.205). She also realized that 'he was not a Rake that made a Trade to delude Women .... but he was really a Gentleman .... a lovely Person indeed; of generous Principles, good sense and of abundance of good Humour'. (pp. 207-8). But he had to leave her in her own interest as he was a highway man with the police after him. So ended Moll's fourth marriage but it was a marriage which was *qualitatively* different from the others. In spite of the initial deception on both sides, she felt that they had developed deep affection and love for each other. He inspired feelings in her which none of her earlier husbands had done.

Moll's fifth marriage to the Bank Clerk comes just in time to save her from financial disaster. It was not altogether a marriage of convenience, as Shirlene Mason claims.[23] The man had known Moll for quite some time and they had also been lovers. He could not marry her earlier as he had a wife. But now he was free and keen to marry her. He met her on her way to London and stopped her there. They decided to stay for the night at an inn before going to London. There he got a parson and asked him to perform the ceremony of marriage. Moll protested against being married 'in an Inn, and at Night too'. But the parson removed her doubts:

> I assure you your Marriage will be as firm here as in the Church; we are not tyed by the Canons to Marry no where but in the Church; .... as for the time of Day it does not at all weigh in this Case; our Princes are married in their Chambers, and at Eight or Ten O'Clock at Night. (p.245).

At last the marriage took place and Moll tells us that she never lived 'four pleasanter Days together in my life' than the days spent on her honeymoon. 'I was a meer Bride all this while', she adds, 'and my new Spouse strove to make me entirely easie in every thing; O could this State of Life have continued! how had all my past Troubles been forgot, and my future Sorrows been avoided! (p.249). When they returned to London,

> I took Possession at once of a House well Furnish'd, and a Husband in very good Circumstances, so that I had a prospect of a very happy Life, if I knew how to manage it; and I had leisure to consider of the real Value of the Life I was likely to live; how different it was to be from the loose ungovern'd part I had acted before, and how much happier a Life of Virtue and Sobriety is, than that which we call a Life of Pleasure (p.250).

She also adds,

> I abhorr'd tne Levity and Extravagance of my former Life, so I chose now to live retir'd, frugal, and within our selves; I kept no Company, made no Visits, minded my Family, and oblig'd my Husband; and this kind of Life became a Pleasure to me. (p.251).

But unfortunately this husband also died after a period of five years. Thus ended Moll's fifth marriage. She was now 48 years of age and knew that at this age she could get neither a husband nor a lover who could maintain her. And yet the problem of sheer survival was as acute now as ever before. She struggled on in 'this dismal Condition' (p.253) for two to three years. Then began a period of her life about which she says:

> O let none read this part without seriously reflecting on the Circumstances of a desolate State, and how they would grapple with meer want of Friends and want of Bread; it will certainly make them think not of sparing what they have only, but of looking up to Heaven for support, and of the wise Man's Prayer, *Give me not Poverty lest I Steal*, (pp. 253-4).

This was her life as a thief and a casual prostitute. At last she was caught stealing two pieces of 'Brocaded Silk' (p. 347) from a warehouse and sent to Newgate. It was here that she met her fourth husband [her Lancashire husband], Jemy, again and discovered that their relationship was as warm as ever, in fact warmer. This is how Defoe describes their meeting in the prison:

> I threw off my Hood, and bursting out into Tears, *my Dear, says I, do you not know me*? He turn'd pale and stood Speechless, like one Thunder struck, and not able to conquer the Surprise, said no more but this, *let me sit down*; and sitting down by a Table, he laid his Elbow upon the Table, and leaning his Head on his Hand, fix'd his Eyes on the Ground as one stupid; I cry'd so vehemently, on the other Hand, that it was a good while e'er I could speak any more; but after I had given some vent to my Passion by Tears, I repeated the same WORDS: MY DEAR, *do you not know me*? at which he answer'd YES, and said no more a good while. (p.375).

They were both transported to Virginia where she discovered that her mother had died and husband/brother had become too old and partially blind but their son was there who received her very warmly. For the first time in her life, she behaves in a manner which was somewhat unusual for a woman of Moll's character. She becomes sentimental and kisses the ground her son had trodden. Ian Watt cannot reconcile this gesture with her normal attitude to her children - 'the majority are mentioned only to be forgotten, and, once left in the care of relatives or foster-mothers, are neither redeemed subsequently nor even enquired after when opportunity permits.[24] One explanation of this unusual behaviour could perhaps be the new situation in which she finds herself. There is another incident where her love for another child is quite real. Before she married the Bank Clerk, she 'was brought to Bed .... and had another brave Boy'. (p.231). This boy was a real hindrance to her marriage and she had to make some arrangement for his maintenance before leaving for London. She claims that

> I was not come up to that pitch of Hardness common to the Profession; I mean to be unnatural, and regardless of the Safety of my Child, and I preserv'd this honest Affection so long, that I was upon the Point of giving up my Friend at the Bank, who lay so hard at me to come to him and Marry him, that in short, there was hardly any room to deny him. (pp.236-7).

VI

Hagstrum in *Sex and Sensibility* describes Defoe as 'an admirable supporter of Woman's advancement and a portrayer of such persistent and invincible lovers as Moll Flanders and Roxana' but he claims that Defoe is

> fundamentally less concerned with either erotic or ideal love than with essentially prudential relationships. His women lovers, for all their experience, do not often—perhaps even—pledge the heart or the body to deep or lasting emotion; they remain the female equivalents of the *homo economicus* Robinson Crusoe.[25]

Roxana's considerations are, of course, always prudential but perhaps there is one case where Moll seems to rise above such considerations. It is difficult to say that her relationship with Jemy is necessarily guided by prudential considerations. In the beginning, of course, their marriage was a fraud on both sides but soon they realized that they were deeply in love with each other. This had never happened to Moll before and she now feels that she cannot afford to lose him. But, as we have seen, he is not in a position to stay with her. So in the interest of Moll herself, he decides to leave her. When the moment of his departure came, she

> 'fell into a vehement fit of crying, every now and then, calling him by Name, which was *James, Oh Jemy! come back, come back*, I will give you all I have, I'll beg, I'll starve with you'. (pp.210-11).

When this was happening he had already travelled about 12 miles from her. He unexpectedly returns and claims that he had heard her crying.

> 'You call'd aloud', he says, 'and said, *O Jemy! O Jemy! come back, come back*' (p.211). (Italics Defoe's).

Perhaps Charlotte Bronte had this scene in mind in *Jane Eyre* when Jane Eyre heard Rochester's call and rushed to meet him.

The case of Roxana is quite different. David Blewett has rightly said:

> The development and final shape of the novel is controlled by Roxana's choice between two paths in life; initially, virtuous poverty or sinful prosperity, then later, a respectable marriage or the glamorous but immoral life of a whore. Throughout the novel Roxana is torn between these alternatives, fatally tempted by wealth and flattery while yearning for respectability. (p.11).[26]

After her husband deserts her, she does not think of marrying again, as Moll Flanders had done even though her marriage was irregular. Novak rightly says that Moll is, 'at best, only half- hearted as a prostitute, always seeking a comfortable marriage as the solution to her problems. 'I understood too well', she remarks, 'by the want of it, what the Value of a settl'd Life was, to do anything to forfeit the felicity of it'. Roxana, on the other hand, becomes the 'Queen of Whores', and after her initial modesty is conquered seems to have been perfectly satisfied to remain in her profession'.[27]

It must, however, be admitted that her plea of necessity is quite genuine. After ruining the flourishing business of his father, her foolish husband had deserted her and her five children in abject poverty. She claims that

> if I had had one Child, or two Children, I would have done my Endeavour to have work'd for them with my Needle, ... but to think of one single Woman not bred to Work, and at a Loss where to get Employment, to get the Bread of five Children, that was not possible, some of my Children being young too, and none of them big enough to help one another. (p.48).

In this situation she is compelled to send four of her children to her husband's reluctant relatives and one to the parish in which he was born. She was not happy to part with her children like this but this was the only way to save them from starvation.

In these circumstances too, she was not willing to become her landlord's mistress. When Amy, her maid-servant, suggested this to ease the situation faced by her, she rejected the suggestion in very sharp terms:

> 'Why, Madam, *says Amy*, I hope you won't deny him, if he should offer it.
>
> What d'ye mean by that, *Hussy, said I*? No, I'd starve first.
>
> I hope not, Madam, I hope you would be wiser; I'm sure if he will set you up, as he talks of, you ought to deny him nothing; and you will starve if you do not consent, that's certain.
>
> What, consent to lye with him for Bread? *Amy, said I*, how can you talk so?
>
> Nay, Madam, *says Amy*, I don't think you wou'd for any

> thing else; it would not be Lawful for any thing else, but for Bread, Madam: why nobody can starve, there's no bearing that, I'm sure. (p.61).

It would, of course, be misleading to suggest that Roxana accepted to become the landlord's mistress without giving thought to the immorality of the action. She had been brought up as a gentlewoman and she knew the rules of conduct laid down for middle class young women in such matters. Such explains:

> Hitherto I had not only preserv'd the Virtue itself, but the virtuous Inclination and Resolution; .... for, without question, a Woman ought rather to die, than to prostitute her Virtue and Honour, let the Temptation be what it will. (pp.62-63).

But her circumstances were such that she had no option but to accept the advice of her maid-servant, Amy:

> he calls you Widow, and such, indeed, you are; for as my Master has left you so many Years, he is dead to be sure; at least, he is dead to you; he is no Husband, you are, and ought to be free to marry who you will; and his Wife being gone from him, and refuses to lye with him, then he is a single Man again, as much as ever; and tho' you cannot bring the Laws of the Land to join you together, yet one refusing to do the Office of a Wife, and the other of a Husband, you may certainly take one another fairly. (p.71).

Later in her life Roxana regretted having followed Amy's advice but she offered the following explanation:

> I had strong Natural Aversions to the Crime at first, partly owing to a virtuous Education, and partly to a Sence of Religion; but the Devil, and that greater Devil of Poverty, prevail'd, and the Person who laid Siege to me, did it in such on obliging, and I may almost say, irresistible Manner, all still manag'd by

> the Evil Spirit; for I must be allow'd to believe, that he has a Share in all such things, if not the whole Management of them. These Circumstances, I say, the Devil manag'd not only to bring me to comply, but he continued them as Arguments to fortify my Mind against all Reflection, and to keep me in that horrid Course, I had engag'd in, as if it were honest and lawful.

Her lack of desire or enthusiasm at the time of her surrender to the landlord is more than evident from the following:

> I had nothing of the Vice in my Constitution; my Spirits were far from being high; my Blood had no Fire in it, to kindle the Flame of Desire; but the kindness and good Humour of the Man, and *the Dread of my own Circumstances* concurr'd to bring me to the Point, and I even resolv'd, before he ask'd, to give up my Virtue to him, whenever he should put it to the Question. (p.75) (Italics mine).

She is, however, clear that she is making the choice of 'sinful prosperity' with open eyes:

> And thus in Gratitude for the Favours I receiv'd from a Man, was all Sence of Religion, and Duty to God, all Regard to Virtue and Honour, given up at once, and we were to call one another Man and Wife, who, in the Sence of the Laws, both of God and our Country, were no more than two Adulterers, in short, a Whore and a Rogue. (p.78).

The landlord is a rich jeweller and life with him not only satisfies all her needs but also her vanity. This is the first time that some one has been in love with her. Her husband had been not only a fool but a 'conceited fool' who was incapable of loving any one but himself. But she is still 'young, handsome' and, as she says, 'vain, and that not a little; and as it was a new thing, so it was a pleasant thing, to be courted, caress'd, embrac'd, and high Professions of Affection made to me by a Man so agreeable, and so able to do me good'. (p.73). He gives evidence of his seriousness of affection by offering

> 'a Contract in Writing, wherein he engag'd himself to me; to cohabit constantly with me; to provide for me in all Respects as a Wife; and repeating in the Preamble, a long Account of the Nature and Reason of our living together, and an Obligation in the Penalty of 7000 l. never to abandon me; and at last, shew'd me a Bond for 500 l. to be paid to me, or to my Assigns, within three Months after his Death. (p.76).

There are times, however, when she regrets that she accepted this kind of life. They, of course, 'liv'd as merrily, and as happily, after this as cou'd be expected, considering our Circumstances; but as much as I was harden'd, and that was as much, as I believe, ever any wicked Creature was, yet I could not help it; there was, and would be, Hours of Intervals, and of dark Reflections which came involuntarily in, and thrust in Sighs into the middle of all my Songs; and there would be, sometimes, a heaviness of Heart, which intermingl'd itself with all my Joy, and which would often fetch a Tear from my Eye; and let others pretend what they will, I believe it impossible to be otherwise with any-body; there can be no substantial Satisfaction in a Life of known Wickedness; Conscience will, and does, often break in upon them at particular times, let them do what they can to prevent it.' (p.83).

We should also remember that her conscience also troubles her because of what she has done to her maid-servant, Amy. She gets so steeped in lust herself that she makes Amy also her sharer in 'sin'. She tells us that one evening '.... I sat her down, pull'd off her Stockings and Shoes and all her clothes, Piece by Piece, and led her to the Bed of him .... I fairly strip'd her, and then I threw open the Bed, and thrust her in'; 'I stood by all the while'. (p.81). Everet Zimmerman has said that 'Roxana's corruption of Amy is the archetypal sin of the book. She destroys Amy's autonomy, making Amy one with her morally and sexually'.[28] He adds: 'In this last novel, evil is obscurely but persistently present .... Her hatred of her daughter Susan and maid Amy's murder of the girl are the final and compelling testimonies to Roxana's identification with the malevolent world that she sees'.[29]

VII

After living as the jeweller's mistress for over two years, she went with him to Paris. There they took a good house and, Roxana claims, she lived 'in a very good Figure, and might have liv'd higher if I pleas'd'. (p.86). But 'in the middle of all this Felicity, a dreadful Disaster' (p.86) took place. Her lover who used to deal with 'some Persons of the First Rank, and to whom he had sold some Jewels of very good Value' (p.85), was robbed and killed when he was going to Versailles to wait upon the Prince of .... After his death Roxana inherited his entire property as she claimed to be his legally wedded wife. Though the jeweller's death was a great blow, it had left Roxana much richer than ever. Moreover, this caused the Prince to visit her to pay his condolences. He was so struck by her beauty that he called her the most beautiful woman in France. Soon they became lovers and this suited Roxana eminently. She has the following explanation to give in her defence:

> I had now no Poverty attending me; on the contrary, I was Mistress of ten Thousand Pounds before the Prince did any thing for me; had I been Mistress of my Resolution; had I been less obliging, and rejected the first Attack, all had been safe, but my Virtue was lost before, and the Devil, who had found the Way to break-in upon me by one Temptation, easily master'd me now, by another; and I gave myself up to a Person, who, tho' a Man of high Dignity, was yet the most tempting and obliging, that ever I met with in my Life. (p.100).

She also adds:

> as it was all irresistable, so it was all lawful; for that Heaven would not suffer us to be punish'd for that which it was not

> possible for us to avoid; and with these Absurdities I kept Conscience from giving me any considerable Disturbance in all this Matter; and I was as perfectly easie as to the Lawfulness of it, as if I had been Marry'd to the Prince, and had had no other Husband. (p.105).

The affair with the Prince came to an end only when the Princess - an unhappy woman - died. This brought about a big change in 'the general Conduct' of the Prince's life. He resolved 'on a Life regulated most strictly by the Rules of Virtue, and Piety; and in a word, was quite another Man'. (p.147). This, of course, was a great loss for Roxana. But she was a very rich woman - very rich indeed - and all she needed was some one who could convey her jewels and bills of money safely to London. Thus she met her third lover, the Duch Merchant.

The affair between Roxana and the Duch Merchant embodies the central theme of the novel. It is partly anticipated by Roxana's reaction to Amy's information that her first husband had died and now she was free to marry again. Roxana emphatically rejects the idea of marriage:

> I had no inclination to be a Wife again. I had had such bad luck with my first Husband, I hated the Thoughts of it; I found, that a Wife is treated with Indifference, a Mistress with a strong Passion; a Wife is look'd upon, as but an Upper-Servant, a Mistress is a Sovereign; a Wife must give up all she has; ... whereas a Mistress makes the Saying true, *that what the Man has, is hers, and what she has, is her own*; (Italics Defoe's) the Wife bears a thousand Insults, and is forc'd to sit still and bear it, or part and be undone; a Mistress insulted, helps herself immediately, and takes another. (pp. 170-1).

She calls these 'Arguments for Whoring' 'wicked', (p.171) but more serious than wicked is the charge that they are absurd. Katherine Rogers has argued that 'Roxana is a helpless victim as long as she remains faithful to her first husband. Only when she has cast off all concern for chastity and reputation is she *completely free to direct her life as she sees fit*'.[30] (Italics mine). But is she *really free* to reshape her life as she chooses? It is true that married women in that period suffered from many disabilities, the chief of them - in Roxana's eyes - being the law that prohibited married women from owning any property. Some women in real distress might have even become 'whores' as Roxana did when her husband deserted her. But how many women in their senses would have preferred the life of a 'whore' to the life of a wife? Roxana herself realizes her folly later on when at one stage she says: 'was ever Woman so stupid to choose to be a Whore, where she might have been an honest Wife?' (p.197).

The real superiority of the life of an honest wife is her *respectability* in her society which Roxana hankers after and which no 'whore', however rich, would ever get. As she admits:

> A Wife appears boldly and honourably with her Husband; lives at Home, and possesses his House, his Servants, his Epuipages, and has a Right to them all, and to call them her own; entertains his friends, owns his Children, and has the return of Duty and Affection from them, as they are here her own, and claims upon his Estate, by the Custom of *England*, if he dies, and leaves her a Widow. (p.171).

But in the case of a 'whore', the real problem is, as in Roxana's own case, that 'If she has any Children, her Endeavour is to get rid of them, and not maintain them; and if she lives, she is certain to see them all hate her, and be asham'd of her'. (p.171). Roxana's children link her to her past and that is precisely what she wants to conceal. In fact, her daughter Susan from her first husband now becomes a real threat to her. She knows that if her past comes to be known to her husband, she would be ruined. Amy and Roxana, therefore, make desperate efforts to hide themselves from the girl. But that is not easy as the girl chases her mother 'as if, like a *Hound*, she had had a hot Scent' (p.366). At last, in sheer desperation, Amy murders her. But this was too much for Roxana who says that it was done without her knowledge. Irrespective of the nature of her involvement in her daughter's murder, 'the Blast of Heaven seem'd to follow the Injury done the poor Girl, by us both'. (p.379). How their unhappy lives ended we are not told but it is clear that we have in this novel 'Defoe's most extreme expression of the isolation'[31] that a human being can be reduced to. Perhaps that is the final fruit of adultery in her society.

In *Roxana*, Defoe raises some disturbing questions about marriage in his times. Roxana claims: 'The opposite Circumstances of a *Wife* and *Whore*, are such, and so many, and I have since seen the Difference with such Eyes, as I cou'd dwell upon the Subject a great-while'. (p.171). But apart from her first marriage in which she is not *shown* as 'a helpless victim', as Katharine Rogers claims, she has known no other marriage. Her first husband was, of course, a fool and he was not capable of running a business. Nor had he the courage to face bankruptcy and disgrace. So, like all cowards, he deserted his wife and five children and escaped to another country. But at no stage is he *shown* as cruel or Roxana as unhappy. Her unhappiness starts only after his desertion - indeed after a year or two when she discovers that she is now faced with starvation. We may ask why after disposing of her children - however painful the decision had been - she chose the profession of a whore. Even if we concede that her need was so great at that point of time that she had no option, but she could have changed her way of life after she had become rich. In fact, after the death of the jeweller, she could have returned to England and settled down as the wife of an English gentleman. Her real weakness seems to be her vanity and her love of glamour. In a perceptive passage, she analyses her case thus:

> *Why am I a Whore now*? Nor indeed, had I any-thing to say for myself, *even to myself*; I cou'd not without blushing, as wicked as I was, answer, that I lov'd it for the sake of the Vice, and that I delighted in being a Whore, *as such*; I say, I cou'd not say this, even to myself, *and all alone*, nor indeed, wou'd it have been true; I was never able in Justice, and with Truth, to say I was so wicked as that; but as Necessity first debauch'd me, and Poverty made me a Whore at the Beginning; so *excess of Avarice for*

> *getting Money, and excess of Vanity*, (Italics mine), continued me in the Crime, not being able to resist the Flatteries of Great Persons; being call'd the finest Woman in *France*; being caress'd by a Prince; and afterwards I had Pride enough to expect, and Folly enough to believe, tho' indeed, without ground, by a Great Monarch: These were my Baits, these the Chains by which the Devil held me bound; and by which I was indeed, too fast held for any Reasoning that I was then Mistress of, to deliver me from. (pp.244-5).

VIII

Moll's attempt at every stage in her life was, as we have seen, to have a settled married life. As she asserted: 'I kept true to this Notion, that a Woman should never be kept for a Mistress, that had Money to make her self a Wife'. As if in direct reply, Roxana announced: 'I added, that whoever the Woman was, that had an Estate, and would give it up to be the Slave of a *Great Man*, that Woman was a Fool, and must be fit for nothing but a Beggar; that it was my Opinion, a Woman was a fit to govern and enjoy her own Estate, without a Man, as a Man was, without a Woman; and that, if she had a-mind to gratify herself as to Sexes, she might entertain a Man, as a man does a Mistress'. (p.188).[32]

Clearly Roxana is demanding something that no married woman was permitted to have in the 18th century - or even today in most societies. A rich woman could, of course, 'govern and enjoy her own Estate, without a Man' but no sexual freedom could be granted to her as it was incompatible with marriage and family life. Men had much greater freedom in this respect. In his *Advice to his Daughter* (1688), Lord Halifax conceded that this double standard was a great injustice to women but he gave an explanation of this 'injustice' which was accepted not only by his own age but has been accepted by most ages and cultures. 'The root and the excuse of this injustice', he said, 'is the preservation of families from any mixture which may bring a blemish to them'.[33] In the 18th century, Dr. Johnson's explanation of the double standard is more or less the same as that of Lord Halifax. He regards female chastity as of the utmost importance because 'upon that all the property in the world depends'. For the preservation of 'property', legitimacy of children is essential and since female adultery causes 'confusion of progeny', 'a woman who breaks her marriage vows is much more criminal than a man who does it'. Man was, of course, 'criminal in the sight of God' but he 'imposed no bastards upon his wife'.[34]

Roxana's protest against the injustice that was done to women by contemporary laws concerning marriage is, of course, perfectly justified:

> That the very Nature of the Marriage-Contract was, in short, nothing but giving up Liberty, Estate, Authority, and everything, to the Man, and the Woman was indeed, a meer Woman ever after, that is to say, a Slave. (p.187).

The Dutch Merchant who wants to marry her agrees with her but defends the institution of marriage in traditional terms:

> that tho' in some Respects it was as I had said, yet I ought to consider, that as an Equivalent to this, the Man had all the Care of things devolv'd upon him; that the Weight of Business lay upon his Shoulders, and as he had the Trust, so he had the Toil of Life upon him, his was the Labour, his the Anxiety of Living; that the Woman had nothing to do, but to eat the Fat, and drink the Sweet; to sit still, and look round her; be waited on, and made much of; be serv'd, and lov'd, and made easie; *especially if the Husband acted as became him*; and that, in general, the Labour of the Man was appointed to make the Woman live quiet and unconcern'd in the World; that they had the Name of Subjection, without the Thing; and if in inferiour Families, they had the Drudgery of the House, and Care of the Provisions upon them; yet they had indeed, much the easier Part, for in general, the Women had only the Care of managing, that is, spending what their Husbands get; and that a Woman had the Name of Subjection indeed, but that they generally commanded not the

> Men only, but all they had; manag'd all for themselves, and where the Man did his Duty, the Woman's Life was all Ease and Tranquillity; and that she had nothing to do but to be easie, and to make all that were about her both easie and merry. (pp. 187-8).

Roxana in a sense covers her own case after her first husband deserted her:

> the Pretence of Affection, takes from a Woman every thing that can be call'd *herself*; she is to have no Interest; no Aim; no View; but all is the Interest, Aim, and View, of the Husband; she is to be the passive Creature you spoke of, *said I*; she is to lead a Life of perfect Indolence, and living by Faith (not in God, but) in her Husband, she sinks or swims, as he is either Fool or wise Man; unhappy or prosperous; and in the middle of what she thinks is her Happiness and Prosperity, she is ingulph'd in Misery and Beggary, which she had not the least Notice, Knowledge, or Suspicion of. (p.189).

Katharine Rogers says:

> Mary Astell and Richardson suggested that a woman might have reason to prefer celibacy to marriage, but only Defoe created heroines who attained true independence - casting off the moral inhibitions laid on women in order to support themselves economically and to control their relationships with men. By setting his female protagonists in situations where they had to fend for themselves, Defoe demonstrated his confidence that they could do so. His heroines remain exhilarating because they live with an independence unequalled in their own time and far from general even in our own.[35]

It is difficult to accept the view that Defoe 'created heroines who attained true independence'. What kind of a true independence it is where a daughter from an earlier marriage has to be killed to save the woman's present marriage? Moreover, these women belong to the underworld and however hard they may try - and however rich they may become - they would never be accepted by society. Moll Flanders was lucky that her son accepted her but that was in a foreign country and her son knew almost nothing about her past. In that age, only marriage could provide financial security to women and if a woman violated her marriage vows and indulged in what we call sexual freedom, she had to deny herself the benefits provided by normal family life.

NOTES

1. Daniel Defoe, *An Essay Upon Projects* (1697), the Facsimile of the original text produced by the Scolar Press, 1969, p.285.
2. Ibid., p.282.
3. Ibid., pp.302-3.
4. Lawrence Stone, *The Crisis of Aristocracy 1558-1641* (Oxford, 1967), (abridged edition), p.298.
5. Sir Keith Thomas, "The Double Standard", *Journal of the History of Ideas*, XX (1959), p.195.
6. See Joseph Crutch, *Comedy and Conscience after the Restoration* (New York, 1924), p.29.
7. See John Robert Moore, *Daniel Defoe: Citizen of the Modern World* (University of Chicago Press, (1958), p.25.
8. Lawrence Stone, *Broken Lives: Separation and Divorce in England 1660-1857* (Oxford, 1993), pp.27-28.
9. *Conjugal Lewdness*, a Facsimile Reproduction with an Introduction by Maximillian E. Novak (1967), p.33. Subsequent references are to this edition.
10. Lawrence Stone, *Uncertain Unions: Marriage in England 1660-1753* (Oxford University Press, 1992), pp. 12-13.
11. *Ibid.*, p.30.
12. *Ibid.*, p.31.
13. *Moll Flanders,* edited by Juliet Michell (Penguin Classics, 1978), p.10.
14. Arnold Kettle's quotation is taken from his piece 'Moll Flanders' in *Of Books and Human Kind* ed. John Butt, London, 1964.
15. Ernest Baker, *The History of the English Novel* (Volume III), 1929, p.191.
16. James Sutherland, *Daniel Defoe: A Critical Study* (Harvard University Press, Cambridge, Mass., 1971), pp.179-180.
17. John Robert Moore, p.244.
18. All quotations are taken from the Penguin Classics edition of *Moll Flanders* ed. David Blewett (1989).
19. Maximillian E. Novak, *Defoe and the Nature of Man* (Oxford University

Press, 1963), pp.100-1.

20. *The Rise of the Novel* (Pelican Book, 1957), p.105.
21. Dorothy Van Ghent, *The English Novel: Form and Function*, (Harper & Row, N.Y., 1961), p. 37.
22. *Ibid.*, p. 34.
23. *Daniel Defoe and the Status of Women* (1978), p. 51.
24. Ian Watt, *The Rise of the Novel* (Pelican Book, 1957), pp.123- 4.
25. Jean H. Hagstrum, *Sex and Sensibility: Ideal and Erotic Love from Milton to Mozart* (University of Chicago Press, Chicago and London, 1980), p.16.
26. *Roxana: The Fortunate Mistress*, ed. David Blewett (Penguin Classics, 1982), p.11.
    All quotations are taken from this edition of *Roxana*.
27. *Op. cit.*, p.83.
28. Everet Zimmerman, *Defoe and the Novel* (Berkeley, 1975), p.169.
29. *Ibid.*, p.156.
30. "The Feminism of Daniel Defoe", *Women in 18th Century and Other Essays* ed. Paul Fritzk and Richard Mortan (Toronto, 1976), p.18.
31. Zimmerman, p.180.
32. See Spiro Peterson, "The Matrimonial Theme of Defoe's *Roxana*", *PMLA* (1955), p.167.
33. *Lord Halifax: Complete Works* ed. J. P. Kenyon (London, 1969), p.279.
34. Cited by Keith Thomas, "The Double Standard", *Journal of the History of Ideas* XX (1959), p.209.
35. Katharine Rogers, pp.23-4.

Chapter III

Samuel Richardson: *Pamela*

In her Introduction to *Pamela* in Penguin Classics (1980), Margaret A. Doody says:

> The novel is revolutionary in its depths, not just on the surface, though there are overt statements which have far-reaching significance. When Pamela says 'my *soul* is of equal importance with the soul of a princess', she is, as Roger Sharrock points out, making an obvious Christian statement, and the statement has social implications. Pamela is threatened by Mr. B., who uses and abuses his power as a man, as an employer, and as member of the governing class. He is the local J. P., so Pamela cannot turn to the law because her oppressor *is* the law. He subjects her to a form of imprisonment, and threatens rape. The novel is constructed out of Pamela's power of defiance. (pp. 8-9).

Richardson shows how far the power of defiance of a maid-servant can go. Her parents are poor who have sent the girl far away from home to serve the mother of Squire B. She is only 15 years of age but she is intelligent and quickly learns her duties. Mr. B.'s mother is so pleased with her that she teaches her many skills - including reading and writing - that only gentlewomen were supposed to learn in that age. Before her death, the old lady tells her son, 'My dear son! .... remember my poor Pamela'.[1]

Even when his mother was alive, Mr. B. was quite struck by

Pamela's beauty, but he was not free to take any liberties with her. After her death, he felt free to make advances to her. After all, it was happening all around him and, as Janet Todd has said, 'numerous maids were deflowered by masters in the first half of the eighteenth century'.[2]

Indeed, it was the assumption of most men in aristocratic families that such girls existed for the 'sexual convenience'[3] of their masters. Janet Todd adds that 'while describing his new pious ideology of service, Richardson uncovered a psychology of servitude that wickedly allowed the social terms - maid, master and mistress - to assume for a while their sexual meaning'.[4] Pamela understands only the social meaning of these terms and she is prepared to play her role as a maid-servant competently.

It is worth recalling that in earlier times, the master was regarded as a benefactor and protector and, in fact, as a substitute for a parent as servants too were often treated as members of the family whose welfare was the responsibility of the head of the family. Even Pamela's parents were of the view that her master had 'the *power* to oblige' and 'a kind of *authority* to command'.[5] Of course, the assumption was that such servants served the family for loyalty and not for pay.

But by the eighteenth century, this view of service had undergone a change. Reverend John Trusler said in the 1780s, that 'to expect attachment from a servant is idle, and betrays an ignorance of the world'.[6] Trusler's statement is prompted by the new view of domestic service where servants worked for pay and not for loyalty. The effect of this was that servants 'stayed on average as little as three or four years with an employer'.[7]

Under the old system where a servant was almost a permanent member of the household, the common view was that the master was a protector of a maid's honour. In *Pamela*, both views of service are present. Pamela has never been paid any regular pay but she has been treated very well and had indeed become a favourite of Mr. B.'s mother. As Mr. B. himself says, '*for my mother's sake*, I will be a friend to you' (Italics mine). Pamela, of course, has no idea that there is a big difference between the old code of conduct of masters and Mr. B.'s code. The moment she realizes that for him the old social terms - master and maid - have acquired a new dimension, a sexual dimension, where the maid also becomes the mistress of the master, she protests.

I

Mr. B's intentions become clear to Pamela when he comes to her in the summer house in the little garden. She hurriedly tries to leave but he stops her:

> 'No, don't go, Pamela; I have something to say to you: and you always fly me when I come near you, as if you were afraid of me.'
>
> I was much out of countenance, you may well think; but said at last, 'It does not become your poor servant to stay in your presence, Sir, without your business required it; and I hope I shall always know my place'.
>
> 'Well,' says he, 'my business does require it sometimes, and I have a mind you should stay to hear what I have to say to you'. (Vol. I, p. 11).

He then asks her whether she would like to go to his sister Lady Davers who had herself told her brother that since there was no lady in the house, she would be safer with her. But before Pamela can reply, he tells her that 'she would not do for you what I am resolved to do, if you continue faithful and obliging'. When she tells him that she would prefer to wait upon Lady Davers, he shouts:

> you are a little fool, and know not what's good for yourself. I tell you I will make a gentlewoman of you, if you be obliging, and don't stand in your own light;' and so saying, he puts his arm about me, and kissed me!
>
> ... I struggled and trembled, and was so benumbed with terror, that I sunk down, not in a fit, and yet not myself; and I found myself in his arms, quite void of strength, and he kissing

> me two or three times with frightful eagerness. At last I burst from him, and was getting out of the summer-house, but he held me back, and shut the door.
>
> I would have given my life for a farthing. And he said, 'I'll do you no harm, Pamela; don't be afraid of me'. I said, 'I won't stay', — 'You won't, hussey!' said he: 'do you know whom you speak to?' I lost all fear and all respect, and said, 'Yes, I do, Sir, too well! Well may I forget that I am your servant, when you forget what belongs to a master'.
>
> I sobbed and cried most sadly — 'What a foolish hussey you are!', said he; 'have I done you any harm?' 'Yes, Sir,' said I, 'the greatest harm in the world: you have taught me to forget myself, and what belongs to me, and have lessened the distance that fortune has made between us, by demeaning yourself, to be so free to a poor servant. Yes, Sir, I will be bold to say, I am honest, though poor: and if you was a prince I would not be otherwise.' (Vol. I, pp. 11-12).

Next time, when he makes another attempt, he again raises the question of her 'duty' to her master:

> I fell down on my knees, and said, 'For heaven's sake, your honour, pity a poor creature, that knows nothing of her duty, but how to cherish her virtue and good name! I have nothing else to trust to; and, though poor and friendless, yet I have always been taught to value honesty above my life'. — 'Here's ado with your honesty', said he, 'foolish girl! Is it not one part of honesty to be dutiful and grateful to your master, do you think?' — 'Indeed, Sir,' said I, 'it is impossible I should be ungrateful to your honour, or disobedient, ... but when your commands are contrary to that first duty which shall ever be the principle of my life'. (Vol. 1, p. 19).

When he 'by force kissed my neck and lips' and 'then put his hand in my bosom' she

> got loose from him by a sudden spring, and ran out of the room; and the next chamber being open, I entered it, shut to the door, and it locked after me: but he followed me so close, he got hold of my gown, and tore a piece off, which hung without the door; for the key was on the inside. .... (Vol. 1, p. 20).

Such conduct on the part of Pamela exasperates him and he decides to give her notice and 'resolved she shall return to the distress and poverty she was taken from'. (p. 24).

It is clear that Mr. B. finds Pamela's conduct inexplicable. Maid servants did not behave the way she did and they did not spurn their master's advances as Pamela had done. Mr. B. calls her 'a strange girl' and claims that he 'knew not what to make of [her]'. He also says that he 'never met with the fellow of her in [his] life' (Vol. 1, p. 26). Mrs. Jervis also says: 'Pretty face, where gottest thou all thy knowledge, and thy good notions, at these years. Thou art a miracle for thy age, and I shall always love thee' (p. 27). Richardson's view of virtue may, of course, be somewhat narrow and too self-righteous and Pamela may also be accused of flaunting her virginity a little too aggressively. But Arnold Kettle's view that '*Pamela* remains only a record of a particularly loathsome aspect of bourgeois morality'[8] is too extreme. It also seems to ignore the historical fact that in that age loss of virginity could be ruinous for girls of all classes.

David Daiches also condemns Richardson for his 'narrow and mechanical view of sex, and indeed of love'. 'The notion of mutual sexual satisfaction', he says, 'never seems to have occurred to him. None of Richardson's rakes seeks such satisfaction; they want to rape; they are not sensualists but competitive collectors of virginities by violence. In *Clarissa*, Lovelace achieves his nefarious purpose on a drugged and passive victim. It is a purely quantitative business, a matter of arithmetic; the more people you can violate, the greater your glory as a rake.'[9]

Pamela's originality as a comic heroine lies in the extraordinary importance that she attaches to her virginity.

Ian Watt has said:

> There is, of course, nothing inherently new in making a fictional heroine regard her chastity as a supreme value; what was new was that Richardson attributed such motives to a servant-girl: for whereas romance had usually exalted feminine chastity, the other forms of fiction which dealt with characters of humbler social origins had tended to take an opposite view of feminine psychology.[10]

Loss of chastity is, of course, a disaster for a middle-class girl but Richardson propounds the view which was quite radical in those times — or even today — that it is no less disastrous for servant-girls. Lawrence Stone says:

> 'Without protection from parents, kin, neighbours, ministers or local opinion, these girls were easy victims of seduction by their masters who then dismissed them when they became pregnant'.[11]

What would happen to these girls then? The babies to whom they gave birth were often killed by them and their bodies thrown into gutters. There is evidence that sometimes dead bodies of babies were picked up by the police from London streets. Or these girls died in child-birth, or committed suicide or became prostitutes. Their families in any case would not accept them and they could not get shelter anywhere else. It need not surprise us that Pamela's pious father says that if his daughter is not honest (i.e., chaste), 'poor as I am, I would not own her'. (Vol. 1, p. 261). Some clever girls did escape such fate. Lawrence Stone mentions the case of Reverend Thomas Goodmin who in 1767 was known to have seduced his maids. One maid left 'alleging that her master had offered her five guineas to sleep with him, and when she refused and gave him a black eye, he offered her ten guineas to keep her mouth shut about the episode'.[12]

II

When Pamela shares with Mrs. Jervis her anxiety about her fate,

Mrs. Jervis tries to comfort her. She knows the master well and she perhaps understands his present state of mind better than any one else:

> My master is a fine gentleman; he has a great deal of wit and sense, and is admired, as I know, by half a dozen ladies, who would think themselves happy in his addresses. He has a noble estate; and *yet I believe he loves you, though his servant, better than all the ladies in the land*; he has tried to overcome it, because you are so much his inferior; and it is my opinion he finds he can't; and that vexes his proud heart, and makes him resolve you shan't stay: and so he speaks so cross to you when he sees you by accident'. (Italics mine) (Vol. 1, pp. 28-9).

But this hardly solves Pamela's problem. She knows that she cannot afford to respond to her master's love as this could ruin her life. So she says:

> 'Well, but, Mrs. Jervis,' said I, 'let me ask you, if he can stoop to like such a poor girl as me, as perhaps he may (for I have read of things almost as strange, from great men to poor damsels), what can it be *for*? He may condescend, perhaps to think I may be good enough for his harlot; and those things don't disgrace men, that ruin poor women, as the world goes. (Vol. 1, p. 29).

In the meantime Mr. B. is quite troubled in mind. When he happens to see her, he asks her:

> 'Pamela!' said he, 'how long are *you* to stay here?' — 'Only, please your honour,' said I, 'till I have done the waistcoat; and it is almost finished.' — 'You might,' says he very roughly, 'have finished that long ago'. — 'Indeed, and please your honour,' said I, 'I have worked early and late upon it: there is a great deal of work in it.' — '*Work in it*!' said he; 'you mind your pen more than your needle; I don't want such idle sluts to

stay in my house'. (Vol. 1, p. 35).

Pamela's comment on her master's impatience makes it clear that she fully understands the situation:

> Is it not strange that love borders so much upon hate? But this wicked love is not like the true virtuous love, to be sure: *that* and *hatred* must be far off as *light* and *darkness*. And how must this hate have been increased if he had met with a base compliance, after his wicked will had been gratified! (Vol. 1, p. 40).

She recognises that the safest course of action for her is to leave for her parents' home. In order to prepare herself for life there, she buys some sad-looking stuff from a farmer's family to prepare a dress for herself. She knows that it would suit her better in her father's house. She put on this new dress 'and looked in the glass, as proud as anything. To say truth, I never liked myself so well in my life'. (Vol. 1, p. 42). Then she went down to Mrs. Jervis who was amazed at this transformation of Pamela. But her master suddenly appeared. He, of course, recognises her but he starts to play with her. He asks Mrs. Jervis:

> "But, pray, what pretty neat damsel was with you? .... I never saw her before. ....
>
> I dropt a low curtsey, but said never a word. I dare say he knew me as soon as he saw my face; but was as cunning as Lucifer. He came up to me, and took me by the hand, and said, "Whose pretty maiden are you? I dare say you are Pamela's sister, you are so like her. So neat, so clean, so pretty! Why, child, you far surpass your sister Pamela!"
>
> I was all confusion, and would have spoken, but he took me about the neck: "Why," said he, "you are very pretty, child: I would not be so free with your *sister*, you may believe; but I must kiss *you*." — "O Sir," said I, "I am Pamela, indeed I am: indeed I am Pamela, *her own-self*!"
>
> He kissed me for all I could do: and said, "Impossible! you

> are a lovelier girl by half than Pamela; and sure I may be innocently free with *you*, though I would not do her so much favour.' .....
>
> He then took me in his arms, and presently pushed me from him. "Mrs. Jervis," said he, "take the little witch from me; I can neither bear nor forbear her!" — Strange words these! — "But stay; you shan't go! — Yet begone! — No, come back again." (Vol. I, pp. 43-44).

But, of course, he does not want her to go. He makes another attempt. But again he is prevented - this time by Mrs. Jervis who tells him:

> "You shall not hurt this innocent," said she; "for I will lose my life in her defence. Are there not," said she, "enough wicked ones in the world, for your base purpose, but you must attempt such a lamb as this?" (Vol. I, p. 50).

He threatens to dismiss Mrs. Jervis and then says what is really insulting that they should both go and 'take a house in London, and let lodgings to us members of Parliament, when we come to town; and such a pretty daughter as you may pass for, will fill her house, and she's to get a great deal of money.' (Vol. I, p. 55). This stings Pamela and she says:

> permit me to say, that if you were not rich and great, and I poor and little, you would not insult me thus. Let me ask you, Sir, if you think this becomes your fine clothes, and a master's station?" — "Why so serious, my pretty Pamela?" said he: "why so grave?" And would kiss me; but my heart was full, and I said, "Let me alone; I *will* tell you, if you were a king, and insulted me as you have done, that you have forgot to act like a gentleman; and I won't stay to be used thus." (Vol. I, p. 56).

It is such situations which make Terry Eagleton's remark very apt:

> *Pamela* is a sickly celebration of male ruling class power; but it is also a fierce polemic against the prejudice that the most inconspicuous serving maid cannot be as humanly valuable as her social superiors.[13]

We might add that 'the most inconspicuous serving maid' *can* be superior to almost all her 'social superiors' as Pamela clearly is. Indeed, against Richardson's avowed intention, he is here not a defender of the status quo. The novel poses a real threat to social hierarchy and those of Richardson's contemporaries who saw a 'leveling' tendency in the novel were not too wrong. As if to protect himself against this charge, Richardson made Pamela say: 'it is my absolute opinion, that degrees in general should be kept up.' (Vol. II, p. 168). But she says it in Part II of the novel by which time, in Eagleton's words, she has been 'snatched into the ruling class and tamed to its sexist disciplines.'[14]

III

Having failed in all his grand designs to seduce her, Mr. B. plans to rape her. Since it is not possible to do so in his present house where all the servants - and specially Mrs. Jervis - would try to protect her, he finally decides to send her to his estate in Lincolnshire. There she is kept like a prisoner under the supervision of the cruel Mrs. Jewkes. The place is safe for rape - so safe indeed that Pamela can get no assistance from any quarter. Indeed, one quarter from which she hoped to get some help is a neighbour - Sir Simon Darnford - whose wife is known to be a good woman and who has got 'two daughters, virtuous young ladies'. But he gives a reply which is shattering: 'Why, what is all this, my dear, but that our neighbour has a mind to his mother's waiting maid! And if he takes care she wants for nothing, I don't see any great injury will be done her. He hurts no *family* by this.' (Vol. I, p. 116). Clearly, according to Sir Simon, the poor have no right to protect their chastity nor indeed are they supposed to have any family honour! It is only proper that Richardson puts this insulting sentiment in the mouth of a vulgar man who earns Pamela's contempt.

In this context, we may recall Pamela's reaction to Mrs. Jewkes' argument that Mr. B., as her master, has a complete control over her and 'to rob him of yourself, would be the worst that could happen to him, in his opinion':

> "And pray", said I, ... "how came I to be his property? What rights has he in me, but such as a thief may plead to stolen goods?" — "Why, was ever the like heard?" says she, "This is downright rebellion, I protest!" (Vol. I, p. 108).

As Margaret Anne Doody says,

> Pamela is a downright rebel. .... It is Pamela's steadfast demand for *freedom*, despite the disabilities involved in being female, poor, and of low station, that makes her such a revolutionary heroine — and aroused the suspicion and hostility of some members of the Establishment.[15]

Brissenden has also emphasised this characteristic of Richardson's heroines. 'Richardson's heroines,' he says, 'are all democracts : their most fundamental desire is that their suitors should 'respect' them; that is, should accord them their rights as individual human beings before beginning to treat them as women.'[16]

Pamela's attitude is clear from what she says to Mr. B.:

> Whatever you have to propose, whatever you intend by me, let my assent be that of a *free* person, and not of a sordid slave, who is to be threatened and frightened into a compliance with measures, which your conduct seems to imply. (Italics mine), (Vol. I, p. 121).

As if in despair, he asks whether she prefers any other man to him. She frankly tells him that she has never given "the least encouragement" to any man. In fact, her problem is:

> 'I know not the man breathing I would wish to marry; and that the only one I could honour more than another, is the gentleman, who, of all others, seeks my everlasting dishonour.' (Vol. I, p. 165).

This makes him believe that she could be tempted by offers of money and land. But she rejects all his offers and tells him:

> I know, Sir, by woeful experience, that I am in your power: I know all the resistance I can make will be poor and weak, and perhaps stand me in little stead: I dread your *will* to ruin me is as great as your *power*: yet, Sir, will I dare to tell you, that I will make no *free will* offering of my virtue. All that I *can* do, poor as it is, I *will* do. (Vol.1, p.167) (Italics mine).

He then tells her that if the terms he had offered

> "are not sufficient, I will augment them to two-thirds of my estate; for," said he, and swore a dreadful oath, "I cannot live without you: and since the thing is gone so far, *I will not!*" (Vol. 1, p.169).

He then plans to rape her. The cruel Mrs. Jewkes is, of course, readily available to help him to violate the poor girl. She catches Pamela's one hand and Mr. B. the other but at this stage,

> I screamed out in such a manner, as never any body heard the like. But there was nobody to help me; and both my hands were secured, as I said. Sure never poor soul was in such agonies as I. "Wicked man!" said I, "wicked abominable woman! — O God! my God! this *time*! this *one time*! deliver me from this distress! or strike me dead this moment." And then I screamed again and again. (Vol.1, pp.178-9).

With 'struggling and terror', she fainted and since she did not recover for some time, 'they both, from the cold sweats that I was in, thought me dying.' (Vol.1, p. 179).

Pamela is, of course, horrified at Mr. B.'s attempt to rape her. But still she finally accepts him gratefully and cheerfully as her husband. Since Richardson's own times, critics have offered different explanations for her conduct. After all, earlier in the novel, she had seen that he was keen to seduce her. She got quite a few opportunities to leave his house and go to her parents but every time she found some excuse or the other not to leave this man. If she was really sincere in saying that she 'would marry a man who begs from door to door, and has no home, rather than endanger my honesty' (Vol.1, p.124), why did she marry a man of Mr. B.'s morals who threatens her 'honesty' time after time?

Amongst modern critics, David Daiches has been most critical of Pamela:

> If a man is a wealthy landowner, and handsome and graceful in manners to boot, he must be considered wholly good so long as he is not being actively bad. Printers do not become angels by merely ceasing to threaten girls with sexual violence, but evidently squires do. Richardson, of course, would have been horrified by such a comment. He claimed that he was showing a genuine reformation of character, wrought by Pamela's virtue in a young man who had the advantage of an excellent moral grounding in childhood. But we know better, and I suspect Pamela did.[17]

The real weakness in this argument is that after marriage Pamela is prepared to renounce everything - his wealth and position - when she finds his conduct unacceptable. So it is clear that she could not have been tempted only by Mr.B.'s wealth and status. Her motive must have been deeper.

Janet Todd's understanding of Pamela's motives is clearly much more convincing. She emphasises the strong element of sado-masochism in the relationship of Pamela and Mr. B.:

> When Mr. B. falls in love largely through her letters, it is the

image of himself and Pamela as tyrant and victim that he finds most ravishing. In the brothel at the heart of the novel, the letters function as overhead mirror, where his encroaching wickedness and her virtuous resistance are constantly reflected. In letters Mr. B. can enjoy his own humbling and re-create again and again the image of his naughty self.

Pamela plays her part of victim so well because she too derives pleasure from the role. Indeed it is Mr. B.'s sadism that wins her. The kindly and pious Parson Williams seems in her view a 'poor gentleman' beside the lordly master, and he has no chance of winning her. Never can she love such a one, she declares, for her heart is quite given to the man who is unrelenting in his persecution, who spurns her as his painted bauble and gewgaw and whose mighty threats of rape prostrate her in a tangle of tears and hair. 'I know not how it came', she remarks of her love for her master, 'nor *when* it began; but crept it has, like a thief, upon me; and before I knew what was the matter, it looked like love' (p. 260). But the reader knows exactly how it came, for it is immediately after Mr. B.'s cruelest treatment that it arrives.[18]

Doody's view is somewhat more sober and it is much more in consonance with the text. According to her, Mr. B. is not *at heart* a rapist. She adds: 'if he were really a man of unbridled lust (as his masculine ego sometimes makes him think he is) or a sadist like Lovelace, her helplessness would have been his opportunity.'[19] Mr. B.'s attempt at rape is an expression of his frustration that all his attempts, including his offer of two-thirds of his estate to her, had made no impression on Pamela though she is only a maid-servant in his house. What is still more revealing of his character is his conduct after this attempt at rape. He is really apologetic and has a feeling of revulsion. He tells her:

"You know I am not a very abandoned profligate: I have hitherto been guilty of no very enormous or vile actions. This confining you thus, may perhaps, be one of the worst. Had I been utterly given up to my passions, I should, before now, have gratified them, and not have shown that *remorse and compassion* for you, which have reprieved you more than once, when absolutely in my power; and you are as involate a virgin as you were when you came into my house." (Vol.1, p.188) (Italics mine).

His real problem is that he desperately needs to secure her as a *mistress*. She has stirred his blood and he regards her as an ideal sexual partner. He is prepared to pay any price for it. But marriage is a different matter. Marriage in eighteenth century England was often a contract involving two families with financial and political considerations. As a father in Susan Ferrier's novel *Marriage* (1818) says to his daughter, 'matrimony was ordained amongst people of birth .... for the aggrandising of [their] family, the extending of their political influence - for becoming, in short, the depository of their mutual interest'.[20]

Mr. B. is worried about how his marriage to his mother's waiting-maid will be received in his circle and how she will conduct herself in her new life as the wife of a Squire. But he loves her and cannot live without her. He is, however, quite uneasy in his mind about marrying her. 'Consider the pride of my condition', he says, and 'the distance between us in the world's judgment'. 'Can I think of making you my wife,' he asks her and then says, 'yet I must have you: I cannot bear the thoughts of any other man supplanting me in your affections.' He also tells her that he admires her intelligence and her 'open, frank and generous mind'. In beauty, of course, he says, 'you excel all your sex, in my eyes.' (Vol. 1, p. 188). But he is not the hero of a romance: he is a realistic person and has to care for public reaction. He needs courage to defy the code of his class. He has to conquer his pride - both personal pride and his family pride - and it is not easy to conquer them. The man who had boasted that 'he will not sue meanly where [he] can command' (Vol. 1, p. 169) feels defeated and he at last decides to send Pamela to her parents.

IV

But now that Pamela is *free* to leave, she realizes that she would not like to leave Mr. B. We have been conscious all along that Pamela is in love with her master. She herself had said that in spite of 'all his ill usage,' she cannot hate him. 'Can you believe it?' She writes to her parents:

> What could be the matter with me, I wonder? I felt something so strange at my heart! I wonder what ailed me! But this was so *unexpected*! - I believe that was all. Yet I am very strange still. Surely I cannot be like the old murmuring Israelites, to long after the onions and garlic of Egypt, when they had suffered there such heavy bondage? - I'll take thee, O contradictory, ungovernable heart, to severe task, for this thy strange impulse, when I get to my dear father and mother's. (Vol. 1, p. 217).

However, she left the house but after she had reached her first stop some miles away, a letter from her master was delivered to her. She was so affected by the letter, that she wrote to her parents: 'My dear parents, forgive me,' she wrote:

> .... my heart was too partial in his favour; but *now*, with so much openness, affection and *honour* too (which was all I had doubted), I am quite overcome. This was a happiness, however, I had no reason to expect. But I must own to you, that I shall never be able to think of any body in the world but him. "Presumption!" you will say; and so it is; but love is not a voluntary thing — *Love*, did I say — But come, it is not, I hope, gone so far as to make me *very* uneasy: for I know not *how* it came, nor *when* it began; but it has crept, like a thief, upon me, before I knew what was the matter. (Vol. 1, p. 220).

Next morning, when the chariot was to leave on their onward journey to her parents' house, there came another letter - in which her master begged her to return. 'But spare me, my dearest girl,' he wrote, 'the confusion of following you to your father's: which I must do, if you persist to go on; for I find I cannot live a day without you.' (Vol. 1, p. 222). Her response to this call is ecstatic:

> O my exulting heart! how it throbs in my bosom ... "But take care thou art not too credulous, neither, O fond believer!.... his pride of heart and condition may again take place; and a man that could, in so *little* a space, first love me, then hate, then banish me his house, and now send for me again, in such affectionate terms, may *still* waver, may *still* deceive thee .... O credulous, fluttering, throbbing mischief! that art so ready to believe what thou wishest; I charge thee to keep better guard than thou hast lately done, and lead me not to follow too implicitly thy flattering and desirable impulses." Thus foolishly dialogued I with my heart; and yet, all the time, this heart is Pamela. (p. 223).

But, of course, 'he has too great hold in my heart, for me to be easy presently, if I should refuse' (p. 224) and so Pamela returns to Mr. B. She later admits that 'I had the less merit in this my return, because I was driven by irresistible impulse to it, and I could not help it if I would.' But Mr. B. has not yet been able to muster courage to make an offer of marriage to her. He is worried about how it will be received by his class and whether she will be well received by women who normally should visit his wife. 'For some company you must keep', he tells her, and warns her that his 'station will not admit it to be with my servants'. The 'ladies will fly your acquaintance, and still, though my wife, will treat you as my mother's waiting-maid'. She is worried about 'the rude jests you will yourself encounter with, for thus stooping beneath yourself' (Vol. 1, p. 233). This self-consciousness is obvious in his conduct when he introduces her to Sir Simon and other guests as his 'pretty rustic' (Vol. 1, p. 253). When before her marriage day, Pamela regrets that in most marriages there is much 'singing, and sealing settlements, and portions, and such like; but now the poor Pamela brings you nothing at all', he comforts her by telling her that she brings as his wife

> what is infinitely more valuable — an experienced truth and well-tried virtue, and a wit and behaviour more than equal to the station you will be placed in: to say nothing of this sweet person, that itself might captivate a monarch; and of the *meekness of temper, and sweetness of disposition*, which makes you superior to all the women I ever saw. (Vol.1, p. 301) (Italics mine).

This 'meekness of temper and sweetness of disposition' is most visible at the time of her marriage. When asked if she knows of any 'impediments', Pamela 'blushed, and said, softly, 'None, Sir, but my *unworthiness*'. Then she curtsied and 'answered to every article of *obey, serve, love and honour.*' (Vol. 1, pp. 308-9). After their marriage, when she is excessively 'grateful' and says she 'shall never be able to deserve all your goodness', he is gracious enough to say: 'But let us talk of nothing henceforth but equality'. (Vol. 1, p. 314).

V

But equality takes time to develop in a case where the concept of equality has been altogether absent. In eighteenth century England, it was universally believed that the first duty of a wife was to obey her husband at all times and in all circumstances whatever her social status before marriage. Pamela's social status had always been that of a maid-servant and whatever her attractions for Mr. B., equality was not easy to establish between her and her master. Critics have, of course, claimed that Richardson is 'a radical feminist'.[21] It is, however, doubtful if he *really* believed in equality between the sexes. Mark Kinkead-Weekes is perhaps correct when he says that this 'greatest feminist of the eighteenth century is no apostle of Women's Liberation'.[22] Whatever interpretations we put on the actions of his heroes and heroines, it is clear that there is no equality between them. In *Pamela* itself it is clear that the heroine has no option but to submit to her husband in all matters. Lady Davers indeed tells her 'if ever you offend, he will not easily forgive' (Vol. 1, p. 392). Though he claims that he 'shan't be a very tyrannical husband' (Vol. 1, p. 401), he warns her that he would 'not allow, that my imperfections shall excuse those of my wife, or make her think I ought to bear faults in her which she can rectify, because she bears greater from me' (Vol. 1, p. 405). Otherwise, too, he is a very exacting husband. Kinkead-Weekes has summarised some of the 'injunctions' that she, as his wife, should keep in mind:

> B. gives her lengthy instructions on her dress, regulation of mealtimes and domestic economy, behaviour to his friends, conduct to himself, the bringing up of children, and so on. Many of these precepts are obviously a challenge to a frivolous society to return to old-fashioned regularity and order. At one point Pamela reduces a curtain-lecture to forty-eight articles to be pondered (Vol. 1, pp. 406-9): we may perhaps concern ourselves only with those which bear on the Whole Duty of Wifely Submission. 'The wife should bear with her husband even when he is in the wrong, should be flexible, should overcome by sweetness and complaisance though not slavishly, should show no reluctance to oblige and obey him, and, if he be set on a wrong thing, should not dispute with him unless it is a really important point, but do it first and expostulate afterwards.[23]

It is important to notice that before marriage Pamela is capable of defying her powerful master, but after marriage she seems to have lost her courage and strength and becomes a very docile and in fact a slavish wife. It is clear that she has learnt to adopt the code of conduct of middle-class eighteenth century women in marriage. But does this new attitude suit her? However it was necessary to do so as the ruling class of which she had now become a member, expected it. Of course, Pamela is fairly successful in playing the middle-class wife and people are charmed by her conduct as the wife of a Squire. She has also realized that her husband is the spoilt son of an ancient and rich family and she hopes to reform him by her obedience. At one stage when she tells him that she will 'endeavour to conform myself in all things, to your will', his reply is prompt:

> "I have no doubt of it; and I'll endeavour to make my will as conformable to reason as I can. And let me say, that this belief of you is one of the inducements I have had to marry at all." (Vol. 1, p. 401).

K.G. Hall has rightly said that in essence Mr. B.'s choice of Pamela as a spouse

> seems to have been based upon her remarkable deference more than her exemplary virtue. Sketching his requirements in a wife - which are considerable - B. frankly admits that he would be unlikely to get the degree of respect and obedience which he demands from a social equal. And B. here makes it plain that whilst he appreciates Pamela's beauty and character, above all else he expects her to obey him and maintain her characteristic subservience. *Pace* K. Rogers, Richardson did not think that marriage was a 'partnership between equals.[24]

Janet Todd is even more emphatic:

> Pamela is a proper wife not despite her servanthood but because of it. In Mr. B.'s required scheme, a wife is the extension of the maid and Pamela is eager to weld the two roles and keep the lowliness which has after all won her lord. So she continues to call her husband master and she curtsies at her wedding. Indeed her reactions are fitting since, in both hierarchies, his and hers, she is now below the man: Mr. B. guards the virtue which she had once used to resist him, for he stands as husband between her and God. 'I should be unworthy, if I could not say, that I can have no will but yours', she sighs and, after some time of marriage, she piously exclaims, 'I will endeavour to conform myself, in all things, to your will'. (p. 470). In fact she delights in the totality of her subservience to her lordly husband and stresses again and again that she is entirely the work of his bounty. As a wife, Pamela fervently asserts that her husband

will always be her master and that she will think herself more and more his servant. The wife becomes more servile than ever the servant has been. 'How dare you approach me', Mr. B. snaps at his new mate, 'without leave, when you see me thus disturbed?' (p. 460), and the once pert Pamela hardly murmurs at the imperious rebuke. So, too, as wife she is prepared to be objectified, to be trotted out for neighbours as the new wonder of the parish where, as a servant, she had rebelled against much degradation. In the novel, then, the servant's pedagogy slides into the wife's handbook, and the maid becomes the mistress by exaggerating servility.[25]

VI

Can this kind of 'servility' become a suitable basis for a happy marriage? Can a wife play the two roles mentioned by Janet Todd - - that of a wife and a servant — successfully? And should a wife be compelled to play these two roles? Miss Darnford writes to Pamela (or, to be correct, to Mrs. B.):

> O these men! Fathers or husbands, much alike! the one tyrannical, the other insolent: so that, between one and t'other, a poor girl has nothing for it, but a few weeks' courtship, and perhaps a first month's bridalry, if that: and then she is as much a slave to her husband, as she was a vassal to her father — I mean if the father be a S'ar Simon Darnford, and the spouse a Mr. B. (Vol. 2, p. 45).

But Richardson would like his parents and husbands to be reasonable. Indeed, his view is perhaps more accurately reflected in Lady Davers' reaction to Mr. B.'s 'curtain-lecture' to Pamela where he had laid down his 'injunctions':

> But what a curtain-lecture hadst thou, Pamela! A noble one, dost thou call it? — Why, what a wretch hast thou got, to expect thou shouldst never expostulate against his lordly will, even

> when in the wrong, till thou hast obeyed it, and of consequence, joined in the evil he imposes! (Vol. 2, p. 58).

Lady Davers' advice is that Pamela need not take everything literally. Her brother, Mr. B., may not be after all too tyrannical. She tells her:

> Thou hast a sensible and a generous Heart to work upon; one who takes no Glory in the blind Submission of a Slave; but, like a true *British* Monarch, delights to reign in a free, rather than in an abject Mind. Yet is he jealous as a Tyrant of his Prerogative: But you have found the way to lay that watchful Dragon asleep....

Pamela takes some time to settle down as a wife. She is still sometimes quite frightened of him. Once when he 'withdraws with a very serious aspect' from the room where Lady Davers and some other ladies were chatting, Pamela says:

> "What shall I do, if I have incurred Mr. B.'s anger by my over-forwardness! Did he not look displeased? Dear ladies, if he be so, plead for me, and I'll withdraw when he comes in; for I cannot stand his anger: I have not been used to it." (Vol. 2, p. 153).

When she argues that it is 'a mother's duty to nurse her own child', Mr. B. prohibits her from doing it and uses his 'prerogative' to do so, she writes to Miss Darnford:

> Could you ever have thought, my dear, that husbands have a dispensing power over their wives, which kings are not allowed over the laws? (Vol. 2, p. 202).

When she raises the point again, he tells her

> "I don't love to speak twice my mind on the same subject; you

> know I don't! and you have really disputed this point with me five or six times; insomuch, that I wondered what was come to my dearest." (Vol. 2, p. 234).

He is, of course, short tempered and hates to be contradicted. But there is no doubt that he loves Pamela and Pamela should bear with these shortcomings. This conversation, for instance, is very revealing:

> "I have, Sir," said I, "obeyed your first kind injunctions as to dressing myself before dinner. But, may be, you are busy, Sir?" He put up the papers he was reading, and said, "I can have no business or pleasure of equal value to your company, my dear. What were you going to say?" — "Only, Sir, to know if you have any more kind injunctions to give me? I could hear you talk a whole day together." — "You are very obliging, Pamela," said he; "but you are so perfectly what I wish, that I might have spared those I gave you; but I was willing you should have a taste of my freedom with you, to put you upon the like with me: for I am confident there can be no friendship lasting without freedom, and communicating to one another even the little caprices, if my Pamela can have any such, which may occasion uneasiness to either." (Vol. 1, pp. 334-5).

Friendship is, of course, the most solid basis of a happy marriage and almost all eighteenth century novelists recognise it. Jean H. Hagstrum, however, claims that sex is the most important element in *Pamela*. On both sides, he says, 'Pamela's no less than Mr. B.'s - there is physical attraction' and their marriage is 'firmly based on potent sexuality.[26] Sex is an important element in most marriages but no marriage can be sustained by sex alone. Sexual passion soon fades and the two partners have to find some more solid props to keep the marriage going. What happens in *Pamela* is most instructive. After the birth of her son, Pamela realizes that Mr. B. has lost interest in her and has started his affair with the Countess. What should she do now? Of course, there was the typical advice that the eighteenth century conduct-books gave to women in that period. Dr. Johnson is categorical that 'wise women don't trouble themselves about infidelity in their husbands'. Man, he says, is, of course, 'criminal in the sight of God' but he 'imposed no bastards upon his wife'. He, however, regards female chastity as of the utmost importance because 'upon that the property in the world depends'. For the preservation of property, legitimacy of children was absolutely vital and since female adultery causes 'confusion of progeny', 'a woman who breaks her marriage vows is much more criminal than a man who does it'.[27] I may say in passing that Boswell challenged this view of Dr. Johnson. He gave the example of a lady who 'argues that she may indulge herself in gallantries with equal freedom as her husband does provided she takes care not to introduce a spurious issue in her family'. Dr. Johnson's retort was, 'this lady of yours, Sir, I think is very fit for a brothel'.[28] But this is evading the issue.

Lord Halifax had told his daughter in 1688 what most women regarded as very sensible:

> 'Do not seem to look or hear that way: if he is a man of sense, he will reclaim himself, the folly of it is of itself sufficient to cure him; if he is not so, he will be provoked, but not reformed.'[29]

Pamela herself says: 'My business is to reclaim, and not to provoke' (Vol. 2, p. 288). So she suffers quietly for some time. Earlier she had quite cheerfully accepted the fact of Mr. B.'s illegitimate daughter. She knew that the child's mother had left the country and her husband was not altogether wholly to blame for what had happened. But now the Countess is a different matter. She is deeply hurt when the Countess calls on them more to show off her superior upper-class breeding and to establish her superiority to Pamela in her husband's eyes. She 'came adorned with every outward ornament' but Pamela 'put on only a white damask gown, having no desire to vie with her in appearance'. She says that 'a virtuous and honest heart is [her] glory' (Vol. 2, p. 293). The

Countess expresses a wish to see their son. Pamela asks her nurse 'to bring *my* Billy down'. '*My*, I said, with an emphasis' and a sense of 'triumph in my heart' (Vol. 2, p. 294). This is after all her superiority: she is a *mother* and at least in this, she was superior to the Countess.

But the situation becomes unbearable when she learns that her husband has taken a house in Tunbridge and he and the Countess intend to live there as husband and wife. She also learns that they both believe in polygamy and that the Countess has in fact told her uncle that 'she had rather be a certain gentleman's second wife, than the first to the greatest man in England' (Vol. 2, p. 289). She cannot keep quiet any more. She has, however, to behave with restraint. She does not want to quarrel with her husband because that would be counter-productive. She, therefore, makes a very reasonable proposal to him: that he should permit her to go to Kent to her parents with her son. She knows that she cannot compete with the Countess:

> 'Tis my misfortune, that she is too lovely, and too attractive: and it is the less wonder, that a fine young gentleman as you are, and a fine young lady as she is, should engage one another's affections'. (Vol. 2, p. 208).

She recognises that she

> 'excels your poor girl in all those outward graces of form, which your kind fancy (more valued by me than the opinion of all the world besides) had made you attribute to me. And she has all those additional advantages as nobleness of birth, of alliance, and deportment, which I want.' (Vol. 2, p. 310).

She tells him:

> "I will never take your name into my lips, nor suffer any other in my hearing, but with reverence and gratitude, for the good I and mine *have* reaped at your hands: nor wish to be freed from

> my obligations to you, except you shall choose to be divorced from me; and if so I will give your wishes all the forwardness I honourably can, with regard to my own character and yours, and that of your beloved baby." (Vol. 2, p. 311).

She also tells him that

> 'if, by any accident, and misunderstanding between you, you should part by consent, and you will have it so, my heart shall be ever yours, and my hopes shall be resumed of being an instrument still for your future good, and I will receive your returning ever-valued heart, as if nothing had happened, the moment I can be sure it will be wholly mine.' (Vol. 2, p. 312).

But she wants to make one thing clear:

> "For, think not, dear Sir, whatever be your notions of polygamy, that I will, were my life to depend upon it, consent to live with a gentleman, dear as , GOD is my witness" (lifting up my tearful eyes) "you are to me who lives in what I cannot but think open sin with another! You *know*, Sir, and I appeal to you for the purity, and I will aver piety of my motives, when I say this, that I *would not*; and as you do know this, I cannot doubt but my proposal will be agreeable to you both. And I beg of you, dear Sir, to take me at my word; and don't let me be tortured, as I have been so many weeks, with such anguish of mind, that nothing but religious considerations can make supportable to me." (Vol.2, p. 312).

She had already told his sister, Lady Davers, earlier that she could not share her husband with another wife:

> I could not have loved, as I love, if I could easily part with my interest in so beloved a husband. — For my interest I *will* part with, and sooner die, than live with a gentleman who has another wife, though I was the first. *Let Countesses, if they can,*

> *and ladies of birth, choose to humble themselves to this baseness. The low-born Pamela cannot stoop to it.* (Vol. 2, p. 302). (Italics mine).

When he asks her whether she can easily part with him, she replies firmly: "I can, Sir, and I will! — rather than divide my interest in you, knowingly, with any lady upon earth. But say not, can I part with you, Sir; it is you that part with me: and tell me, Sir, tell me but what you had intended should become of me?" (Vol. 2, p. 312).

VII

Doody rightly says that for Richardson marriage is 'a relationship of love, and can be maintained only by real communication. Practical calculations, even well-intentioned dissimulations, can kill both friendship and love in marriages.'[30] Pamela cannot accept any compromise, whatever the consequences. Doody says that Pamela realizes that if 'Mr. B. is tired of her, she has lost everything'. Doody adds:

> Like all of Richardson's heroines, Pamela is at her best when defying the world. All the maxims of prudence are against her; according to them, and to general opinion, she ought to keep tight hold on her new-found status, and her marital position, preserving her good name and worldly advantage by treating her husband with aloof courtesy whenever he condescended to leave his mistress and visit her, and clutching her allowance, her carriage, and her diamonds. If she left Mr. B. she would create a scandal of which she would be the victim. A divorced woman, or one separated from her husband, was (unless of supremely high rank, or a member of what has been called 'Cafe Society') a social outcast. Mr. B. would still be accepted; his wife would have lost all claim to notice, and would be blamed, not pitied. Pamela possesses courage.[31]

Pamela's outburst, however dignified and restrained it is, stuns

Mr. B. He had not realized that Pamela could take such a stand. Most women in the eighteenth century accept the fact of infidelity on their husbands' part with equanimity. But this low-class girl is a fighter. Mr. B. has to surrender. And it is not a temporary surrender. He recognises Pamela's natural superiority.

He was moved and 'he came round', Pamela tells us, and 'took me in his arms':

> "Exalted creature!" said he: "noble-minded" Pamela! Let no bar be put between us henceforth! No wonder, when one looks back to your first promising dawn of excellence, that your fuller day should thus irresistibly dazzle such weak eyes as mine. Whatever it costs me, and I have been inconsiderably led on by blind passion for an object too charming, but which I never thought equal to my Pamela, I will (for it is yet, I bless God, in my power), restore to your virtue a husband all your own." (Vol. 2, p. 314).

He is so overwhelmed that he says:

> "You are virtue itself, my dearest life; and from this moment I will reverence you as my tutelary angel. I shall behold you with awe, and implicitly give up myself to all your dictates: for what you *say*, and what you *do*, must be ever right. But I will not, my dearest life, too lavishly promise, lest you should think it the sudden effects of passions thus movingly touched, and which may subside again, when the soul, as you observed in your own case, sinks to its former level: but this I promise (and I hope you believe me, and will pardon the pain I have given you, which made me fear more than once, that your head was affected, so *uncommon*, yet so like *yourself*, has been the manner of your acting,) that I will break off a correspondence that has given you so much uneasiness: and my Pamela may believe, that if I can be as good as my word in this point, she will never more be in danger of any rival whatever." (Vol. 2, pp. 314-15).

He then explains to her that it was his vanity and pride which had led him astray. He also tells her that her 'unwonted reception' of him at home gave him a feeling of 'disgust' and so he went to the Countess who was 'ever cheerful and lively'. But, of course, he has now realized his mistake and she need not harbour any anxiety on account of the Countess.

He then begs her forgiveness:

> "But say, my dear love," added he, "say you forgive me; and resume but your former cheerfulness, and affectionate regards to me, else I shall suspect the sincerity of your forgiveness: and your shall indeed go to Kent, but not without me, nor your boy neither." (Vol. 2, p. 315).

The Countess also visits Pamela and explains the very superficial nature of her relationship with Mr. B. She also informs her that she is now going to France and 'shall pass a year or two in Italy, and then I shall, I hope, return as solid, as grave, as circumspect, though not so wise, as Mrs. B.' (Vol. 2, p. 370).

In conclusion, we may say that Pamela is a genuinely revolutionary character. In this she has the advantage of her poor birth. Middle class women are keen to compromise because they do not want to lose the advantages of married status. But Pamela is different. In Doody's words, 'the virtue that is rewarded is in large measure the virtue of rebellion'.[32] Hence she has been called by Brissenden 'the first real heroine in English fiction'![33]

NOTES

1. Samuel Richardson, *Pamela*, Everyman's Library, 2 Volumes, (London, 1950), Vol. 1, p. 1.
2. Janet Todd, "*Pamela* or the bliss of servitude", *Gender, Art and Death* (Polity Press, Cambridge, 1993), p. 71.
3. A phrase of Margaret A. Doody, Introduction to *Pamela*, p. 14.
4. op. cit., p. 63.
5. Cited by Janet Todd, p. 64.
6. Ibid., p. 64.
7. Ibid., p. 64.

8. Arnold Kettle, *An Introduction to the English Novel* (Harper Torchbooks, N. York, 1960), I, pp. 64-65.
9. David Daiches, "*Samuel Richardson*", *Twentieth Century Interpretations of Pamela*, ed. Rosemary Cowler (Prentice-Hall, 1969), pp. 24-25.
10. *The Rise of the Novel* (1957), pp. 187-8.
11. Lawrence Stone, *The Family, Sex and Marriage in England 1500-1800* (London, 1977), p. 642.
12. Ibid., p. 642.
13. Terry Eagleton, *The Rape of Clarissa* (Oxford, 1985). p.37.
14. Ibid., p. 37.
15. Margaret Anne Doody, *A Natural Passion: A Study of the Novels of Samuel Richardson* (Clarendon Press, Oxford, 1974), p. 60. (Italics mine).
16. R. F. Brissenden, *"Pamela", Twentieth Century Interpretations of Pamela* ed. Rosemary Cowler, (Prentice-Hall, 1964), p.54.
17. op. cit., p. 21.
18. Janet Todd, "*Pamela*: or the bliss of servitude", *Gender, Art and Death* (Polity Press, Cambridge, 1993), p. 71.
19. *A Natural Passion*, p. 47.
20. Susan Ferrier, *Marriage, A Novel* (1818), ed. Herbert Foltinek (Oxford, 1971), p. 2.
21. See Katharine Rogers, "Richardson's Empathy with Women", *The Authority of Experience: Essays in Feminist Criticism*, edited by Avlyn Diamond and Lee R. Edwards (Amherst University of Mass., 1977), p. 119.
22. Mark Kinkead-Weekes, *Samuel Richardson: Dramatic Novelist* (London, 1973), p. 63.
23. Ibid., p. 62.
24. "Samuel Richardson: *Pamela*", *The Exalted Heroine and the Triumph of Order: Class, Women and Religion in the English Novel, 1740-1800* (London, 1993), p. 43.
25. "*Pamela*, or the bliss of servitude," *Gender, Art and Death* (Polity Press, Cambridge, 1993), pp. 68-69.
26. Jean H. Hagstrum, *Sex and Sexuality: Ideal and Erotic Love from Milton to Mozart* (University of Chicago Press, London, 1980), p. 192.
27. Cited by Keith Thomas, "The Double Standard", *Journal of the History of Ideas*, XX (1959), p. 209.
28. Ibid., p. 209.
29. *Complete Works*, edited by J. P. Kenyon (London, 1969), p.279.
30. Doody, *A Natural Passion*, p. 96.
31. Ibid., pp. 94-95.
32. Introduction to *Pamela* in Penguin Classics (1980), p. 9.
33. R. F. Brissenden, op.cit., p. 55.

Chapter IV

Fanny Burney: *Evelina* (1778)

Eva Figes has claimed that 'whilst Richardson was deeply conservative with a veneer of liberalism, Burney, as a woman, had a self-protective veneer of die-hard conservatism under which lurked much more liberal, questioning attitudes which dared not find full expression'.[1] These 'liberal' and 'questioning' attitudes are seen at their best in her approach to marriage. Most marriages in her society were mercenary marriages and whatever women's personal preferences, they had no option but to accept such marriages for reasons of economic security. Social reformers did, of course, condemn the practice but at a time of fast economic changes, the rise of the unromantic bourgeois marriage was inevitable. Dr. Johnson strongly condemned mercenary fathers who decked out their daughters for sale and deprecated the young women who themselves participated in the "prostitution of the modern marriage market" (*Rambler*, 1:92). But both parents and daughters were helpless in the existing situation.

Fanny Burney highlights in her *Diary* the dilemma that women faced. She attaches great importance to marriage in a woman's life and indeed believes that marriage alone can give woman a real sense of fulfilment, but she also knows that a mercenary marriage may bring no happiness to her and indeed may cripple her personality. Before she wrote *Evelina*, she wrote in her diary that she needed '*particular inducements*' to unite herself 'for life with one who must have full power to make me miserable, and perhaps none to make me happy - for it is such chance'.[2] For Sarah Pennington the risk is even greater. She describes it in the following words: 'Happy is her Lot, who in an Husband, finds [an] invaluable Friend! Yet, so great is the Hazard, so disproportioned the Chances, that I could almost wish the dangerous Die was never thrown for any of you!'[3] It is, of course, too pessimistic a view. Marriage is a risk in any society but that does not mean that we should not take the risk at all. It is, however, true that in view of women's economic dependence on their husbands, the risks in eighteenth century were certainly much greater than in later periods.

In her *Early Diary*, Burney mentions how she felt when she witnessed a young woman's wedding: 'O how short a time does it take to put an eternal end to a woman's liberty!' In a later passage she says, 'Tis preparing one to lead a long journey, to know the path is not altogether strew'd with roses .... she [the bride] may not find the road it leads her to very short; be that as it may, she must trudge on'.[4] Parents too were conscious of the risk that their daughters were taking. But what could they do? No father can guarantee his daughter's happiness in marriage. Dr. John Gregory in his *A Father's Legacy to his Daughters* (1774), reminds them of the uncomfortable truth: 'Your whole life is often a life of suffering; you cannot plunge into business, or dissipate yourselves in pleasure and riot, as men often do, when under the pressure of misfortunes; you must bear your sorrows in silence, unknown and unpitied' (p.12). Hestor Chapone in her *Letters* (1773) goes so far as to say that 'the calamities of an unhappy marriage are so much greater than can befall a single person, that the unmarried woman may find abundant argument to be contented with her condition'.[5] But life of a single woman was no better. The fact is that most women in the period were caught up in a situation from which there was no escape.

Yet women with courage and intelligence could successfully flight against the most adverse circumstances and achieve a happy marriage. Fanny Burney proves it in her own case. When in 1775, one Mr. Thomas Barlow proposed to her, she rejected him on the ground that she did not love him. In her *Early Diary* (8th May,

1775), Burney describes Mr. Barlow as 'rather short but handsome'. She adds: 'He is very well-bred, good tempered and sensible young man .... and he is highly spoken of for disposition and morals'. He was also known to be rich and in the eyes of her family members very eligible as a husband for Fanny. Mr. Crisp, her mentor, urged her to accept him in order to avoid "the situation of an unprotected, unprovided woman" (*ED*, 2:54). Her father also asked her not to be '*peremptory*' in her refusal of the proposal. Crisp went so far as to warn her that

> "The opportunity [of marriage] is never to be recover'd; the tide is lost, and you are left in shallows, fast a-ground, and struggling in vain for the remainder of your life to get on, - doom'd to pass it in obscurity and regret. Look round you Fan; look at your aunts! *Fanny Burney* won't always be what she is now!" (Ed, 2:54).[6]

She knew that spinsterhood might cause regret, but a non-romantic bourgeois marriage for economic security did not seem a very attractive proposition. Her pessimism about women's role in the institution of marriage must have been validated later in her life by her sister Susan's grim marriage and early death, brought on, in Burney's view, by her husband's cruelty.

Margaret Anne Doody on the basis of Burney's *Early Diary*, describes the Barlow episode in the following words:

> After one evening's acquaintance, at a party at her grandmother Burney's, Barlow had sent a letter declaring that "the Affability, Sweetness, and Sensibility, which shone in your every Action, lead me irresistibly to Love and Admire". She found the epistle absurd, and its author dull (and also short). She gives them a splendid comic (and novelistic) dialogue. Barlow, the naive male, is sentimental about marriage; his interlocutor is not:
>
> "...but is it possible that you can have so bad an opinion of

> the Married State? It seems to me the only state for happiness!"
>
> "Well, Sir, you are attracted to the married life - I am to the single - therefore every man in his humour - do you follow your opinion - and let me follow mine."
>
> ...
>
> "What - what can I do?" cried he very sorrowfully.
>
> "Why - go and ponder upon this affair for about half an hour. Then say - what an odd, queer, strange creature she is - and then - think of something else."

Burney was able to write very firmly to Crisp, "I AM QUITE FIXED." She made it plain that even his injunctions and emotive threats could not prevail in this case, and was strong enough to make his threats and her firmness into a comical matter:

> And so it is all over with me! - and I am to be given up - to forfeit your blessing - to lose your good opinion - to be doomed to regret and the horrors - because I have not a mind to be married."[7]

But when she had a mind to be married, she married the man of her choice despite all opposition and all handicaps. When she was almost forty years of age, she met a middle-aged military man, a year younger than herself, M. Alexandre d'Arblay. He was an émigré from France and had been an officer of the army of Louis XVI. He had escaped to England along with a few friends and settled in a colony of French émigrés in the neighbourhood of the Burneys. It was here that Fanny also met Mme. de Staél, the well-known French writer. Staél admired Fanny's novels and wanted to visit her house. But Fanny's father prohibited her developing any relation with that 'wicked' woman. He hated the French and regarded all of them as revolutionaries and a bad influence on his daughter. Fanny was sad but she could not disobey her father. But he could not prevent her meeting d'Arblay between whom and Fanny a warm friendship developed. Clearly there was mutual admiration which could develop into love. Doody's comment is worth quoting on this relationship:

> Hesitant because of his lack of means and of all status in England, he began to indicate his feelings in a manner that would allow Frances to withdraw or to ignore them, but, as she told Susanna [her sister] in April, "to such a Man .... I could not be so unjust, so ungenerous, so false, as to disguise my whole sentiments'. The bilingual courtship can now be read in the "Courtship Journal" like a story; it may remind us of the relation between Lucy Stowe and M. Paul in Charlotte Bronte's *Villette*, but this story was to have a happy ending - despite Charles Burney [her father]'s opposition.[8]

I

It is difficult to accept Mona Scheurmann's view that the world of *Evelina* is 'a morally comfortable world'.[9] How can a world be 'morally comfortable' where the heroine's 'predominant emotion seems to .... be an acute anxiety which is painful, real and powerful'.[10] It seems to me a cruel world, at once snobbish, conventional and misogynistic. It is specially hostile to women who are not protected by the status of their families or their wealth. As Judy Simons says: 'For, like Cecilia and Juliet in *The Wanderer*, Evelina is a girl without parental support, unprotected in a powerful and exclusive society. How can she best survive? That is the question posed by all the novels, as Burney's heroines try to adopt their intuitive sense of value to the practical demands of existence that confront them.'[11]

To fully understand Evelina's situation we have to go back to her grandfather's disastrous marriage. Mr. Villars, who is at present Evelina's guardian, tells us that her grandfather, Mr. Evelyn had gone on travels with him as his tutor. On his return, against his advice and 'entreaties of all his friends', he married Madame Duval, who was 'a writing girl in a tavern'. She was a 'vulgar and illiterate' woman but Mr. Evelyn was 'too weak to resist the allurements of beauty, which nature, though a niggard to her in every other boon, had with a lavish hand hestowed' on her. (p. 14).[12] Out of shame, he left England and settled in France with his wife. After about two years, he died leaving an infant girl behind. Before his death, he had realized that Madame Duval was 'by no means a proper companion or guardian for a young woman'. She was 'at once uneducated and unprincipled; ungentle in her temper, and unamiable in her manners.' (p. 13). So Mr. Evelyn entrusted 'the sole guardianship of his daughter's person till her eighteenth year' to Mr. Villars, 'conjuring [him] in the most affecting terms, to take charge of her education till she was able to act with propriety.' He left him 'a legacy of a thousand pounds.' (p. 14).

When Miss Evelyn was eighteen, Madame Duval 'sent for her to Paris' and at the instigation of her husband 'earnestly, or rather tyrannically, endeavored to effect a union between Miss Evelyn and one of his nephews'. When Evelyn resisted this, Madame Duval 'threatened her with poverty and ruin' (p. 15). Evelyn, out of despair, 'rashly, and without a witness, consented to a private marriage with Sir John Belmont, a very profligate young man'. He had promised to take her profligate young man'. He had promised to take her to England but discovering that she had no money, 'he infamously burnt the certificate of their marriage, and denied that they had ever been united'. Evelyn flew to Villars for protection and died after giving birth to her daughter. As Villars says, 'Thus it happened that the education of the father, daughter, and grand-daughter, has devolved on me'. (p. 16).

Mr. Villars tells us that Evelina has been 'educated in the most secluded retirement in the countryside'. She 'has a virtuous mind, a cultivated understanding, and a feeling heart' but otherwise she is totally ignorant of the ways of the world. Her real misfortune is that she is 'a young woman of obscure birth', but of 'conspicuous beauty' — a combination that is fatal for a young woman in her society. Naturally when this woman enters society, she is described as a 'nobody' and treated as a bastard. 'The social destiny of such an attractive, well-bred female bastard', in the words of Doody, 'would seem inevitably to be some upper-class man's kept mistress, as Sir Clement Willoughby implicitly believes.'[13] This was the natural fate of girls who 'had too much beauty to escape notice .... [but] too little wealth to be sought with propriety by men of the fashionable world' (p.19).

Two small incidents - though not too small either when it comes to their social significance - may also be mentioned to show how insensitive this society is to the feelings of others. Madame Duval is, of course, a despicable character but is it necessary to humiliate her the way Captain Mirvan does when he masquerades as a highway thief and attacks her? She ends up wigless in a ditch with her feet tied together and the rope attached to a tree:

> The ditch, happily, was almost quite dry, or she must have suffered still more seriously; yet, so forlorn, so miserable a figure, I never before saw. Her head-dress had fallen off, her linen was torn; her negligee had not a pin left in it, her petticoats she was obliged to hold on; and her shoes were perpetually slipped off. She was covered with dirt, weeds, and filth, and her face was really horrible, for the pomatum and powder from her head, and the dust from the road, were quite *pasted* on her skin by her tears, which, with her *rouge*, made so frightful a mixture, that she hardly looked human. (pp. 159-160).

Another example of the gross insensivity of this society is to be noticed in the case of the 'bet' between Lord Merton, the future husband of Lord Orville's sister, Lady Louisa, and Jack Coverley. The bet is for one hundred pounds and it is to 'be settled by a race between two old women, one chose by each side, and both of them to be proved more than eighty, though, in other respects, strong and healthy as possible' (p. 317). Neither Lord Orville nor any one else sees any cruelty in the scheme. For them it is only a joke. Evelina alone feels the 'sensation .... of pity at the sight' of the old women (p. 335). But no one shares her feelings. Indeed, when the women came forward, 'they were greeted with a laugh from every beholder, Lord Orville excepted, who looked very grave during the whole transaction' (p. 335). But Lord Orville also did not intervene to stop this mockery of the old and the poor, though he claimed that he was 'no friend of gaming.' (p. 318). For Evelina, of course, it is a crude and vulgar display of the power of the rich over the poor:

> When the signal was given for them to set off, the poor creatures, feeble and frightened, ran against each other, and, neither of them able to support the shock, they both fell on the ground.
>
> Lord Merton and Mr. Coverley flew to their assistance. Seats were brought for them, and they each drank a glass of wine. They complained of being much bruised, for, heavy and helpless, they had not been able to save themselves, but fell, with their whole weight upon the gravel. However, as they seemed equal sufferers, both parties were too eager to have the affair deferred.
>
> Again, therefore, they set off, and hobbled along, nearly even with each other, for some time, yet frequently, and to the inexpressible diversion of the company, they stumbled and tottered; and the confused hallowing of '*Now Coverley*!' '*Now Merton*!' rung from side to side during the whole affair.
>
> Not long after, a foot of one of the poor women slipt, and, with a great force, she came again to the ground. Involuntarily, I sprung forward to assist her, but Lord Merton, to whom she did not belong, stopped me, calling out 'No foul play! no foul play!'.
>
> Mr. Coverley, when repeating the same words, went himself to help her, and insisted that the other should stop. A debate ensued; but the poor creature was too much hurt to move, and declared her utter inability to make another attempt. Mr. Coverley was quite *brutal; he swore at her with unmanly rage, and seemed scarce able to refrain even from striking her*. (Italics mine). (pp. 335-6).

II

Evelina's education is clearly incomplete in various ways. In her times, it was absolutely essential for any young woman entering fashionable life to be familiar with 'forms' and 'manners'. Knowledge of proper etiquette and social codes was indeed a much more essential feature of eighteenth century education for women than a cultivated understanding. In upper-class society, women were valued for their social graces rather than their intellectual qualities. Her very first experience of high life, therefore, causes embarrassment to Evelina. She attends a private ball in the company of Mrs. Mirvan and her daughter and commits a social blunder. She refuses an offer of a dance with the first person who approaches her and accepts the offer of a second person. This is clearly a breach of ballroom etiquette. The first person is, of course, a fop and the second a noble lord and the hero of the novel. But the fop is perfectly justified in denouncing her. He accuses her of 'ill-breeding' and is surprised that 'a person who is nobody, [should] give herself such airs' (p. 38). At a later stage in the novel, Mrs. Selwyn advises Evelina to '*pay my court* to this Mr. Lovel; 'for .... though he is malicious, he is fashionable, and may do you some harm in the great world' (p. 317). But, of course, Evelina cannot do it, as she says: 'I should disdain myself as much as I do him, were I capable of such a duplicity, as to flatter a man whom I scorn and despise' (p. 317).

Burney makes it clear that it is a man's world and women - specially unprotected women - cannot feel safe here. In the very first scene where she commits the mistake of offending Mr. Lovel, there is another man, and a more dangerous one, Sir Clement Willoughby, who poses a threat to her. She is lucky that the noble lord, Lord Orville, with whom she danced first, is a powerful man but even his first impression of Evelina is not a very favourable one. He is, of course, greatly attracted by her beauty but he admits that he is confused about her: "Whether ignorant, or mischievous, I will not pretend to determine, but certain it is, she attended to all I could say to her, though I have really fatigued myself with fruitless endeavours to entertain her, with the most immovable gravity; but no sooner did Lovel begin his complaint, than she was seized with a fit of laughing, first affronting the poor beau, and then enjoying his mortification' (p. 39). Sir Clement Willoughby is keen to find out the extent of Lord Orville's interest in her as he would not like to antagonise him. So he proceeds cleverly and asks Lord Orville:

> 'Why, my Lord, what have you done with your lovely partner!'
>
> 'Nothing!' answered Lord Orville, with a smile and a shrug.
>
> 'By Jove,' cried the man, 'she is the most beautiful creature I eve saw in my life!'
>
> Lord Orville, as he well might, laughed, but answered, 'Yes, a pretty modest-looking girl'.
>
> 'O my Lord!' cried the madman, 'she is an angel!'
>
> 'A *silent* one,' returned he.
>
> 'Why ay, my Lord, how stands she as to that? She looks all intelligence and expression.'
>
> 'A poor weak girl!' answered Lord Orville, shaking his head.
>
> 'By Jove', cried the other, 'I am glad to hear it!' (pp. 37-8).

Sir Clement is happy that Lord Orville holds a rather low opinion of Evelina and the field is clear for him. But he is mistaken.

Lord Orville soon realizes that the girl is too innocent and perhaps also too weak to protect herself from fops like Mr. Lovel and libertines like Sir Clement Willoughby. Mr. Lovel is, of course, not much of a difficulty; one snub from Lord Orville can assure his good conduct but Sir Clement is a crafty man and Lord Orville suspects that he has designs on Evelina. His delicacy does not permit him to warn her about it but when she uses his name to escape dancing with an undesirable person, he assures her: 'Be not distressed, I beseech you; I shall ever think my name honoured by your making use of it' (p. 51). It is merely an indication that she can depend on his protection. Later, when he learns that she is leaving London, he came to her, 'and took [her] hand, saying: 'I *do* think, that whoever has once seen Miss Anville, must receive an impression never to be forgotten' (p.78). This indicates that his interest in her is somewhat deeper than that of a mere good-natured protector. Evelina is thrilled by this and what she writes to her guardian about

Lord Orville clearly shows her response to him:

> The conversation of Lord Orville is really delightful. His manners are so elegant, so gentle, so unassuming, that they at once engage esteem, and diffuse complacence. Far from being indolently satisfied with his own accomplishments, as I have already observed many men here are, tho' without any pretensions to his merit, he is most assiduously attentive to please and to serve all who are in his company; and, though his success is invariable, he never manifests the smallest degree of consciousness.
>
> I could wish that *you*, my dearest Sir, knew Lord Orville, because I am sure you would love him; and I have felt that wish for no other person I have seen since I came to London. I sometimes imagine, that, when his youth is flown, his vivacity abated, and his life is devoted to retirement, he will, perhaps, resemble him whom I most love and honour. His present sweetness, politeness, and diffidence, seem to promise in future the same benevolence, dignity, and goodness. But I must not expatiate upon this subject. (pp. 78-9).

It is not safe to say that Evelina has fallen in love with Lord Orville, though it is certainly correct that she is strongly drawn towards him. In her times, girls brought up well were advised not to fall in love with strangers and Lord Orville is still more or less a stranger. He is also a nobleman of high standing in society and Evelina is acutely conscious of her low status. She has neither a name nor a family. These her father alone can give her but he must be persuaded first to own her. But she is happy that Lord Orville has taken some interest in her, though it hardly amounts to more than a desire to protect a helpless girl. This itself is something as she needs protection. In the country-side she felt safe with her guardian but in London she feels that she is alone and threatened from various quarters.

Judy Simons has indeed said that 'Evelina's panic, lost in the subliminally sinister dark alleys at Vauxhall dramatises women's basic fear of personal violation. Evelina is 'terrified to death', 'frightened exceedingly', 'distracted with terror'. Attacked by a group of strange men who see her as legitimate sexual game, she is rescued by another who, under the guise of friendship, tries to seduce her and proves to be equally as treacherous. It seems as if there is no escape'.[14] To feel the full horror of the situation, it is best to see Burney's description of the scene:

> By the time we came near the end, a large party of gentlemen, apparently very riotous, and who were hallowing, leaning on one another, and laughing immoderately, seemed to rush suddenly from behind some trees, and, meeting us face to face, put their arms at their sides, and formed a kind of circle, that first stopped our proceedings, and then our retreating, for we were presently entirely enclosed. The Miss Branghtons screamed aloud, and I was frightened exceedingly: our screams were answered with bursts of laughter, and, for some minutes, we were kept prisoners, till, at last, one of them, rudely, seizing hold of me, said I was a pretty little creature.
>
> Terrified to death, I struggled with such vehemence to disengage myself from him, that I succeeded, in spite of his efforts to detain me; and immediately, and with a swiftness which fear only could have given me, I flew rather than ran up the walk, hoping to secure my safety by returning to the lights and company we had so foolishly left; but, before I could possibly accomplish my purpose, I was met by another party of men, one of whom placed himself so directly in my way, calling out, 'Whither so fast, my love?' — that I could only have proceeded, by running into his arms.
>
> In a moment, both my hands, by different persons, were caught hold of; and one of them, in a most familiar manner, desired to accompany me in a race, when I ran next; while the rest of the party stood still and laughed.
>
> I was almost distracted with terror, and so breathless with running, that I could not speak, till another advancing, said, I was as handsome as an angel, and desired to be of the party. I

running, that I could not speak, till another advancing, said, I was as handsome as an angel, and desired to be of the party. I then just articulated, 'For Heaven's sake, Gentlemen, let me pass!'

Another, then, rushing suddenly forward, exclaimed, 'Heaven and earth! what voice in that?—'

'The voice of the prettiest little actress I have seen this age', answered one of my persecutors.

'No, — no, — no, —' I panted out, 'I am no actress, — pray let me go, — pray let me pass —.'

'By all that's sacred,' cried the same voice, which I then knew for Sir Clement Willoughby's, ' 'tis herself!'

'Sir Clement Willoughby!' cried I, 'O Sir, assist — assist me — or I shall die with terror! —'

'Gentlemen,' cried he, disengaging them all from me in an instant, 'pray leave this lady to me.'

Loud laughs proceeded from every mouth, and two or three said, '*Willoughby has all the luck*!' But one of them, in a passionate manner, vowed he would not give me up, for that he had the first right to me, and would support it.

'You are mistaken', said Sir Clement, 'this lady is — I will explain myself to you another time; but I assure you, you are all mistaken.'

And then, taking my willing hand, he led me off, amidst the loud acclamations, laughter, and gross merriment of his impertinent companions.

As soon as we had escaped from them, Sir Clement, with a voice of surprise, exclaimed, 'My dearest creature, what wonder, what strange revolution, has brought you to such a spot as this?'

Ashamed of my situation, and extremely mortified to be thus recognized by him, I was for some time silent, and when he repeated his question, only stammered out, 'I have, — I hardly know how, — lost myself from my party, —'

He caught my hand, and eagerly pressing it, in a passionate voice, said, 'O that I had sooner met with thee!'

And then I saw, what the perturbation of my mind had prevented my sooner noticing, that he had led me, though I know not how, into another of the dark alleys, instead of the place whither I meant to go.

'Good God!' I cried, 'where am I? — What way are you going?—'

'Where,' answered he, 'we shall be least observed.'

Astonished at this speech, I stopped short, and declared I would go no further.

'And why not, my angel?' again endeavouring to take my hand.

My heart beat with resentment; I pushed him away from me with all my strength, and demanded how he dared treat me with such insolence?

'Insolence! repeated he.

'Yes, Sir Clement, *insolence*; from you, who know me, I had a claim for protection, — not to such treatment as this.' (pp. 212-14).

III

It is not Sir Clement's first attempt to seduce Evelina nor is it his last. He continues tormenting her almost throughout the novel. When she was returning from the opera, he trapped her in his chariot on the pretence of taking her to the place where she was staying with Mrs. Mirvan. On realizing that he was taking her elsewhere, she tried to jump out of her chariot. He tried to calm her: 'Whence this alarm, my dearest angel? — What can you fear? — my life is at your devotion, and can you, then, doubt my protection?' 'And so saying, he passionately kissed my hand'. She realized the danger and cried: 'If you do not intend to murder me,' .... 'for mercy's, for pity's sake, let me get out!' (p. 107). Anyway, he dropped her near her residence and even apologised to her. Later, he chased her to Bristol where she was staying in Mrs. Beaumont's house. As usual he started flirting with her and pleaded that she should 'look upon [him] with pity -- if not with favour!;

> 'Suffer me, Sir,' said I, very gravely, 'to make use of this occasion to put a final conclusion to such expressions. I entreat you never again to address me in a language so flighty, and so unwelcome. You have already given me great uneasiness; and I must frankly assure you, that if you do not desire to banish me from wherever you are, you will adopt a very different style and conduct in future.' (p. 371).

He was still pleading with her for 'pity' when Lord Orville arrived on the scene. He saw them and 'was hastily retiring; — but I called out, 'Lord Orville! — Sir Clement, release me, — let go my hand!' Lord Orville intervened: 'Sir Clement, you cannot wish to detain Miss Anville by force!' (p. 372).

The moment has come now for a final confrontation between Lord Orville and Sir Clement which Lord Orville has been avoiding all along. He tells Sir Clement that though Evelina

> 'seems alone, and, in some measure, unprotected, is not entirely without friends; she has been extremely well educated, and accustomed to good company; she has a natural love of virtue, and a mind that might adorn *any* station, however exalted: is such a young lady, Sir Clement, a proper object to trifle with? — for your principles, excuse me, Sir, are well known.' (p.373).

He asks Sir Clement what his intentions towards Evelina are. Sir Clement is quite frank about them:

> 'My intentions,' cried he, 'I will frankly own, are hardly known to myself. I think Miss Anville the loveliest of her sex, and, were I a *marrying man*, she, of all the women I have seen, I would fix upon for a wife, but I believe that not even the philosophy of your Lordship would recommend to me a connection of that sort, with a girl of obscure birth, whose only dowry is her beauty, and who is evidently in a state of dependency.' (pp. 374-75).

It is curious that before embarking on his travels on the continent, Sir Clement writes a letter to Evelina explaining his conduct, more particularly his role in creating a prejudice in her mind against Lord Orville. He confesses that he had forged the letter which had made Evelina suspect Lord Orville of evil intentions towards her. In a state of despair, she had then written to Miss Mirvan: 'I cannot but lament to find myself in a world so deceitful, where we must suspect what we see, distrust what we hear, and doubt even what we feel!' (p. 281). She had also told Mr. Villars to his surprise: 'I hate Lord Orville, — he is the last man in the world in whose favour I should be prejudiced.' (p. 289). Sir Clement does not, of course, offer an apology but his confession of a wrong that he had done to Evelina reminds us of the Countess' last visit to Pamela to explain her conduct. It is clear that Fanny Burney is greatly influenced by Richardson. Pamela and Evelina are, of course, placed in different circumstances and their backgrounds and unbringing are also quite different. But both are facing a hostile world. Pamela, as we know, is a fighter but Evelina too is a fighter though her technique is different. She uses her helplessness as a weapon. Julia Epstein calls her appeal to Lord Orville as 'cunning':

> There is no young creature, my Lord, who so greatly wants, or so earnestly wishes for, the advice and assistance of her friends, as I do; I am new to the world, and unused to acting for myself, — my intentions are never wilfully blameable, yet I err perpetually! — I have, hitherto, been blest with the most affectionate of friends, and, indeed, the ablest of men, to guide and instruct me upon every occasion; — but he is too distant, now, to be applied to at the moment I want his aid; — and *here*, — there is not a human being whose counsel I can ask![15]

The fact, however, is that, as Judy Simons says, it is only in her 'public behaviour' that she 'persists in an attitude of helplessness, reliant on male advice'. Judy Simons adds:

Evelina is easily the most astute and reliable character around but she remains subservient to the cardboard figures who masquerade as men, asking them to 'think for me, my dearest Sir, and suffer not my doubting mind that knows not which way to direct its hopes to be guided by your wisdom and unerring counsel.' Evelina surely needs no-one to think for her; her quizzical intelligence selects and discriminates on every page of the novel. Rather albeit unconsciously, she is playing a double game.[16]

IV

Evelina is threatened not only by Sir Clement Willoughby but by others too. Almost every man in her society is a threat to women. Most men believe that women exist only for men's sexual gratification. Even the vulgar Mr. Smith who comes from a lower middle class home but who has pretentions of being a 'gentleman' tries to flirt with Evelina. When she snubs him, he replies:

> 'My dear Ma'am, you must be a little patient; I assure you I have no bad designs, I have not upon my word; but, really, there is no resolving upon such a thing as matrimony all at once; what with the loss of one's liberty, what with the ridicule of all one's acquaintance, — I assure you, Ma'am, you are the first lady who ever made me even demur upon this subject; for, after all, my dear Ma'am, marriage is the devil!'
>
> 'Your opinion, Sir,' answered I, 'of either the married or the single life, can be of no manner of consequence to me, and therefore, I would by no means trouble you to discuss their different merits.'
>
> 'Why, really, Ma'am, as to your being a little out of sorts, I must own I can't wonder at it, for, to be sure, marriage is all in all with the ladies; but with us gentlemen it's quite another thing! Now only put yourself in my place, — 'suppose you had such a large acquaintance of gentlemen as I have, — and that you had always been used to appear a little — a little smart

among them, — why now, how should you like to let yourself down all at once into a married man?' (p. 243).

The aristocrats, of course, regard it as a part of their normal culture to entice young women. Lord Merton who is regarded as 'the standard 'bad' aristocrat of the story'[17] says to a young lady: 'And how can one sit by you, and be good?' .... 'when only to look at you is enough to make one wicked, or wish to be so?' (p. 120). He is also the speaker of the notoriously memorable line: 'I don't know what the devil a woman lives for after thirty; she is only in other folks way' (p. 295). This need not surprise us as even Maria Edgeworth 'wryly commends the "wish of a celebrated beauty" not to live past twenty-nine as "good sense".'[18] The fact, of course, is that for aristocrats like Lord Merton women are mere sex-objects and they cannot see the very important role that women play in life after attaining maturity. In this respect, Lord Orville is altogether different from Lord Merton and his circle. He speaks of Mrs. Mirvan, a middle-aged lady, 'in terms of most just praise'. 'She is gentle and amiable', he says, 'a true feminine character' (p. 311). She is a genuinely affectionate and cultured lady and it is not surprising that she treats Evelina almost as her own child. She tries to protect her from Mrs. Duval and writes to her mother, Lady Howard, that she should not bring Mrs. Duval to Howard Grove as she would try to take away Evelina to her undesirable relations. Evelina rightly says: 'This dear lady seems eternally studying my happiness and advantage'. (p. 112).

Lord Merton is described as 'a professed admirer of beauty, but a man of most licentious character; that among men, his companions consisted chiefly of gamblers and jockies, and among women, he was rarely admitted' (p. 297). But he is going to marry Lord Orville's sister. The brother did oppose the march but 'now that she is near being at her own disposal, is tolerably quiet' (p. 297). What is extraordinary is that Lord Merton can misbehave to other women even in the presence of Lady Louisa, Lord Orville's sister. Evelina tells us that in the presence of Lord Orville and his sister, Lord Merton 'attached himself to me .... with a freedom of gallantry that put me extremely out of countenance. He paid me the most high-flown compliments, and frequently and forcibly seized my hand, though I repeatedly, and with undissembled anger, drew it back. Lord Orville, I saw, watched us with earnestness, and Lady Louisa's smiles were converted into looks of disdain.' (p. 337). After she got herself released, she tried to escape him but 'hastily following, [he] caught my hand, and saying the *day was his own*, vowed he would not let me go.'

> 'You *must*, my Lord,' cried I, extremely flurried.
>
> 'You are the most charming girl in the world,' said he, 'and never looked better than at this moment.'
>
> 'My Lord,' cried Mrs. Selwyn, advancing to us, 'you don't consider, that the better Miss Anville looks, the more striking is the contrast with your Lordship; therefore, for your own sake, I would advise you not to hold her.' (p. 337).

At last Mrs. Beaumont intervenes: 'My Lord', said Mrs. Beaumont,

> 'I must beg leave to interfere; I know not if Lady Louisa can pardon you, but, as this young Lady is at my house, I do not chuse to have her made uneasy.'
>
> 'I pardon him!' cried Lady Louisa, 'I declare I am monstrous glad to get rid of him'. (p.338).

One may ask, then why is she marrying him and what kind of marriage it is going to be? It is also a grave reflection on Lord Orville that all this can happen in his presence and he dare not intervene. His assurance to Evelina a few moments later somehow sounds hollow:

> 'My *dear* Miss Anville,' cried he, warmly, 'allow me to be your friend; think of me as if I were indeed your brother, and let me entreat you to accept my best services, if there is any thing in which I can be so happy as to shew my regard,—my respect for you!' (p.339).

In Lord Merton's circle, women are generally regarded with contempt. That Lady Louisa does deserve contempt is beyond doubt. She is an affected and empty-headed girl. Her only merit is that she is an heiress. When Lord Merton asks her 'if she should *take the air before dinner*,' she gives an irritatingly affected reply:

> 'Really,' answered she, 'I don't know; — I'm afraid it's monstrous hot; besides,' (putting her hand to her forehead) 'I a'n't half well; it's quite horrid to have such weak nerves! — the least thing in the world discomposes me: I declare, that man's oddness has given me such a shock, — I don't know when I shall recover from it. But I'm a sad weak creature, — don't you think I am, my Lord?'
>
> 'O, by no means,' answered he, 'your Ladyship is merely delicate, — and devil take me if ever I had the least passion for an Amazon.'
>
> 'I have the honour to be quite of your Lordship's opinion,' said Mr. Lovel, looking maliciously at Mrs. Selwyn, 'for I have an insuperable aversion to strength, either of body or mind, in a female.'
>
> 'Faith, and so have I,' said Mr. Coverley; 'for egad I'd as soon see a woman chop wood, as hear her chop logic.'
>
> 'So would every man in his senses,' said Lord Merton; 'for a woman wants nothing to recommend her but beauty and good-nature; in every thing else she is either impertinent or unnatural. For my part, deuce take me if ever I wish to hear a word of sense from a woman as long as I live!' (p. 390).

Mrs. Selwyn's retort to all this nonsense is most apt:

> 'It has always been agreed,' said Mrs. Selwyn, looking round her with the utmost contempt, 'that no man ought to be connected with a woman whose understanding is superior to his own. Now I very much fear, that to accommodate all this good company, according to such a rule, would be utterly impracticable, unless we should chuse subjects from Swift's hospital of idiots.' (p. 390).

Evelina should enjoy this retort. Inwardly she herself is capable of this retort. She has the same aversion to male arrogance and stupidity. But outwardly, of course, she has to adopt a more appropriate feminine style. She has already heard Lord Orville praising Mrs. Mirvan for her truly 'feminine character' and her aim seems to be to do all that can win Lord Orville's approval. Of course, Mrs. Selwyn has an assured social standing in society and she can afford to ignore public opinion. Evelina does find her a little too aggressive but are we sure that she disapproves of her character as she claims for the benefit of Mr. Villars? 'Mrs. Selwyn's is very kind and attentive to me,' she says. She also admires her intelligence but believes that

> 'her understanding, indeed, may be called *masculine*; but, unfortunately, her manners deserve the same epithet; for, in studying to acquire the knowledge of the other sex, she has lost all the softness of her own. In regard to myself, however, as I have neither courage nor inclination to argue with her, I have never been personally hurt at her want of gentleness; a virtue which, nevertheless, seems so essential a part of the female character, that I find myself more awkward, and less at ease, with a woman who wants it, than I do with a man. She is not a favourite with Mr. Villars, who has often been disgusted at her unmerciful propensity to satire.' (p. 292).

Perhaps Fanny Burney is herself not clear what attitude to adopt towards Mrs. Selwyn. Mrs. Selwyn is a liberated woman and she is clearly superior to almost all characters in the novel (whether male or female) in both intelligence and courage. She confronts Evelina's father boldly and solves a problem that had baffled Mr. Villars and Lady Howard for such a long time. Judy Simons says that 'we are presented with two models of female behaviour and Mrs. Selwyn must be seen as a necessary compliment to Evelina'. The novel, in Judy Simons' words, 'demonstrates that active interference produces results just as effectively as the heroine's modest submissiveness secures the attentions of the desirable Lord Orville.[19]

V

Since most novels of the period were regarded as Cinderella stories, Anthea Zaman declares that with Fanny Burney's *Evelina*,

> 'Suddenly the reader was in a world where Cinderella's views on footwear mattered as much as Prince Charming's; where hair was not golden tresses but something which needed a hairdresser. *Evelina* tore a certain set of conventions to shreds once and for all, and there was no hope whatever that they could ever be patched up again.'[20]

The most important convention that Burney rejected was the romantic view that Cinderella stories had encouraged. She is a realist and she reminded her women readers that no Princes were waiting for them and that they had to prepare themselves to face a hostile world in order to survive. She propounded the view that young women needed a rational attitude to life and warned them of the consequences of uncontrolled emotion. She describes the heroine of *Camilla* in a situation in which 'the ardour of her imagination .... shook her judgement from its .... unsteady seat, and left her at the mercy of wayward Sensibility - that delicate but irregular power.'[21]

In *Evelina* itself, at one stage Mr. Villars reminds Evelina that in her love for Lord Orville she is also 'at the mercy of wayward Sensibility:

> Young, animated, entirely off your guard, and thoughtless of consequences, *imagination* took the reins, and *reason,* slow-paced, though sure-footed, was unequal to a race with so eccentric and flighty a companion. How rapid was then my Evelina's progress through those regions of fancy and passion whither her new guide conducted her! — She saw Lord Orville at a ball, — and he was *the most amiable of men*! — She met him

again at another, — and *he had every virtue under Heaven*! (p. 332).

Lord Orville makes a powerful impression on Evelina's mind in her first meeting with him. After all, it was natural that a seventeen year old girl coming to London for the first time and mixing in high society should be dazzled when a Lord treats her with extra politeness. She writes to her guardian, Mr. Villars, that she wished that he knew him 'because I am sure you would love him; and I have felt that wish for no other person I have seen since I came to London' (p. 79). Later she wrote to Miss Mirvan with whom she had stayed in the earlier part of her visit:

> Tell me, my dear Maria, do you never re-trace in your memory the time we past here when together? to me, it recurs for ever! And yet, I think I rather recollect a dream, or some visionary fancy, than a reality. — That I should ever have been known to Lord Orville, — that I should have spoken to — have danced with him, — seems now a romantic illusion: and that elegant politeness, that flattering attention, that high-bred delicacy, which so much distinguished him above all other men, and which struck us with such admiration, I now re-trace the remembrance of, rather as belonging to an object of ideal perfection, formed by my own imagination, than to a being of the same race and nature as those with whom I at present converse. (p. 186).

But Burney knows that 'ideal perfection' is created only by imagination and it is not the stuff of which marriages are made. Lord Orville is, of course, a mature person and though he is greatly attracted by Evelina's beauty, he is not wholly clear in his mind about her. We have already seen that he formed a somewhat low opinion of her intelligence when he first met her. He, in fact, described her as 'a poor weak girl'. When she was described as an angel, he merely retorted, 'a *silent* one' (p. 38). But as time passed and he saw her in various situations - some of them very embarrassing ones - he started taking more interest in her. He is shocked when he sees her in the company of two prostitutes. He can't understand why a girl of her beauty, superior culture and breeding should be mixing in such company. He is by nature reserved but he can't help finding out the truth though, of course, he hesitates to ask her a direct question:

> 'I should be extremely sorry to appear impertinent,—yet hardly know how to avoid it.'
>
> 'Impertinent! O my Lord,' cried I, eagerly, 'that, I am sure, is impossible!'
>
> 'You are very good,' cried I,
>
> 'You are very good,' answered he, 'and encourage me to be ingenuous—'
>
> Again he stopped; but my expectation was too great for speech: at last, without looking at me, in a low voice and hesitating manner, he said, 'Were those ladies with whom I saw you last night, ever in your company before?'
>
> 'No, my Lord,' cried I, rising and colouring violently, 'nor will they ever be again.' (p. 260).

The forged letter of Sir Clement Willoughby does, of course, create serious doubts in Evelina's mind about Lord Orville's character. In fact she goes so far as to say: 'I hate Lord Orville, — he is the last man in the world in whose favour I should be prejudiced' (p. 289). She writes to her friend, Miss Mirvan:

> As a sister I loved him, — I could have entrusted him with every thought of my heart, had he deigned to wish my confidence; so steady did I think his honour, so *feminine* his delicacy, and so amiable his nature! I have a thousand times imagined that the whole study of his life, and whole purport of his reflections, tended solely to the good and happiness of others: — but I will talk, — write, — think of him no more! (p. 284).

She meets Lord Orville again when she goes to Bristol with Mrs. Selwyn. She is not sure how he would conduct himself and is, in fact, unhappy that she has to meet him again. But she finds him behaving exactly as he had behaved earlier, with proper politeness and consideration. Evelina is delighted and writes to Mr. Villars:

> Oh Sir, Lord Orville is still himself! still, what from the moment I beheld, I believed him to be, all that is amiable in man! and your happy Evelina, restored at once to spirits and tranquillity, is no longer sunk in her own opinion, nor discontented with the world; — no longer, with dejected eyes, sees the prospect of passing her future days in sadness, doubt, and suspicion! — with revived courage she now looks forward, and expects to meet with goodness, even among mankind; — though still she feels, as strongly as ever, the folly of hoping, in any *second* instance, to meet with *perfection.* (p. 299).

Though Lord Orville is no more a perfect man in her eyes, Evelina is quite impressed by the interest that he takes in her welfare. She attributes this interest to Lord Orville's feeling that he 'seems to regard [her] as a helpless stranger, ... entitled to his good offices and protection' (p. 319).

In their relationship, Mr. Macartney also creates difficulties. He is really Evelina's half-brother but Evelina does not know this. She had met him at Branghtons' house and had prevented him from committing suicide. She had also helped him with some money. In Bristol, he saw her and tried to meet her. She could not invite him to come to Mrs. Beaumont's house but he came uninvited and requested a private meeting with her for a few minutes. Lord Orville happened to see him talking to Evelina and became curious. He asked her why he was insisting on a private meeting. Evelina merely said: 'He is a gentleman, and has been very unfortunate, — but I am not, — I think not, — at liberty to say more' (p. 329). This excites Lord Orville's curiosity still further. He explained his curiosity by telling her that he was deeply interested 'not only in all your concerns, but in all your actions.' 'This speech' Evelina calls 'the most *particular* one Lord Orville had ever made to me' (p. 343, Italics mine). She was so struck by it that she could not make an answer. A little later, he again asked her when she would see, Mr. Macartney:

> 'Indeed, my Lord,' cried I, 'I know not, but I would give the universe for a few moments conversation with him!' I spoke this with a simple sincerity, and was not aware of the force of my words.
>
> 'The universe!' repeated he, 'Good God, Miss Anville, do you say this to *me*?
>
> 'I would say it,' returned I, 'to any body, my Lord.' (p. 343).

Lord Orville was disturbed by this but he wisely chose to trust Evelina:

> 'This meeting, you say is essential to your repose?'
>
> 'I did not say *that*, my Lord; but yet I have the most important reasons for wishing to speak to him.'
>
> He paused a few minutes, and then said, with warmth, 'Yes, you *shall* speak to him! — I will myself assist you! — Miss Anville, I am sure, cannot form a wish against propriety, I will ask no questions, I will rely upon her own purity, and uninformed, blindfold as I am, I will serve her with all my power!' (p. 344).

VI

Then Evelina receives Mr. Villars' letter in which he asks her to 'quit' Lord Orville as 'his sight is baneful to your repose, his society is death to your future tranquillity' (p. 333). He is obviously warning her not to fall in love with Lord Orville as it would hurt her. He is convinced that whatever a girl's merit, no lord would marry her in her present circumstances. She promises to leave Lord Orville though she realizes that it is not easy to do so:

> The more I consider of parting with Lord Orville, the less fortitude do I feel to bear the separation; — the friendship he has

> shewn me, — his politeness, — his sweetness of manners, — his concern in my affairs, — his solicitude to oblige me, — all, all to be given up! (p. 347).

She writes to Mr. Villars:

> — for never, never can I cease to regret that I have lost the friendship of Lord Orville! — Oh Sir, I have slighted, have rejected, — have thrown it away! — No matter, it was an honour I merited not to preserve, and I now see, — that my mind was unequal to sustaining it without danger.
>
> Yet so strong is the desire you have implanted in me to act with uprightness and propriety, that, however the weakness of my heart may distress and afflict me, it will never, I humbly trust, render me wilfully culpable. The wish of doing well governs every other, as far as concerns my conduct, — for am I am not *your* child? — the creature of your own forming? — Yet, oh Sir, friend, parent of my heart! — my feelings are all at war with my duties; and, while I most struggle to acquire self-approbation, my peace, my hopes, my happiness, — are lost! (p. 362).

The decisive moment comes when she hears the conversation that takes place between Lord Orville and Sir Clement Willoughby. This is the moment when Lord Orville asks Willoughby about his 'intentions' towards Evelina. Willoughby asks Lord Orville what authority he has to ask him such a question when he is nothing to her — neither a father, nor a brother, nor a lover. Lord Orville admits that he has 'not the right of enquiry which any of those three titles bestow, and yet I confess the warmest wishes to serve her, and see her happy' (p. 373). When Willoughby calls Lord Orville's attitude 'extraordinary', Lord Orville replies:

> 'It may be so,' said Lord Orville; 'but this young lady seems to be peculiarly situated; she is very young, very inexperienced, yet appears to be left totally to her own direction. She does not,

> I believe, see the dangers to which she is exposed, and I will own to you, I feel a strong desire to point them out.' (p. 373).

He also praises her 'understanding' though he recognises that 'she is too young for suspicion, and has an artlessness of disposition that I never saw equaled.' He also admits that

> She is not, indeed, like most modern young ladies, to be known in half an hour; her modest worth, and fearful excellence, require both time and encouragement to shew themselves. She does not, beautiful as she is, seize the soul by surprise, but, with more dangerous fascination, she steals it almost imperceptibly. (p. 374).

After hearing all this, Evelina writes to Mr. Villars: 'tell me, my dear Sir, what *you* think of him? — tell me if he is not the noblest of men? (p. 375).

VII

When Lord Orville hears that Evelina is going to her guardian in Berry Hill, he rushes to her:

> 'You are going, then,' cried he, taking my hand, 'and you give me not the smallest hope of your return! — will you not, then, my too lovely friend! — will you not, at least, teach me, with fortitude like your own, to support your absence?
>
> 'My Lord,' cried I, endeavouring to disengage my hand, 'pray let me go!'
>
> 'I will,' cried he, to my inexpressible confusion, dropping on one knee, 'if you wish to leave me!'
>
> 'Oh, my Lord,' exclaimed I, 'rise, I beseech you, rise! — such a posture to me! — surely your Lordship is not so cruel as to mock me!'
>
> 'Mock you!' repeated he earnestly, 'no, I revere you! I esteem and I admire you above all human beings! — you are the

> friend to whom my soul is attached as to its better half! you are the most amiable, the most perfect of women! and you are dearer to me than language has the power of telling!' (p. 379).

Evelina informs Mr. Villars: 'my dear Sir, I was not proof against his solicitations — and he drew from me the most sacred secret of my heart!' (p. 380). This secret, of course, is her love for him.

But Evelina is realistic enough to recognise that she is not Lord Orville's equal. He has everything — family, wealth, name and status in society whereas she has nothing. When Lord Orville asks her to share her griefs with him and tells her not to 'withdraw [her] esteem' and not to 'repent the goodness you have shewn me' (p. 396), his generosity overpowers her and she weeps 'like an infant'. She is afraid that if Lord Orville knew everything about her, a man of his standing would not marry her. And yet she would not like to marry any one - far less a noble man like Lord Orville - by hiding her real situation from him. Moreover, his tenderness emboldens her and she says:

> 'My Lord,' said I, when I was able to speak, 'you little know what an outcast you have honoured with your choice! — a child of bounty, — an orphan from infancy, — dependent, even for subsistence dependent, upon the kindness of compassion! — Rejected by my natural friends, — disowned for ever by my nearest relation, — Oh, my Lord, so circumstanced, can I deserve the distinction with which you honour me? No, no, I feel the inequality too painfully; — you must leave me, my Lord, you must suffer me to return to obscurity, — and there, in the bosom of my first, best, — my only friend, — I will pour forth all the grief of my heart! — while you, my Lord, must seek elsewhere —'
>
> I could not proceed; my whole soul recoiled against the charge I would have given, and my voice refused to utter it.
>
> 'Never!' cried he, warmly; 'my heart is yours, and I swear to you an attachment eternal! — You prepare me, indeed, for a tale of horror, and I am almost breathless with expectation, —

> but so firm is my conviction, that, whatever are your misfortunes, to have merited them is not of the number, that I feel myself more strongly, more invincibly attached to you than ever! — 'Tell me but where I may find this noble friend, whose virtues you have already taught me to reverence, — and I will fly to obtain his consent and intercession, that henceforward our fates may be indissolubly united, — and then shall it be the sole study of my life to endeavour to soften your past, — and guard you from future misfortunes!' (p. 397).

In *Evelina* too we have a novel in which 'virtue' is 'rewarded' as Samuel Richardson had done more than forty years earlier. In modern times, happy endings have become suspect but surely Burney has made the ending as realistic as she could. She is not, of course, Jane Austen but there is no doubt that she anticipates Jane Austen. Jane Austen herself recognised it. There is every possibility - indeed probability - that the marriage of Lord Orville and Evelina, the daughter of Sir John Belmont (who finally owns her), would be a happy one.

NOTES

1. Eva Figes, *Sex and Subterfuge: Women Novelists to 1850* (London, 1982), p. 33.
2. *The Early Diary of Frances Burney* (1768-1778), ed. Annie Raine Ellis, 2 Vols., New York (1971), Vol. 2, p. 88.
3. *An Unfortunate Mother's Advice to her Absent Daughters in a letter to Miss Pennington* (1761), pp.49-50. Cited by Kristina Straub, *Divided Fictions: Fanny Burney and Feminine Strategy* (University Press of Kentucky, Lexington, 1987), p. 64.
4. *The Early Diary of Frances Burney*, Vol.1, p. 17 and p.49.
5. See Kristina Straub, p. 227.
6. Cited by Kristina Straub, p. 69.
7. Margaret Anne Doody, *Frances Burney: The Life in the Works* (Rutgers University Press, New Brunswick, New Jersey, 1988), pp. 42-3.
8. Margaret Anne Doody, op. cit., p. 200.
9. Mona Scheurmann, *Social Protest in the Eighteenth Century English Novel* (Ohio University Press, Columbus, 1985), p.70.
10. Susan Staves, *"Evelina: or Female Difficulties"*, *Modern Philology* (Vol.

73, 1975-6), p. 368.

11. Judy Simons, *Fanny Burney* ('Women Writers'), Macmillan, 1987, p.25.
12. Page references are to the 1992 reprint of *Evelina or The History of a Young Lady's Entrance into the World* (Bantam Books, New York) with an Introduction by Angeline Goreau (1992).
13. Margaret Anne Doody, op. cit., p. 40.
14. Judy Simons, *op. cit.*, p. 36.
15. Julia Epstein, *The Iron Pen: Frances Burney and the Politics of Women's Writings* (University of Wisconsin Press, Madison, 1989), p.110.
16. Judy Simons, p. 51.
17. K.G. Hall, *The Exalted Heroine and the Triumph of Order: Class, Women and Religion in the English Novel, 1740-1800* (Macmillan, 1993), pp. 110-111.
18. See Kristina Straub, p. 10.
19. Judy Simons, p. 55.
20. Anthea Zaman, *Presumptuous Girls: Women and their World in the serious woman's novel.* (London, 1977), pp. 12-13.
21. Cited by Jean Hagstrum, *Sex and Sensibility: Ideal and Erotic Love from Milton to Mozart* (University of Chicago Press, 1980), p. 271.

Chapter V

Susan Ferrier's View of a Happy Marriage

These days very few people read Susan Ferrier's *Marriage, a Novel* (1818) though it was quite popular in the 19th century. Even in the 20th century it has not been wholly neglected. Indeed, it has been constantly in print and has the prestige of having been included in the Oxford English Novels.

Herbert Foltinek, the editor of the novel in the Oxford Series (1971), describes the central theme in the following words: "The ideal of a happy marriage, of which the novel offers so singularly few examples, comes as an ultimate reward to the long-suffering heroine who has proved her good sense, fine sentiment, and strength of character" (Introduction, p. XV). It is perhaps best to quote the author herself to see her conception of a happy marriage. In the last paragraph of the novel she says:

> in a virtuous attachment, [husband and wife] found happiness as earth's pilgrims ever possess, whose greatest felicity must spring from a higher source. The extensive influence which generally attends upon virtue joined to prosperity, was used by them for its best purposes. It was not confined either to rich or poor, to cast or sect; but all shared in their benevolence whom that benevolence could benefit. And the poor, the sick, and the desolate, united in blessing what heaven had already blessed - this happy Marriage. (p. 468).[1]

It is picture of a virtuous life where happiness springs from a higher source and where benevolence is the most important feature of human conduct. A modern reader may, however, ask whether in this picture there is enough scope for *companionship in marriage* between man and woman. It is interesting that the mother of Col. Lennox (the man who is going to marry the heroine) feels compelled to say to her son: 'Young people now,' she says, 'are diffirent from what they were in my day. There is no such thing as falling in love now, you are all so cautious'. (p.298). To what age is she referring? The novel's date is 1818 but it clearly reflects an earlier period. One wonders whether Mrs. Lennox is referring to early 18th century or even the Restoration age. One thing is, of course, clear: the heroine of Ferrier's novel would greatly improve if she had had a touch of the Restoration heroine's sparkle. Elizabeth Bennet of Jane Austen's *Pride and Prejudice* (which appeared in 1813) certainly has some of that sparkle and it is no accident that what charms Darcy is 'the intelligent .... and beautiful expression of her dark eyes' and more particularly, her 'easy playfulness.' It is also not without significance that Elizabeth starts flirting with Darcy the moment she notices his special interest in her and later does not hesitate to make fun of him immediately after marriage. Can Ferrier's heroine do so? But the heroine of Ferrier's novel is not, of course, Elizabeth Bennet and consequently the ideal of a happy marriage in her case is somewhat flawed - too religiously dogmatic and hence limited and deficient.

I

It is, of course, true that in the context of the various marriages that the novelist presents, the heroine's marriage does shine quite brightly. First we have her own mother's disastrous marriage. Lady Juliana, the mother, is the daughter of an earl and inherits all the weaknesses of the 18th century fashionable upbringing. The emphasis in her upbringing has been only on elegance of manners and the cultivation of her mind and character has been completely neglected. Surprisingly, she has not been given even the slightest religious instruction. That may explain why she has developed almost an aversion to religion. She, of course, never visits a church herself but it is surprising that when Mary seeks her permission to go to church, she is forbidden to do so. Mary pleads that she has 'always been accustomed to attend church' at her aunt, Mrs. Douglas's place, but Lady Juliana retorts: 'That is a sufficient reason for my choosing that you should not attend it here'. (p. 248).

Lady Juliana's ideas of love and marriage were moulded by contemporary romantic fiction. Her father, of course, had an altogether different approach. His own marriage had been a wholly mercenary one. As Lady Maclaughlan tells Lady Juliana in her very first meeting with her, her 'mother was an heiress' and her 'father married her for money, and she married him to be a countess'. The conflict of views about marriage between father and daughter is reflected in their conversation in the very first chapter:

> 'As I can give you no fortune', said the Earl, ... 'you have perhaps no great pretensions to a very brilliant establishment.'
>
> 'Oh! none in the world, papa,' eagerly interrupted Lady Juliana; "a mere competence with the man of my heart" -
>
> "The man of a fiddlestick!" exclaimed Lord Courtland in a fury; "what the devil have you to do with a heart, I should like to know! There is no talking to a young woman now about marriage, but she is all in a blaze about hearts, and darts, and - and - but heark ye child, I'll suffer no daughter of mine to play the fool with her heart, indeed! She shall marry for the purpose for which matrimony was ordained amongst people of birth - that is, for the aggrandisement of her family, the extending of their political influence - for becoming, in short, the depository of their mutual interest. These are the only purposes for which persons of rank ever think of marriage." (p.2).

The father then suggests a suitable husband for Lady Juliana. He asks her with 'exultation and delight' what she thinks of 'Duke of L -.'

The Duke of L -?, repeated Lady Juliana, with a scream of horror and surprise; 'surely, papa, you cannot be serious; why, he's red haired and squints, and he's as old as you'.

'If he were as old as the devil, and as ugly too,' interrupted the enraged Earl, 'he should be your husband; and may I perish if you shall have any other!' (p.3).

The Earl is, of course, serious in his resolve as his belief is that 'it was very well for ploughmen and dairy maids to marry for love; but for a young woman of rank to think of such a thing, was plebian in the extreme!' (p.4). In this he reflects the views of his class which educated its daughters 'for the sole purpose of forming a brilliant establishment, of catching the eye, and captivating the senses,' of some suitable youngmen of their class. The "cultivation of [their] minds[s], or the correction of [their] temper" did not form a part of their education (p.4.). Any girl with some commonsense would have thought of some way of bringing her father round to her point of view, but Juliana has neither commonsense nor patience and so, in a fit of passion, she elopes to Scotland with her lover who was as 'young, thoughtless, and enamoured as herself'. (p.5).

It is no surprise that this marriage leads to disaster. Indeed, 'at the end of two months, ... the enamoured husband began to suspect, that the lips of his 'angel Julia' 'could utter very silly things; while the fond bride, on her part, discovered that though her 'adored Henry's' 'figure was symmetry itself, yet it certainly was deficient in a certain air - a *je ne scais quoi* - that marks the man of fashion'. (pp. 5-6).

Lady Juliana's expectations from marriage are clearly contradictory. In addition to the adventure of romance, she also wants the fashionable life of London which only a 'brilliant establishment' could provide. Henry can provide the adventure of romance but not a life of fashion in London. All that he can do is to take her to his ancestral home in the Highlands, Glenfern Castle. She, however, despises the place and its inmates. She indeed hates everything Scottish. When breakfast is served, she refuses to touch the "barley meal scones", home-made cakes or pease-meal or cakes made of oat meal provided by Henry's aunts and instead demands 'some muffin and chocolate'.(p.33). Her husband has to remind her that she is not in London. The real problem here is that she has lived a wholly superficial upper-class life in London and has neither any understanding of things outside that fashionable circle nor any capacity for adjustment. She had got infatuated by Henry's figure when she saw him in his glittering military uniform of an A.D.C. to a high military dignitary. Now, of course, he has been deprived of his commission too on account of absence from duty without leave.

It is to be noted that Lady Juliana's marriage defies all the wisdom that contemporary conduct books contained on the question of love and marriage. Eighteenth century warned its daughters to beware of passion which Mary Astell had described as an 'irregular Appetite' in her famous pamphlet on *Reflections upon Marriage* (1700). This passion, it was widely believed, was prompted by nothing more solid than more sexual attraction. This attraction, experience showed, soon subsided leaving the woman to a life of drudgery. It was also the parents responsibility to teach their daughters the duties that they would have to perform as wives and as mothers and also the various skills that they needed in order to run a household. But Juliana has no notion of any of these things and it is extraordinary that she cannot even dress herself without the assitance of her woman. When Henry asks her to come down from her room to meet his elder brother and his wife, Juliana bluntly refuses: 'O, not now, I don't feel equal to the encounter; besides, I must dress. But what shall I do; since that vile woman [whom they had picked up on their journey to be Juliana's maid] is gone, I can't dress myself. I never did such a thing in my life, and I am sure, it is impossible that I can". (p.19).

Juliana is a stupid and selfish woman and totally unfit to marry almost any one. The picture that Ferrier paints of this marriage somehow does not seem convincing. When Juliana presents 'to the house of Douglas - not, alas, the ardently desired heir to its ancient consequence, but twin-daughters' (116), her behaviour strikes us as almost unnatural. Henry, of course, is delighted and rushes to his wife's room and 'kneeling by her side, he press[es] her hands to his lips with feelings of the deepest emotion'! But the mother is not pleased at all and blurts out:

> 'How very provoking! I hate girls so - and two of them - oh!'

And when Henry kisses the babies, she exclaims:

> "How can you kiss them, Henry! They are so ugly, and they squall so! Oh do, for heaven's sake, take them away'. (pp. 117-8).

It is only after 'pressing solicitations of her husband, [that] the fashionable mother was prevailed upon to attempt nursing one of the two starving infants'. A wet-nurse was procured but 'she refused to undertake both children' and the second baby was left in the care of Henry's aunts. (p.118).

This second baby was 'weak and delicate' by birth and it soon started losing its strength. Luckily Mrs. Douglas, the wife of Henry's elder brother, happened to visit them at this stage. She congratulated Juliana on the birth of her daughters, but Juliana told Mrs. Douglas that she hates girls - and 'cannot stand her crying all the while'. 'I wish', she says, 'I could send her out of my hearing altogether, for her noise will be the death of me.' Mrs. Douglas is shocked to hear it but she has no children of her own and she offers to take away the girl to nurse her and bring her up. Juliana is pleased to be relieved of 'the little plague'. (p.120). Mrs. Douglas' husband, though pleased at what his wife has done, is outraged by Juliana's conduct as a mother. 'The mother is such a fool', he says but Mrs. Douglas indignantly describes her as very much 'worse than a fool .... for she hates and abjures this her unoffending babe'. (p.121).

II

Mrs. Douglas is, of course, an altogether different kind of woman from Juliana and so is her marriage. This is how she is introduced by the author:

> Mrs. Douglas was, on the maternal side, related to an English family. Her mother had died in giving birth to her; and her father, shortly after, falling in the service of his country, she had been consigned in infancy to the care of her aunt. Lady Audley had taken charge of her, on condition, that she should never be claimed by her Scottish relations, for whom that lady entertained as much aversion as contempt. A latent feeling of affection for her departed sister, and a large portion of family pride, had prompted her wish of becoming the protectress of her orphan niece. (pp. 73-4).

Under her aunt's care, the orphan niece, Alicia Malcolm, grew up as a 'rational, cheerful, and sweet-tempered girl' (74). She was, of course, lucky in her governess who was a 'woman of strong understanding and enlarged mind' and who 'instilled' in the girl's mind 'a deep and strong sense of religion' (p.74). Lady Audley's son was also more or less of the same age as Alicia. They grew up together and by the time he was nineteen years of age and she was eighteen, their friendship had ripened into love. Lady Audley realized it only when Alicia rejected a proposal of marriage from 'a gentleman of large fortune and brilliant connexions who resided in their neighbourhood'. He was also an 'heir to an earldom' and 'member of the county'. (pp. 76-7). Lady Audley rejoiced at such an excellent match for Alicia and she was determined that Alicia should become the man's wife. But Alicia's rejection of the match made Lady Audley suspect that there must be some hidden reason for it. But Alicia only pleaded with her aunt 'to waive the subject, as she found it impossible ever to consent to such an union' (p.78). Lady Audley's son, Sir Edmund Audley, who by nature was 'ardent, impetuous and passionate' (p.75) at last mustered up sufficient courage to tell his mother of his desire to marry Alicia himself. His mother was shocked but he declared that he was determined to marry her 'as soon as he was of age' (p. 79). When his mother threatened him by her show of authority, he left the house 'to allow his mother time to reconcile herself to the misfortune of beholding him the husband of Alicia Malcolm". (p.79).

He also left a letter for Alicia in which he told her that 'two years must relapse before I can become legally my own master' and expressing full 'confidence .... in her constancy' (p. 80). Alicia who had always felt the deepest sense of gratitude towards her aunt, handed the letter to Lady Audley. Lady Audley was furious and made it clear that 'while she had life, she would never give her consent and approbation to her son's marriage' to Alicia (p.81). She also decided to send Alicia immediately to her grand- father, Sir Duncan Malcolm, who had often written to Lady Audley that he wanted to see his grand-daughter before he died. Before Alicia was ready to leave, Lady Audley insisted that she give her a promise 'mever to unite herself to Sir Edmund unsanctioned by his mother' (p.83). Out of her sense of gratitude to her aunt, she gave the promise in all sincerity. She also wrote a letter to Sir Edmund before her departure indicating her resolve to keep the promise given to his mother:

> Forget, I entreat you, this inauspicious passion. Resolve, like me, to resign yourself, without murmuring, to what is now past recall; and, instead of indulging melancholy, regain, by a timely exertion of mind and body, that serenity which is the portion of those who have obeyed the dictates of rectitude. (p. 84).

Sir Edmund was not, of course, the kind of person who could so easily obey the dictates of rectitude. So when, after travelling for four days, Alicia stopped at an inn for the night, a chambermaid came to her and informed her that she was wanted below. Thinking that Lady Audley must have sent for her, she followed the girl who conducted her to another part of the building where she found herself not in the presence of Lady Audley, 'but in the arms of Sir Edmund' (p.85). He now told her that they were in Scotland, 'the land of liberty' and he had 'a clergyman waiting'. So, he said, 'in five minutes, you shall be my own beyond the power of fate to sever us' (p.86). Pleading with her to speak the word, he knelt at her feet when sudenly Lady Audley entered the room. Instead of venting her anger at her son, she accused Alicia of 'deceit and treachery' (p.86) and indignantly told her son: "Go, marry her; but first hear me swear, solemnly swear.... that my malediction shall be your portion!" Hearing this, Alicia exclaimed: "Dear Edmund! .... never for me shall your mother's malediction fall on you! Farewell for ever!" (87). And she left the mother and son.

But Edmund did not stop chasing her. She was now living with her grand-father when she received a letter from Edmund. He informed her that two years had passed since they had parted and that he was now of age. He also told her that he would visit her at her grand-father's house. Realizing that she could not stop Edmund from pursuing her unless she 'bestowed her hand on some one else' (p.90), she decided to marry Major Douglas, eldest son of Mr. Douglas of Glenfern. He had been courting her for some time and 'he was pleasing in his person; quiet and simple in his manners; and his character stood for integrity, good temper, and plain sense' (p.91). Soon he resigned his commission and se up as a gentleman-farmer on a small estate bequeathed to him by an uncle in the neighbourhood of Glenfern.

Mrs. Douglas' motive for marrying Major Douglas need not seem extraordinary to us if we remember that her character is moulded on contemporary conduct books. She had given a word to Lady Audley that she would not marry her son without her consent and she had told Edmund that 'never for me shall your mother's malediction fall on you'. Marrying Major Douglas was perhaps the best method of fulfilling both these promises. The writer is conscious that it is not an ideal marriage but she knows that such marriages have as good a chance of succeeding as any other. "An eternal constancy", she says, "is a thing [too] rare to be met with". (p.91). Hence all of us, not women alone, have to adjust to the circumstances in which we have been thrown. Instead of 'indulging in lovelorn pensiveness', Mrs. Douglas 'diligently strove, not only to make up her mind to the lot which had devolved to her, but to bring it to such a frame of cheerfulness, as should enable her to contribute to her husband's happiness' (p.91). In Ferrier's times, and perhaps even today, often it is the husband's 'happiness' which becomes a wife's chief concern. Specially in traditional societies a good wife is expected to think of her husband's happiness first and of her own happiness only secondarily. In most religions and cultures this indeed has been regarded as the most solid basis of a happy marriage. Even in advanced countries, this attitude still persists in one form or another.

Ferrier, of course, does not fail to remind us that in her attempt to provide happiness to her husband, Mrs. Douglas lost 'the buoyant spirit of youth, the bright and quick play of fancy, yet a placid contentment crowned her days; and, at the end of two years, she would have been astonished had any one marked her as an object of compassion' (p.92).

Juliana can neither understand nor appreciate this kind of 'placid contentment'. Indeed, she is amazed to learn that Mrs. Douglas had lived in London: "'You lived in London?' ..... 'And how then can you contrive to exist here?'" Mrs. Douglas' reply is simple and straightforward: "'I not only contrive to exist but to be extremely contented with existence!'..... I possess health, peace of mind, and the affections of a worthy husband; and I should be very undeserving of these blessings, were I to give way to useless regrets, or indulge in impious repinings, because my happiness might once have been more perfect, and still admits of improvement.'" (p.72).

Lady Juliana finds this attitude incomprehensible. Her life is one of constant regrets and 'repinings'. When she happens to see in an old London newspaper the description of the marriage of 'Miss D— to his Grace the Duke of —', 'Envy, regret, self-reproach and resentment, all struggled in the breast of the self-devoted beauty.' (p.110). She cannot think of happiness except in terms of glamour and glitter of high life in London. Later on, when, in spite of her husband's remonstrance, she decides to attend her sister-in-law's masked ball in London, she comes home so disgusted with her own life that she cannot help commenting on the kind of luxurious life that her brother can provide to her sister-in-law:

> there was nobody in the world so much to be envied as Lady Lindore. Such jewels! such dresses! such a house! such a

> husband! so easy and good natured, and rich and generous! She was sure Lindore did not care what his wife did. She might give what parties she pleased; go where she liked; spend as much money as she chose; and he would never trouble his head about the matter. She was quite certain Lady Lindore had not a single thing to wish for; *ergo*, she must be the happiest woman in the world! (p. 145).

The author's general comment on Juliana's attitude is perhaps to be interpreted in the light of the fact that within a few days the news comes that Lady Lindore, 'the happiest woman in the world' according to Juliana, has eloped with 'her favourite St. Leger'. This news makes Juliana's father fall in an 'apoloplectic fit' which causes his death. It does not surprise any one except Lady Juliana that her 'name was not even mentioned in her father's will'. (p. 149).

III

We have discussed two marriages neither of which can be described as really happy in the full sense of the term and neither is based on genuine love. Mrs. Douglas' is clearly a marriage of convenience. It is true that 'eternal constancy' is not easy and perhaps need not even be aimed at. But a marriage which lacks the element of passion altogether and where a woman has to strive 'diligently' to bring herself in 'such a frame of cheerfulness, as should enable her to contribute to her husband's happiness' can hardly be described as successful in the true sense of the term though, of course, as mentioned earlier, such marriages can provide contentment to a woman whose expectations from marriage are not too high. Mrs. Douglas is, of course, a sensible woman and though she has no children of her own, she would perhaps be happy to bring up one of Juliana's daughters. Her husband is also a kind, considerate and, as she claims, a loving and affectionate man. So the compromise seems to be working well. It always does in cases where, to quote Charlotte Lucas of Jane Austen's *Pride and Prejudice*, the woman is not 'romantic' and where she can be satisfied with a 'comfortable home' and a husband whose 'character, connections, and situation in life' offer her a fair 'chance of happiness' - as fair indeed as 'most people can boast on entering the marriage state' (chapter 22). An attempt to seek any kind of resemblance between Charlotte Lucas' marriage with Mr. Collins and that of Alicia with Mr. Douglas is clearly most unfair to Mr. and Mrs. Douglas but all compromises do somehow remind us of that classic compromise.

Juliana's is, of course, a most hopeless case. She is so selfish and self-centred that she is not capable of establishing and maintaining an affectionate and stable relationship with any one, whether husband or children. She is a foolish woman of fashion who needs a husband only to support her in her profligate tastes. Perhaps it would have been better for her if she had accepted her father's advice and married 'the Duke of L'. She would have, of course, missed the adventure of high romance - however short-lived - in eloping with 'adorable Henry' whose 'figure was symetry itself'. But, as her father had said, it would have been no 'mighty sacrifice .... when repaid with a ducal coronet, the most splendid jewels, the finest equipages, and the largest jointure of any woman in England'. (p.3). Henry is a decent fellow but he is so infatuated by Juliana's beauty that he gave no thought to the consequences of his action.

With two daughters and an expensive wife to support, Henry realized that he must do something. He knew that he could not any longer continue being a burden on his family nor could he accept his father's proposal to live the life of a farmer. In sheer despair he wrote to 'the friend and patron of his youth', General Cameron, to help him. The General had felt quite unhappy at Henry marrying 'a lady of quality' whom he knew he could not afford. He is, however, willing to forget it and gets Henry 'reinstated in his former rank in the army' and is also willing to 'settle seven hundred per annum on him, till he saw how matters were conducted' (p.124). This is an excellent offer and the moment Juliana hears it, in her typical manner, she jumps at it:

"Seven hundred pounds a year! ... Heavens! What a quantity of

> money! Why, we shall be quite rich, and I shall have such a beautiful house and such pretty carriages, and give such parties and buy so many things - O dear, how happy I shall be!" (p.125).

Soon they get settled in London but in the very first visit that General Cameron pays to their London house, he realizes that things cannot go right in this house. Not only that he is kept waiting for more than an hour, but he is also made to feel that she has no time to waste on him. Indeed she is too busy talking to the trades people and in ordering all kinds of fancy things in fashion in London society. Henry tries to check her but she has no patience with him. The General sees all this and leaves after advising Henry to ask his wife to seek reconciliation with her father and himself "try to exchange into a marching regiment; for a fellow like you, with such a wife, London is the very devil!" (p.136).

Henry himself had been quite concerned for some time about the future as, after their return to London, Juliana had also given birth to a son. But nothing seemed to affect Juliana. He had often asked her to write to her father but her social life was too hectic to leave her any time for such a trifling matter. This drives Henry to desparation and he shouts in indignation:

> 'Can I not make you understand, that you are ruining yourself and me; that we have nothing to depend upon but the bounty of that man whom you disgust by your caprice, extravagance, and impertinence; and that if you don't get reconciled to your father, what is to become of you? You already know what you have to expect from my family, and how you like living with them.' (p.138).

All this only increases Juliana's defiance and soon enough, 'the fatal blow came. Horses - carriages - everything they could call their own, were seized' by the creditors. The term for which they had held the house had also expired and 'they found themselves on the point of being turned into the street'. Juliana at last expressed the 'desire of being conveyed to her brother's house. A hackney coach was procured, into which the hapless victim of her own follies was carried. Shuddering with disgust, and accompanied by her children and their attendants, she was set down at the noble mansion from which she had fled two years before' (pp. 149-50).

Henry who had stayed with a fellow officer was soon arrested for debts. Juliana's brother obtained his release, took upon himself the discharge of his debts and procured 'leave for him to exchange into a regiment', 'then under orders for India' (p. 154). 'Henry who had never doubted her readiness to accompany him' was shocked when Juliana refused to leave 'all her friends', and 'go to live amongst savages'. This led to a violent scene which 'terminated in an eternal farewell' (p. 155). Some years later we learn that he died in India. Juliana's only regret was that during the period of mourning, she would have to put on black which did not suit her very much!

IV

The only marriage in the novel which is described by the writer as a 'happy Marriage' (p. 468), is that of Mary, Juliana's daughter, whom Mrs. Douglas had taken from her mother in infancy and brought up in the Highlands according to her own principles. We have already seen that 'a deep and strong sense of religion' had been 'instilled' in the mind of Mrs. Douglas herself in her childhood. So 'to engraft into [Mary's] infant soul the purest principles of religion' became the 'chief aim' of Mrs. Douglas. (p.138). Mrs. Douglas' own experience had taught her that 'Happiness is not a plant of this earth ..... but God gives peace and tranquillity to the virtuous in all situations, and under every trial'. She, therefore, decided that she must 'strive to make Mary virtuous, and leave the rest to Him who alone knoweth what is good for us!' (p.164). This kind of upbringing was bound to make Mary very different from the mother and her sister who were living in London and moving in London high society.

This is seen most clearly when she is sent to stay in London for a few months with her mother and sister. She was about eighteen years of age and had never seen any member of her family all these years. All that she had learnt was that her father 'remained in a distant station in India; and was seldom heard of' and that her 'brother was gone to sea'. She had 'written repeatedly to her sister' but 'her letters remained unreplied'. (p. 181). Mrs. Douglas was not happy to send her to London at all but Mary's health had been causing some anxiety to her relations in Scotland and the idea was that a stay in London for some time might do her good. So when a letter was sent to Lady Juliana about Mary's arrival in London, the expectation was that she would recognise her 'alienated daughter's claim upon her care and affection' and be happy to receive her. But Juliana felt 'bitter indignation' at the 'base ingratitude and hypocrisy of her sister-in-law' (p. 188). For one thing, she did not believe that the girl was ill. Moreover, she hated everything Scottish. 'What can I do with a girl who has been educated in Scotland?', she exclaimed. 'She must be vulgar - all Scotchwomen are so.... Then, to hear the Scotch brogue - oh, heavens! I should expire every time she opened her mouth!'(p. 189). Even her daughter, Adelaide, who is described by the author as at once 'heartless and ambitious' and 'beautiful and accomplished' (p.187) has the decency to intervene. 'Perhaps my sister may not speak so *very* broad', she 'kindly suggested' in her 'sweetest accents'. (p. 189). But Juliana is determined not to receive her daughter at her house. Her real fear, of course, is that the girl might distract people's attention from Adelaide for whom she is now expecting some very brilliant offers of marriage. Lady Emily, the daughter of Lady Juliana's brother, who is not very fond of either her aunt or her cousin, is quite indignant that the mother is refusing to receive her daughter simply because of her fear that the girl might have acquired a somewhat Scotch accent. So she intervenes: 'If a person speaks sense and truth, what does it signify how it is spoken? And whether your Ladyship chooses to receive your daugher here or not, I shall, at any rate, invite my cousin to my *father's house*'. It is important to remember that the house is not really Juliana's at all. She had come here and received hospitality from her brother - Emily's father - after she had made a mess of her life. She did feel 'highly incensed at this freedom of her niece', but she realized that she had no option except 'to write a decently civil sort of letter to Mrs. Douglas, consenting to receive her daughter for a *few months*'. In her own mind, of course, she was determined that she would conceal the girl 'from all eyes and ears while she remained,' and send her back to her 'Scotch relations early in the summer'. (p.190).

At last Mary arrived in London and she could not understand why her mother disliked her and her sister despised her. She tried hard to receive 'one kind word from [her] mother's lips' and 'one kind glance from [her] sister's eye' (p. 229) but all her efforts to win their love and affection were spurned at and she was advised, ostensibly in the interest of her health, to stay in her apartment. She found a friend only in Lady Emily who went to see her in her apartment and 'embraced her again and again' and 'assured her' that 'she loved her already' as 'she was so like her dear Edward' (p.223), Mary's brother, whom Emily intended to marry whenever he returned from the sea.

Juliana was determined that Mary should not move in society and so she decided that she 'should be confined to her own apartment during the winter'. The excuse, of course, was that she would 'get quite well and strong against spring. As to visiting, or going into company, that of course must be out of the question' (p. 236). Mary, therefore, was not allowed freedom of any sort. But in Juliana's absence, Emily sometimes took her out though her regret was that Mary did not sufficiently assert herself. Once when Emily had taken her to meet someone, they happened to meet the Duke of Altamont and his mother. Emily realized that the Duke and his mother were taking too keen an interest in Mary. Indeed, when they were leaving, the Duke's mother said to Lady Emily: 'What a charming intelligent countenance your cousin has!' The Duke, to Emily's surprise, also could not help paying a compliment to her: 'What a very sweet modest looking girl, Miss Douglas was!' (p. 314).

Next day the message came that the Duke and his mother were going to call on them. Emily immediately understood the reason for the visit and told Mary that the Duke was going to propose to her.

Mary had not been much impressed by the Duke and so she deliberately absented herself to avoid meeting them. This upset Emily who knew that in her situation the best thing that Mary could do was to make herself the Duchess of Altamont. Mary, however, had no interest in being a Duchess 'with ninety thousand a year' (p.318). Lady Emily, who despised Lady Juliana and Adelaide for the way they treated Mary, tells Mary that becoming a Duchess would be the best way to escape 'the torments of Lady Juliana's authority'. But Mary makes it clear that 'for the sake of shaking off a parent's authority', she would not impose on herself 'chains still heavier and even more binding'. She also makes it clear that she would not marry any one, however exalted his status in life, unless she felt real love for him.

> "Can you suppose I would so far forfeit my honour and truth, as that I would swear to love, honour, and obey, where I could feel neither love nor respect; and where cold constrained obedience would be all of my duty I could hope to fulfil?"

This surprises Emily. 'Love! did you say?, she exclaims:

> 'I thought that had only been for naughty ones, such as me; and that saints like you would have married for any thing and every thing but love! Prudence, I thought, had been the word with you proper ladies - a prudent marriage! Come, confess, is not that the climax of virtue in the creed of your school?' (p.319).

Emily correctly reflects the normal assumptions of the age about contemporary successful marriages. Such marriages were invariably guided by prudence and not by love or passion which the age regarded as unsafe guides in the case of marriage. Mary, however, demands love - not the kind of love for which her mother eloped with her father - but love based on mutual understanding and respect. Hence, without any second thoughts she rejects Emily's simplistic view. When Emily insists on knowing what Mary had been taught by Mrs. Douglas regarding love, Mary replies that Mrs.

Douglas had always warned her to beware of that

> 'passion, which was very fashionable, and which .... was the result of indulged fancy, warm imaginations, and ill-regulated minds; that many had fallen into its snares, deceived by its glowing colours and alluring name'. (p.320).

Emily sarcastically calls this 'a very good sermon' and then offers her own views on marriage. These views basically are not too different from those of Mary though all that we are being told is not what love is but what it should not be *confused with*:

> 'Cupid has many counterfeits going about the world, who pass very well with whose minds are *capable of passion, but not of love*. (Italics mine). These Birmingham Cupids have many votaries amongst boarding school misses, militia officers, and milliners' apprentices; who marry upon the mutual faith of blue eyes and scarlet coats: have dirty houses and squalling children, and hate each other most delectably. Then there is another species for more refined souls, which owes its birth to the works of Rousseau, Goethe, Cottin, &c.: its success depends very much upon rocks, woods, and waterfalls: and it generally ends in daggers, pistols, poison or Doctors' Commons.' (pp.319-20).

Emily is, of course, making fun of the fashionable views of love held both by the ignorant and the immature as also by those who are victims of contemporary romantic views of human sensibility.

Mary rejects both the approaches mentioned by Emily and tells her that what Mrs. Douglas had taught her was that

> 'there was a love which even the wisest and most virtuous need not blush to entertain - the love of a virtuous object, founded upon esteem, and heightened by similarity of taste, and sympathy of feelings, into a pure and devoted attachment.'

'Unless I feel all this', she declares, 'I shall never fancy myself in love.' (pp. 320-21). Emily continues in her usual bantering tone:

> 'Humph! I can't say much as to the similarity of tastes and sympathy of souls between the Duke and you, but surely you might contrive to feel some love and esteem for a coronet and ninety thousand a year'.

'Suppose I did', Mary says with a smile, deliberately insisting on the literal meaning of the marriage oath, 'the next point is to honour; and surely he is as unlikely to excite that sentiment as the other'. (p.321).

Mary may seem to be treating the marriage vow as somewhat too literally but the fact is that for her marriage is a sacred institution. She believes that one should not enter the married state without being absolutely clear about one's feelings. When Juliana, for instance, asks her to marry Mr. Downe Wright, Mary frankly tells her that she cannot receive the addresses of a man who is 'almost a stranger to her'. Juliana rebukes her for this foolishness and tells her that he is 'a man of family and future, heir to a title .....' etc. and what more she would wish to know? Mary candidly replies that she would 'wish to know something of his character - his principles - his habits - temper, talents - in short, all those things on which my happiness would depend'. (p.346). All this is, of course, wholly incomprehensible to Juliana. 'Character and principles!' she exclaims, 'one would suppose you were talking of your footman!' (pp. 346-7). This was a natural reaction of an age when all that one needed to know about the man one was marrying was his wealth and fortune. Adelaide is a tragic victim of this attitude. Mary, however, has an altogether different approach and so when a proposal from Mr. Downe Wright, who has now become Lord Glenallan, is received, she has no difficulty in declining it. She is fully conscious that it is not in 'splendour and distinction that I shall find happiness; it is in the cultivation of the domestic virtues - the peaceful joys of a happy home, and a loved companion, that my felicity must consist.' (p.382).

V

But this is a sentiment with which neither her mother nor her sister would have any sympathy. They demand 'splendour and distinction' rather than 'domestic virtues' which in any case are not the concern of aristocratic ladies. Such ladies also do not treat the marriage vows too seriously and would be quite keen to shower honour - and love and esteem too - on any one who could provide them 'a coronet and ninety thousand a year'. It is best seen in the conduct of Lady Juliana and Adelaide. When they learn that the Duke of Altamont and his mother are coming to dine at their place, they get ready to receive them. Mary, of course, deliberately absents herself from the dinner and instead goes to meet Mrs. Lennox whom she had been meeting for sometime and who is very fond of her and has even expressed the wish that she should marry her son, an officer in the Navy. On her return home, Mary learns from Emily that the Duke had been received by Adelaide who was 'so sweet - so gracious - so beautiful - [that] the poor gull was caught, and is now .... as much in love as it is in the nature of a stupid man to be' (p. 343). This shocks Mary who, like others, had all along believed that Adelaide was in love with Lord Lindore, Emily's brother. Emily cannot contain her indignation and tells Adelaide that she abhors 'all traps, whether for the poor mouse .... or for the dull elderly gentleman who falls asleep with a star on the breast'. (p.351). She leaves Adelaide in no doubt that she has contempt for her - or indeed for any woman like her - who is in 'love with one man, and at the same time [is] laying snares for another' (p.351).

Adelaide's mother is, of course, thrilled when the Duke's proposal for marriage comes. She is sure that 'as a matter of course, [she] would be invited to accompany her daughter upon her marriage' (p.366). But unfortunately she could not 'extort' such an invitation from her daughter. The Duke indeed proposed to Adelaide that she might invite her sister 'who was always in good humour - always gentle and polite' and in whose company he 'felt more at ease .... than with anybody else'. Such a proposal could hardly be considered seriously by Adelaide who 'coldly rejected' it. (p.366).

Adelaide's marriage, though very cleverly manipulated, was destined to end in disaster. The Duke was very proud of his position in society and he expected his wife to conduct herself exactly as he wished. Adelaide found some of the restrictions imposed upon her as altogether too unbearable but it was too late to recognise that 'of all yokes, the most insupportable is the yoke of an obstinate fool'. It was, therefore, natural that at the end of six weeks, 'the Duchess of Altamont most heartily hated and despised the man she had so lately vowed to love and obey' (p.396). The writer tells us that 'she had the finest house, jewels, and equipages in London, but she was not happy' (p.426). She was reluctant to 'acknowledge, even to herself' that she had done wrong to marry a man whom she despised while her preference was decidedly in favour of another' (p.427). In sheer despair, she thought of 'a separate establishment, carried on in the same house' but 'his Grace had stubborn notions on that score also, and plainly hinted that any separation must be final, and decided'. This Adelaide was not willing to do in 'the first year of her marriage' (p.428). As Lord Lindore was a frequent visitor at Altamont House, Adelaide could not help contrasting 'the elegant, impassioned lover' with 'the dull, phlegmatic husband' and so 'in something less than a year from the time of her marriage', she 'eloped with Lord Lindore, vainly hoping to find peace and joy amid guilt and infamy'. (p.432).

VI

Adelaide's marriage is even a greater disaster than that of her mother's. Juliana's marriage had at least the merit of an impetuous and passionate love affair, however short-lived it might have been. Adelaide's marriage was wholly mercenary. For the novelist, only Mary's marriage is satisfactory from all points of view. She loves Colonel Lennox and very wisely takes some time to be sure of his feelings towards her as also of her own feelings towards him. Misunderstanding had been caused when she overheard Mrs. Lennox praising her to her son and describing her as an ideal wife for him. This did disturb Mary as she felt that she was being 'recommended to the love of a man who was indifferent to her'. 'Could there be such a humiliation', she said to herself, 'such a degradation' (p.335). Her mind is finally cleared by Lady Emily's rebuke:

> You happen to overhear Mrs. Lennox, good old soul! recommending you as a wife to her son - What could be more natural? except his refusing to fall head and ears in love before he had time to pull his boots off. And then to have a wife recommended to him! and all your perfections set forth, as if you had been a laundry maid: an early riser, neat worker, regular attendance upon church! Ugh! - I must say, I think his conduct quite meritorious. I could almost find in my heart to fall in love with him myself, were it for no other reason than because he is not such a Tommy Goodchild as to be in love at his mamma's bidding - that is, loving his mother as he does - for I see he could cut of a hand, or pluck out an eye, to please her, though he can't or won't give her his heart and soul to dispose of as she thinks proper. (pp. 341-2).

Emily also admires him for his looks and finds it 'quite refreshing to see a handsome man that is neither a fool nor a coxcomb' (p.354). When Lady Juliana tries to belittle him by declaring that he 'wants that air *distingué*, which, indeed, belongs exclusively to persons of birth', even Adelaide has the grace to say that 'he has perfectly the air of a man of fashion'. (p.355). Mary's admiration for him increases when she discovers that his 'turn of mind seemed so similar to her own'.(pp. 360-1). But it is only after his return from the battle of Waterloo that Mary sees that she was 'beloved with all the truth and ardour of a noble ingenuous mind, too upright to deceive others, too enlightened to deceive itself'. (p.445).

It is, of course, true that Colonel Lennox's

> 'fortune was small; but, such as it was, it seemed sufficient for all the purposes of rational enjoyment. Both were aware, that wealth is a relative thing, and that the positively rich are not those who have the largest possessions, but those who have the

fewest vain or selfish desires to gratify. From these they were happily exempt. Both possessed too many resources in thier own minds to require the stimulus of spending money to rouse them into enjoyment, or give them additional importance in the eyes of the world; and, above all, both were too thoroughly Christian in their principles, to murmur at any sacrifices or privations they might have to endure in the course of their earthly pilgrimage'. (p.445).

Soon, in spite of some difficulties created by Lady Juliana and her Scottish relations, Mary married Colonel Lennox and the assumption is that they shall live happily ever after. It is interesting, however, to hear Lady Maclaughlan's sceptical words to remind us that no one can be sure about the future. It was she who had introduced Mary to Mrs. Lennox. Now, she comes to tell her that she is glad that she and Colonel Lennox are marrying: 'I'm glad of it. I wished you to marry him. Whether you'll thank me for that twenty years hence, I can't tell - *you* can't tell - *he* can't tell - God knows!' (p. 463).

VII

No one can, of course, be sure how one would feel about one's marriage after twenty years. But Mary is not expected to feel any regrets as she is almost completely modelled on the popular conduct books of the period. In her caste, everything seems to have been dictated by contemporary moralists. The one person in the novel who feels exasperated at her constant attempt to conform to the moral code laid down for women is Lady Emily. She regards such conduct as unnatural as it lacks spontaneity. She does not, of course, accuse Mary of insincerity but she believes that most women who adopt the moral code laid down for them often have to act against their natural inclinations. Emily cannot, for instance, see why women should *naturally* subscribe to Milton's doctrine that man's loyalty is to God only but a woman's loyalty is to 'God in him'. She is surprised when she sees that Mary is 'in some danger of becoming one of these idolatresses'. (p.385). Mary herself claims that the man she would like to marry should be one 'on whose judgment I could rely for advice and assistance, and for whom I could feel a certain deference, that I consider due from a wife to her husband' (p.364). Emily may not seriously object to a woman seeking her husband's advice and assistance or her feeling a certain deference for him, but she despises women who overdo this role. She mentions the case of a woman 'who has such a deference for the judgment of her better half, that she consults him even about tying of her shoes'!

Mary, of course, is not that silly but she has no sympathy with what she calls 'the sect of Independents in the marriage state' (p.385). She gives the example of a woman 'who by all strangers is taken for a widow, such emphasis does she lay upon the personal pronoun - with her, 'tis always *I* do this, or *I* do that, without the slightest reference to her husband; and she talks of *my* house, *my* gardens, *my* carriage, *my* children, as if there were no copartnery in the case' (p.385). Emily agrees with Mary that this woman 'is a fool, as every woman must needs be, who thinks she can raise herself by lowering her husband' (p.385). She has no sympathy with what she calls 'the sect of the Wranglers, whose marriage is only one continued dispute'. She then claims that 'I see it reserved for me to set a perfect example to my sex in the married state' (p.385).

This perfect example she sets by insisting that wife and husband should have 'a more equitable division; for, though man is a reasonable being, he shall know and own that woman is so too - sometimes. All things that man ought to know better I shall yield; Whatever may belong to either sex, I either seize upon as my prerogative, or scrupulously divide; for which reason, I should like the profession of my husband to be something in which I could not possibly interfere' (p.384). She particularly dislikes men 'who are perfect Joves in their own houses - who speak their will by a nod, and lay down the law by the motion of their eye-brow - and who attach prodigious ideas of dignity to frightening their children, and being worshipped by their wives'. (pp. 384-5).

Mary also may not like a husband who frightens his children and browbeats his wife but she does believe that a husband should be superior to his wife in most respects. Her regret is that men often do not care to cultivate their intelligence as they believe that their sphere of action requires other qualities. But Mary would like her husband's 'genius' to be at least as bright as her own. She is clearly distressed that her brother, Edward Douglas, who is in the Navy and whom Emily wants to marry, is not intelligent enough to deserve a girl like Emily. She is surprised that Emily should love a young man who is so ignorant and so immature. She attributes it to Emily's impetuosity and even 'want of early culture' (p. 406). But Mary does not see that Edward has qualities which some women can find very attractive. He is 'a perfect model of youthful beauty, and possessed of all the high spirits of happy *insouciance*, which can only charm at that early period' (p.443). Moreover, he 'loved his profession and had already distinguished himself in it.

It is, of course, true, and Emily herself recognises that he is 'not clever'. Mary regards it as too serious a defect and she fears that Emily's love for him may not last. Emily is sharp-eyed enough to see what is troubling Mary and so she says:

> You were thinking how strange, how passing strange it is, that I, who am (false modesty avaunt!) certainly cleverer than Edward, should yet be so partial to him, and that my lynx eyes should have failed to discover in him faults, which, with a single glance, I should have detected in others. Now, can't you guess what renders even these very faults so attractive to me?'

Mary, of course, is totally incapable of guessing any such thing. She merely believes that Emily too is a victim of blind passion. But Emily is not such a fool and she explains that she knows Edward's faults very well but she loves him

> with my whole heart, faults and all. In the first place, they are the faults with which I have been familiar from infancy; and therefore they possess a charm (to my shame be it said) greater than other people's virtues would have to me. They come over my fancy like some snatch of an old nursery song, which one

loves to hear in defiance of taste and reason, merely because it is something that carries us back to those days, which, whatever they were in reality, always look bright and sunny in retrospection. In the second place, his faults are real, genuine, natural faluts; and, in this age of affectation, how refreshing it is to meet with even a natural fault! I grant you, Edward talks absurdly, and asks question, a *faire dresser les cheveux* of a Mrs. Bluemits. But that amuses me; for his ignorance is not the ignorance of vulgarity or stupidity, but the ignorance of a light head, and a merry heart - of one, in short, whose understanding has been at sea when other people's were at school'. (pp. 443-4).

There is no doubt that Emily has a kind of charm that Mary cannot claim to possess. It is not safe to speculate but would it be altogether absurd to claim that her marriage has a better chance of succeeding, of being happier and much more satisfying than that of Mary's? She possesses a richer personality and an infectious capacity for enjoyment. Mary is too cautious, even suspicious, and given too much to moral reflection. She is somewhat too 'saintly' and unfortunately often too conscious of the kind of role that she has to play. Emily, on the other hand, can relax and walk through life cheerfully almost totally unmindful of the impression that she might create on others. Her high birth is, of course, responsible for this kind of conduct. In her limited sphere, Mary got hardly any chance to flower and blossom as Emily has done.

Emily's high spirits frighten 'saintly' Mary who fears that she might end up in great unhappiness. She sees that Emily's mind is 'open to the reception of every image that brought pleasure along with it; while, in the same spirit, she turned from every thing that wore an air of seriousness or self-restraint; and even the best affections of a naturally good heart were borne away by the ardour of her feelings, and the impetuosity of her temper'. (p. 406). If one were not an eighteenth century moralist, one could ask how such a mind and such capacity for enjoyment of things in life hurt one? Mary is grieved 'to see the graces of a noble mind thus running wild for want of early culture'. But is there any evidence that Emily's conduct has been even slightly immoral in any sense of the term? Indeed, there is enough evidence to show that her mind does not run wild. She did feel attracted towards Colonel Lennox but she soon realized that it was wrong to do so both because of the Colonel's interest in Mary - and also because it would be a betrayal of Edward Douglas. And she told all this to Mary and even asked for her forgiveness. Mary's difficulty is that she is not able to see that even though Emily grew up in the same house and environment as Adelaide, she is altogether different from Adelaide. Mary also perhaps suffers - though only slightly - from the narrow outlook that Mrs. Douglas tried to instil in her in the name of religion.

VIII

Perhaps the novelist realizes that Emily has a subversive effect on the theme of her novel which ostensibly was to 'inculcate morality'. It is interesting to see that she tries to undo the damage by putting some words of repentence in Emily's mouth at the time of her marriage. As the day of Lady Emily's marriage arrived, the writer tells us, Emily 'found her in a more serious mood than she had hitherto appeared in' (p. 464) and she tells Mary: 'The icy bonds of matrimony are upon me already: I feel myself turning into a fond, faithful, rational, humble, meek- spirited wife! Alas! I must now turn my head into a museum, and hang up all my smart sayings inside my brain, there to petrify, as warnings to all pert misses. Dear Mary! if ever I am good for any thing, it will be to you I owe it!' (p.465).

But knowing her and the man she is marrying, as we do, we need have no fears that she would lose her vivacity of temperament and 'dwindle' into an 'humble, meek-spirited wife'. Her husband is described as 'almost provokingly boyish and unthinking, and possessed of a flow of animal spirits as inexhaustible as they were sometimes over-powering'. (p.444). Emily will be found more than his equal and there is no danger of her being over-powered. Indeed, the danger, if any, could be in her being too dominant. But this danger too need not be there because Emily is an intelligent woman and she should know - as intelligent women have known all along - that there are ways of handling a husband which are so clever and subtle that they never become visible to husbands.

Emily's conduct when Mrs. Downe Wright comes to pay a visit to them - clearly with the intention of mocking the Douglas family on Adelaide's elopement - is worth watching as it throws light on Emily's vast intellectual resources. Mary, of course, is totally incapable of facing Mrs. Downe Wright and even blushes when that lady makes a reference to her family but Emily's 'quick tact was presently aware of her design and she prepared to take the field against her' (p.435).

Mrs. Downe Wright has, of course, come to taunt and so almost every topic that she touches is full of innuendoes. But Emily is more than her equal every time. When she derides the army and the navy as inferior professions which 'spoilt a man for domestic life', Emily retorts that the best men suitable for domestic life are indeed those who are 'stupid and idle'. Mrs. Downe Wright can easily see that the reference is to her own son whom Mary had earlier rejected. So she decides to launch a direct attack on Emily by declaring that the worst wife is a woman who is a 'wit or a genius' or a 'clever woman, so called'. Emily accepts the challenge and gives a reply that completely baffles Mrs. Downe Wright:

> 'There is nothing more insupportable than one of your clever women, so called. They are generally under-bred, consequently vulgar. They pique themselves upon saying good things coute qu'il coute. There is something, in short, quite professional about them; and they wouldn't condescend *to chat nonsense as you and I are doing at this moment* (Italics mine) - oh! not for worlds! Now, I think one of the great charms of life consists in talking nonsense. Good nonsense is an exquisite thing; and 'tis an exquisite thing to be stupid sometimes, and to say nothing at all. Now, these enjoyments the clever women must forego. Clever she is, and clever she must be. Her life must be a greater drudgery than that of any actress. She [the actress] merely frets

her hour upon the stage; the curtain dropped, she may become as dull as she chooses; but the clever woman must always stage it even at her own fireside.'

Mrs. Downe Wright does not know how to interpret Emily's comments on clever women. She is indeed surprised that Lady Emily - a clever woman herself - should be saying all this. She merely says with some bitterness:

> 'Lady Emily Lindore is certainly the last person from whom I should have expected to hear a panegyric on stupidity'.

Mrs. Downe Wright's remarks clearly show that she has not fully understood the purpose of Emily's 'panegyric on stupidity'. Emily's retort is sharp and revealing:

> 'Stupidity! - oh, heavens! my blood curdles at the thought of real, genuine, downright stupidity. No! I should always like to have the command of intellect, as well as of money, though my taste, or my indolence, or my whim, perhaps never would incline me to be always sparkling, whether in wit or in diamonds'. (p.439).

The writer tells us that there was 'an airy, high-bred elegance in Lady Emily's impertinence' and so Mrs. Downe Wright's 'coarse sarcasm' was thrown to 'an immeasurable distance'. Clearly Mary is utterly incapable of this 'airy, high-bred impertinence'. But that is not her fault. Her upbringing and her early culture do have their limitations. Mary represents middle class culture as against Emily who is an aristocrat. Emily, however, is entering middle class by marrying a young officer in the Navy who has no fortune of his own. But Emily is not worried. Nor is she worried about Edward's lack of intelligence and aristocratic culture. She will teach him, if he has not yet learnt it already, that 'Good nonsense is an exquisite thing', and 'tis an exquisite thing to be stupid sometimes, and to say nothing at all'. (p.439). These words were spoken ironically to Mrs. Downe

Wright but surely in a happy relaxed marriage there should be scope for some 'nonsense' and even for some 'stupidity'. Mary, of course, would not approve of it though there is a possibility that Colonel Lennox might. But he is destined not to hear the cheering prattle of Emily.

NOTE

1. All quotations are taken from this edition of the novel.

Chapter VI

Women with Small Fortune in Jane Austen

I will begin with a statement that Selma James, an ardent English feminist, made during the course of a lecture that she delivered on Jane Austen at the Cheltenham Library Festival on November 4, 1979. This is what she said:

> Seeing Jane Austen as she is doesn't mean agreeing with all she says. It is appropriate for me to note here that I disagree with her profoundly on a fundamental matter. The conclusion she reached in her last novel, *Persuasion*, is that we have to make the best of the tragic circumstances of our lives; we are not mistaken to allow ourselves to be persuaded by authority. Now I don't think we have to make the best of it, and I don't for a second believe in giving in to authority. I think we have to entirely transform this society which makes our lives a tragedy. But I think she is a great artist because she said our lives *were* a tragedy and that we could be much more than they allowed us to be. May I repeat this: there is not one 'tragedy' in any of her novels. None of the women is exploited as servant, mill-hand or even governess, who were to become the embodiment of exploited womanhood in 19th century literature. In addition, all the novels have happy endings. But her fury at the polite brutality that surrounded her and her use of comic irony to regulate her hatred of much about the world she knew, sprang from a deep and pervasive assumption that the circumstances of the lives of her characters were tragic.[1]

There is no doubt of Jane Austen's 'fury at the polite brutality that surrounded her' and her use of comic irony to regulate her hatred of much about the world she knew. It is also true that she recognised that the contemporary social system prevented most women from achieving a sense of fulfilment. However, there is no evidence to support the view that Jane Austen or any of her woman characters ever thought of transforming their society. Of course, during Jane Austen's time there was a ferment in the air and forces had emerged in England which demanded a transformation of society. It is, for instance, no accident that it was during this period - in 1792, to be precise - that Mary Wollstencraft's revolutionary book, *A Vindication of the Rights of Woman*, was published. This book combined the feminist cause with political radicalism and demanded an overhauling not only of the social system but also of the political system. Such demands, however, had exactly the opposite effect in England. People were so frightened by the happenings in France that the hold of conservative forces in England became much stronger not only on the upper and middle classes but on the lower classes as well. The feminist cause also suffered a set-back and, as Warren Roberts has said, the obedient and wholly passive Victorian wife "was born, so to speak, during the time of the French Revolution and Napoleonic wars."[2]

Although it would be erroneous to search for resemblances between Jane Austen's heroines and the obedient and wholly passive wives of Victorian fiction, it would be equally erroneous to regard them as feminists who are in revolt against their society. They do, of course, take a stand whenever it becomes necessary to do so but by and large they try to adjust to their circumstances as best as they can. Attempts to trace the influence of Mary Wollstencraft's ideas on Jane Austen are also perhaps not altogether justified. For one thing, there is no evidence that Jane Austen read Mary Wollstencraft's *Vindication*. There is only one reference to William Godwin in the whole of Jane Austen and it is not a complimentary one. Jane Austen's view clearly is that women should make the best of their lives, however tragic the circumstances, and should not hesitate to be persuaded by authority if circumstances so demand.

It is, of course, true that the society that Jane Austen depicts is a cruel one and it is particularly hostile to women with small fortune. All Jane Austen's heroines, except Emma, have only a small fortune and they have to face in one form or another the cruelties inherent in a mercenary social system. The basic cruelty, of course, flows from their economic situation. At a time when no honourable professions were available to middle- class girls to earn their living, marriage alone could provide them economic and social security. Mary Astell lamented that the contemporary woman regarded marriage as her "only preferment, the sum total of her endeavours, the completion of all her hopes".[3] Mary Astell could, of course, afford to adopt a high and mighty attitude as she was a respected member of an elitist group and could afford to live the life of an independent scholar. It should not, however, be forgotten that even she had to face humiliation and it was after a grim struggle that she won her independence. For the average girl in 17th and 18th century England the only option available was a respectable marriage.

But a respectable marriage was no easy matter. Perhaps the most serious obstacle was the shortage of marriageable young men in the period. This shortage might have been caused by the depletion of the male population owing to wars and migration to the colonies. But population experts have noticed a more serious cause for the decline of the male population in 18th century England. In an influential article on "European Marriage Patterns in Perspective", Hajnal has said: "It is probable that in eighteenth century Europe .... the ratio of male to female population at the prime marriageable ages .... was much less favourable to women's chances of marriage than in many non-Western populations."[4] That this had a profound impact on the marriage patterns in the age is evident from what Lawrence Stone says in his well-known book *The Family, Sex and Marriage in England, 1500-1800* (1977):

> "the proportion of recorded daughters of the gentry who reached the age of 50 and never married rose from ten per cent in the sixteenth century .... to nearly twenty-five per cent between 1675 and 1799."[5]

In earlier periods, surplus daughters could, at some cost, be sent to the nunneries but in this period that option too was closed to English girls.

I

In such a situation, the value of a bridegroom in the marriage market was bound to rise very considerably. As is well-known, dowry remained a major problem in England till almost the end of the 19th century. This social evil did, of course, come under attack from the very beginning but it was perhaps in the 18th century that the criticism became really constructive. It was in this period, for instance, that some social reformers thought of creating institutions which might help dowerless girls to achieve economic independence. Defoe's Moll Flanders and Roxana, whatever their morals, were wholly correct in thinking that without economic self-sufficiency, a woman had no place in society. A character in *Moll Flanders* bluntly states that the marriage market

> is against our sex .... and if a young woman have beauty, birth, breeding, wit, sense, manners, modesty, and all these to an extreme, yet if she have not money, she's nobody, she had as good want them all, for nothing but money now recommends a woman. (*Moll Flanders*, 1722, Penguin Classics (1989), edited by David Blewett, p.58).

Defoe was also one of the first to plead that daughters of gentlemen should be taught some skills and crafts which would help them to earn at least their living in times of adversity. He also suggested - and he was perhaps the first to do so - that "a marriage office" be set up which would serve "as a kind of clearing house for eligible bachelors", and for girls (usually "old maids"), who were finding it difficult to get suitable husbands.[6] Economic independence was, of course, the best assurance for women whatever their chances in the marriage market. But to offer only two options to girls, either to 'catch' rich husbands or become dependent on their families who regarded them as a burden, was cruel indeed.

Their effort to make women economically self-sufficient was perhaps the greatest contribution that 18th century reformers made to the women's cause. Voices had, of course, been raised in the 17th century too and efforts made that some practical skills should be taught to women but it is in the 18th century that quite elaborate schemes were suggested for their betterment. It is interesting that an anonymous writer in the *Gentleman's Magazine* in 1739 suggested that young women without dowries should be "put Apprentices to genteel and easy Trades, such as Linnen or Wollen Drapers, Haberdashers of small Wares, Mercers, Glovers, Perfumers, Grocers, Confectioners, Retailers of Gold and Silver Lace, Buttons, etc." He asked:

> "Why are not these as creditable Trades for the Daughters of Gentlemen as they are for their Sons; and all of them more proper for Women than Men? Is it not as agreeable and becoming for Women to be employ'd in selling a Farthing's Worth of Needles, a Half-penny Lace, a Quarter Yard of Silk, Staff, or Cambrick, as it is absurd and ridiculous to see a Parcel of young Fellows, dish'd out in their Tie-Wigs and Ruffles, the Lords of the Creation, as Men affect to be call'd, busied in Professions so much below the Honour and Dignity of their Sex .... If Women were train'd up in Business from their early Years, 'tis highly probable they would in general be more industrious, and get more Money, than Men; and if so, what Woman of Spirit would submit to be a slave, and fling herself away, as many are forc'd to do, merely for a Maintenance, because she cannot stoop to be a servant, and can find no reputable Business to go into?"[7]

The situation of women who were not able to 'fling' themselves away merely for a maintenance and who were forced to live the lives of 'old maids' was quite pitiable in this period. William Hayley's *A Philosophical, Historical and Moral Essay on Old Maids* which appeared in 1786 says that while "it is the natural wish and expectation of every amiable girl to settle happily in marriage," some of them could not achieve this goal for lack of fortune. Even when there was no lack of fortune, inability to marry in one's own class left a deep scar on the women's minds. As Dr. Gregory has said in his *A Father's Legacy to his Daughters* (1774), the real problem of such women was - and has always been in all times, including the present - the 'great difficulty of making a transition with dignity and cheerfulness, from the period of youth, beauty, admiration, and respect, into the calm, silent, unnoticed retreat of declining years'. (p.105). When there was lack of fortune, the situation was almost desperate. William Hayley describes the case of a girl who had been well brought up and who had spent "the sprightly years of youth in the comfortable mansion of an opulent father", but after her father's death, had been "reduced to the shelter of some contracted lodging in a country town, attended by a single female servant, and with difficulty living on the interest of two or three thousand pounds, reluctantly, and perhaps irregularly, paid to her by an avaricious or extravagant brother."[8]

The situation described by Hayley was possible only in the case of a girl whose thoughtful father had left some money specifically for her use, though often under a brother's over-all supervision. But what about those unfortunate girls who were entirely dependent on the bounty of their brothers? "These brothers", Mary Wollstencraft says in an important passage in her *Vindication of the Rights of Woman* (1792), "are, to view the fairest side of the question, good sort of men, and give as a favour what children of the same parents had an equal right to. In this equivocal humiliating situation, a docile female may remain sometime with a tolerable degree of comfort. But when the brother marries .... from being considered as the mistress of the family, she is viewed with averted looks as an intruder, an unnecessary burden on the benevolence of the master of the house and his new partner.... The wife, a cold-hearted, narrow-minded woman .... has recourse to cunning to undermine the habitual affection which she is afraid openly to oppose; and neither tears nor caresses are spared till the spy is worked out of her home, and thrown on the world, unprepared for its difficulties; or sent as a great effort of generosity, or from some regard to propriety, with a small stipend .... into joyless solitude."[9]

II

There is no case in Jane Austen where a brother and his wife send an unmarried sister "into joyless solitude". But the situation in *Sense and Sensibility* comes closest to this situation. It is the story of two sisters whose father is dead and who, along with their widowed mother and younger sister, have to leave the house in which they have lived. The house and the estate are inherited by their brother, John Dashwood, from an earlier marriage. He had given a pledge to his father that he would look after his step- mother and his sisters and would not let them suffer deprivation. Though he is a thoroughly selfish person with no feelings towards "anybody beyond himself, his wife, and their child", he is prepared, in deference to his father's wishes, to contribute three thousand pounds towards their maintenance. But his wife is shocked that he should "take away three thousand pounds from the fortune of their dear little boy" "impoverishing him to the most dreadful degree." Husband and wife then rationalize their innate desire to do nothing for them and justify their conduct:

> 'Well, then let something be done for them; but that something need not be three thousand pounds .... Five hundred pounds would be a prodigious increase to their fortunes .... I do not know whether upon the whole it would not be more advisable to do something for their mother while she lives .... something of the annuity kind, I mean .... A hundred a year would make them all perfectly comfortable..... But then, if Mrs. Dashwood should live fifteen years, we shall be completely taken in..... A present of fifty pounds, now and then, will prevent their ever being distressed for money; and will, I think, be amply discharging my promise to my father.... As to your giving them more, it is quite absurd to think of it. They will be much more able to give you something.' (chapt. 2).

As Donald Greene acidly adds, "they end by making designs on the widow's set of breakfast china which is 'twice as handsome as what belongs to this house'," and points out further that "by contrast with this monstrosity, Aunt Norris's little meannesses in *Mansfield Park* and General Tilney's frank acquisitiveness in *Northanger Abbey* seem trifling."[10]

This 'monstrosity', however, is not exceptional in the novel. Mrs. Ferrars, the mother-in-law of John Dashwood, is even worse than her son-in-law and her daughter. It is indeed she who symbolizes the brutality of this society in its extremest form. She attaches importance only to wealth and social status and does not hesitate to publicly insult those who lack them. The reason why Mrs. Dashwood and her daughters have to hurriedly leave their ancestral home is in fact to be traced to her conduct. Edward Ferrars, her elder son, comes for a short holiday from Oxford to stay with his sister, John Dashwood's wife. The sister who inherits all the evil tendencies in her mother's character discovers that Edward is getting friendly with Elinore, the eldest of the Dashwood sisters. He is, of course, not much of a catch for Elinore who is superior to him in almost all respects but he happens to be rich and Elinore is not well provided for. Mrs. John Dashwood, therefore, intervenes sharply and warns Elinore's mother that Edward has "great expectations" and that his mother, Mrs. Ferrars, is determined that he should "marry well". Indeed, she makes a pointed reference to "the danger attending any young woman who attempted *to draw him in*" (Italics Jane Austen's) (chapter 4). The self-respecting Mrs. Dashwood finds this aspersion on her daughter very insulting and she and her daughters decide immediately to shift to another part of the country.

In their new home, Sir John Middleton, their landlord, suggests to Elinore's mother that Mr. Willoughby, a young man who is visiting his aunt in the neighbourhood, is "very well worth catching". The word 'catching' hurts Mrs. Dashwood and she replies firmly that Mr. Willoughby would not be "incommoded by the attempts of either of *my* daughters towards what you call *catching him*. It is not an employment to which they have been brought up.

Men are very safe with us, let them be ever so rich". (chapt. 9). The sharpest rebuke on this question of poor girls trying to *catch* rich husbands comes from Marianne, Elinore's younger sister. When Sir John teases her about Willoughby and says: "I see how it will be. You will be setting your cap at him now, and never think of poor Brandon".

"That is an expression", said Marianne warmly, 'which I particularly dislike. I abhor every commonplace phrase by which wit is intended; and 'setting one's cap at a man', or 'making a conquest', are the most odious of all. Their tendency is gross and illiberal; and if their construction could ever be deemed clever, time has long ago destroyed all its ingenuity". (chapt. 9).

No one in Jane Austen's world, however, is willing to believe that a pretty girl with a small fortune would not try to use her arts to make a 'conquest' of a man of property. Unlike Mrs. Dashwood, most parents of the time found nothing wrong in their daughters trying to catch rich husbands. Indeed the entire education of young women in this period was directed towards teaching them how to play this game with tact and finesse.

Jane Austen's heroines, however, rarely exploit their physical charm and invariably act with propriety and decorum. But even so they become targets of nasty attacks from the rich relations of the heroes. In *Pride and Prejudice*, Darcy's aunt accuses Elizabeth Bennet of using her "arts and allurements" to "draw him in" (chapt. 56). In *Northanger Abbey*, the father of the hero, General Tilney, adopts a most insulting attitude towards Catharine the moment he comes to know that she has no fortune. He had himself invited her to stay in Northanger Abbey, but discovering the true facts about her financial status, "to turn her from the house seemed the best, though to his feelings an inadequate proof, of his resentment towards herself, and his contempt of her family" (chapt. 30). Lucy Steele in *Sense and Sensibility* is, of course, not a heroine and otherwise too she is a very unpleasant and mercenary character but the reason for her and her sister's being thrown out of her house by Mrs. John Dashwood is the same as General Tilney's. Mrs. Dashwood invites the Sheela sisters merely to spite Elinore and her sister who, as her husband's half-sisters, have a better claim on her hospitality in London. But the moment she learns from Lucy's sister that Lucy is secretly engaged to her brother Edward, she declares "they should not stay a minute longer in the house" and they are forced to leave immediately even though they do not have the fare to travel to London.

III

In such a society what options do women have except to make the best of their circumstances? What is important, however, is that Jane Austen's heroines do not buckle under these circumstances and never, even for a moment, lose their self-respect merely to secure a husband. At a time when husband-hunting was regarded as a normal part of a girl's accomplishments, it is significant that none of Jane Austen's heroines is "a designing coquette". Indeed, "they say 'no' when they mean 'no' and 'yes' when they mean 'yes'."[11] Whether the man is the foolish Mr. Collins or the great Mr. Darcy, Elizabeth Bennet demands the right to be treated as a 'rational creature speaking the truth from her heart'. (chapt. 19).

This dignified attitude, however, does not prevent them from being harassed. Again it is *Sense and Sensibility* which provides the worst case of harassment. It is painful to the two sisters, Elinore and Marianne, to be constantly reminded that since they are too poor to attract suitable matches, they must use feminine guile to do so. It is humiliating that John Dashwood, whose responsibility it is to secure suitable matches for his sisters, asks Elinore to use "those little attentions and encouragements which ladies can so easily give" to Colonel Brandon. He callously reminds her that though Colonel Brandon's friends may not regard it as a suitable match for him because of her small fortune, she should, by her own cleverness, "fix him in spite of himself." (chapt. 33).

The point is that women in Jane Austen are under "obligation to marry, no matter whom, to survive."[12] From this Frances Beer has concluded that Jane Austen's view of society is negative, particularly as seen in the case of the Dashwood and the Bennet sisters and also in "the melancholy and quiet desperation of Fanny Price, or Jane Fairfax, or Anne Elliot".[13] But while all women do face difficult circumstances, what Jane Austen is really trying to do - which indeed is her real theme - is to ensure that her heroines do not abandon their 'toughness on the question of personal responsibility; or .... justify the extremes of rebellion or despair'.[14] The main thing is that they must not panic and lose their sense of proportion. Whatever the risk and however difficult the situation, they must behave with propriety and dignity.

This is best seen in her small fragment, *The Three Sisters*. It was perhaps written by Jane Austen when she was only 18 years of age. The three sisters are Mary, Sophia and Georgiana with different approaches to marriage. The eldest sister, Mary, is the weakest and most panicky. She is most anxious to marry before any of her younger sisters. Their mother, like Mrs. Dashwood, is a widow in straitened circumstances and is anxious that her daughters should get settled soon. The fragment which is in epistolary form opens with a letter that Mary writes to a friend informing her that she is "the happiest creature in the world for she has received an offer of marriage from Mr. Watts".[15] Mary's letter to her friend continues:

> He [Mr. Watts] is quite an old man, about two and thirty, very plain, so plain that I cannot bear to look at him. He has a large fortune and will make great settlements on me; but then he is very healthy. In short I do not know what to do. If I refuse him he as good as told me that he should offer himself to Sophia and if she refused him to Georgiana, and I could not bear to have either of them married before me.

It is a pathetic letter. She knows that this marriage has no chance of succeeding and that she would be miserable for the rest of her life. But she seems to have no option as she lacks courage and is mortally afraid of being an old maid. Her mother is happy that one of her daughters is so "advantageously" settled. (p.87). Her sisters also encourage her to accept Mr. Watts lest their mother should compel either of them to marry him. Sophia is, of course, sorry that their "sister may accept a man who cannot make her happy". But Georgiana perhaps knows Mary better. She concedes that Mr. Watts cannot make Mary happy "but his fortune, his name, his house, his carriage will". She has no doubt that "Mary will marry him". He is "rather plain sure," she adds, "but then what is beauty in a man?" (pp.88-89). Her own views about marriage are altogether different. She firmly states: "However, whether Mary accepts him or not, I am resolved. My determination is made. I never would marry Mr. Watts were beggary the only alternative". (p.89). Finally, of course, Mary accepts him and we accept it on a sombre note. Here we cannot help feeling that Jane Austen presents a negative picture of life.

Q. D. Leavis has claimed that Georgiana resembles Elizabeth Bennet and Sophia Jane Bennet.[16] Perhaps Mary is a much less sympathetic Charlotte Lucas. We indeed tend to feel in her case that if a woman can marry an obnoxius man like Mr. Watts simply because he promises "a new carriage .... a new saddle horse .... and an infinite number of most valuable jewels," (p.91), she deserves her fate.

And yet, this is perhaps too harsh a judgement on her. Frances Beer raises a pertinent question: "the problem of what to do with Mr. Watts is deadly serious: *Someone* is going to get stuck with him, and it is an appalling social reality that forces a family of girls with a widowed mother of slender means into this grotesque corner". Mary may have vices and may even be "beyond sympathy", yet "she is also presented as a victim, the warped product of a warping system."[17] *The Three Sisters* clearly presents a society in which a woman is a prisoner with no options for escape.

IV

It is significant that Jane Austen should have chosen this subject in one of her earliest works. It is even more significant that this subject should have haunted her all her life. Georgiana, of course, is still very young and she has no notion of what "beggary" really means. Nor does she realize the pitiable situation of daughters who failed to marry in that period. But the question is whether a woman should feel compelled to accept any kind of marriage, however miserable its consequences.

Jane Austen's later heroines, like Georgiana, wholly reject the view that any kind of marriage is better than no marriage at all. Jenny Calder has rightly said: "Perhaps the highest praise we can award Jane Austen's heroines is that in almost every case we can believe that they might not have married, like Jane Austen herself, and yet lived, within the narrow limits of their confining society, purposeful and interesting lives".[18]

There are, of course, other women in her novels who lack the strength to face the life of an old maid. Almost all women in her novels marry irrespective of whether the marriages are happy or not. It is no accident that except for the solitary case of Miss Bates in *Emma*, there are no old maids in Jane Austen. Jean B. Kern has claimed that in men's novels in the eighteenth century old maids came to be treated as 'sex-starved, frustrated and disagreeable stereotypes described by Defoe as 'a set of despicable characters'.' Bridget Allworthy and Tabitha Bramble who harass their bachelor brothers in *Tom Jones* and *Humphrey Clinker* are presented as models. But the women novelists 'were more sensitive to the problems of old maids rejected by the society in which they must live'. One reason for this may have been that many of these novelists were themselves unmarried, such as Jane Barker, Sarah Fielding, Jane Austen; some married when they were already past forty, such as Fanny Burney. Jane Austen feels somewhat diffident while dealing with Miss Bates. Miss Bates was, like Jane Austen, the daughter of a clergyman, and hence a gentlewoman. But she is in straitened circumstances. Emma should know, as Mr. Knightley does, that though she has lost her status, she has not lost her *class*. She is still a gentlewoman and she cannot be treated as one belonging to the working classes. She is, of course, conceived by Jane Austen as a foolish and garrulous old maid anxious to please those whom she regards her social superiors. But, as Kern rightly says, she is "even made a key figure in the education of the self-willed heroine". When Emma publicly makes fun of her on the Box Hill excursion, she draws a sharp rebuke from Mr. Knightley: "How could you be so unfeeling to Miss Bates? How could you be so insolent in your wit to a woman of her character, age, and situation? Emma, I had not thought it possible". Though Emma tries to defend herself, she realizes that she is guilty not only of gross bad manners but also of gross insensitivity and arrogance. From this moment, Emma starts mending herself.[19]

Jane Austen does not, of course, sentimentalize the case of Miss Bates - or of Anne Elliot or of Jane Fairfax, who might have ended as old maids. But she does quite realistically depict the anxieties of the daughters who knew that after their parents' death their might be none to support them. It may be noted that Jane Austen's own situation was no different. Her niece Caroline tells us that her aunts, Jane Austen and Cassandra, "had very small fortunes, and on their father's death, they and their mother would be, they were aware, but poorly off". "I believe," Caroline adds, "most young women so circumstanced would have gone on trusting to love after marriage".[20] The mention of love after marriage refers to an arranged marriage in the case of such women because they were not likely to secure a husband on their own owing to their small fortune. Unfortunately, this also happened in the case of Jane Austen.

We learn from her letters that when she was 20 years of age, she started taking interest in Tom Lefroy, a recent graduate of Trinity College, Dublin, currently reading law at the Inns of Courts in London and more or less of the same age. He was staying with his aunt in the neighbourhood of the Austens. Jane danced a few times with him at a private ball and he also visited her at her house. Realizing that Tom was taking too serious an interest in someone who had no fortune of her own, the aunt immediately sent him to London and put an end to what might have blossomed into a deep relationship and perhaps marriage. Another opportunity to get married occurred when Jane Austen was about 27. We know that on 25th November, 1802, Cassandra and Jane Austen arrived at Manydown, the home of their friends, the Biggs, for a short visit. A week later, on 2nd December, the son of the house, Harris Biggs Withers, proposed marriage to Jane Austen. There had been no courtship of any kind and the proposal was most unexpected.

Surprisingly, Jane Austen accepted the proposal even though Harris was six years her junior. It is reported that on the night of her betrothal, she "found that she was miserable and that the place and fortune that would certainly be *his*, could not alter the *man*".[21] So the very next morning, she broke the engagement.

Oliver MacDONAGH has asked: "Why did she accept his offer?"[22] But the more important question is: "Why did she change her mind within 24 hours and rejected the offer?" Accepting the offer was, of course, a normal thing. The fact is that however considerate her family, her future as an "old maid" could be very bleak. Moreover, this offer was approved by her sister Cassandra, her mentor, and by Biggs Wither's sisters, who were Jane Austen's oldest and dearest friends. As things were, her marriage would have been a great relief to her family for as an old spinster she would have been a burden on her brothers - and her mother and sister. But here was a test for Jane Austen. Should she behave like Elizabeth in *Pride and Prejudice* or like Charlotte Lucas? In the end, she chose to take a correct stand, though a difficult one, and preferred to stay single. It is significant that all her heroines have to face this test though they do not have to stay single. Let us see how the situation in *Pride and Prejudice* is anticipated in her unfinished piece, *The Watsons.*

This piece has four sisters, Emma being the youngest and the prettiest. She has just returned from her aunt where she had been staying since her childhood. Only one of her sisters, Elizabeth, is at home to receive Emma as the other two sisters, Margaret and Penelope, are away.

Taking advantage of their absence, Elizabeth confesses to Emma that she loved a young man named Purvis, took Penelope into confidence and Penelope set Purvis against her with a view to gaining him herself. The result is that they both lost him to some one else. This makes Elizabeth very bitter against Penelope whose treachery, she says, has ruined her happiness. Elizabeth and Penelope tried for the attention of another handsome young man in the neighbourhood, Tom Musgrove, but he is "a great flirt and never means anything serious", and Elizabeth bitterly tells Emma that Penelope 'thinks everything fair for a husband'.[23]

She herself claims that she is now quite resigned but adds:

> "You know, we must marry - I could do very well single for my own part - A little company, and a pleasant ball now and then, would be enough for me, if one could be young for ever, but my father cannot provide for us and it is very bad to grow old and be poor and laughed at." (p. 109).

Emma, who is only 19, is not only shocked to learn that there can be such "Rivalry, treachery between sisters" (p. 109), but also hurt about Penelope's attitude to marriage:

> 'I am sorry for her anxieties, but I do not like her .... opinions .... To be bent on marriage - to pursue a man merely for the sake of situation - is a sort of thing that shocks me; I cannot understand it. Poverty is a great evil, but to a woman of education and feeling it ought not, it cannot be the greatest - I would rather be a teacher at a school (and I can think of nothing worse) than marry a man I did not like.
>
> 'I would rather do anything than be a teacher at a school' - said her sister. 'I have been at school, Emma, and know what a life they lead you; *you* never have. - I should not like marrying a disagreeable man any more than yourself. - but I do not think there *are* very many disagreeable men; - I think I could like any good humoured man with a comfortable income, - I suppose my aunt brought you up to be rather refined.' (p. 110).

Emma is, of course, refined in the best sense of the term and in *The Watsons*, which is an unfinished piece, it seems clear that in Emma, Jane Austen is creating another Elizabeth Bennet. This is evident from the way Emma treats Tom Musgrove at the ball. To his surprise, he finds her 'calm courtesy' 'very unlike the encouraging warmth he had been used to receive from her sisters' (p. 126) and her declining his offer of a ride in his curricle cuts him to size. When she tells Elizabeth that she finds him 'very vain, very conceited, absurdly anxious for distinction, and absolutely contemptible in some of the measures he takes for becoming so,' Elizabeth exclaims: 'My dearest Emma! - you are like nobody else in the world.' (p. 133). Later Emma refuses to be patronised by her sister-in-law, her brother Robert's wife, and refuses their invitation to go to Croydon. It is a pity that Jane Austen did not complete the story but she is reported to have told her sister Cassandra 'something of the intended story'. After her father's death, Emma was -

> 'to become dependent for a home on her narrow-minded sister-in-law and brother. She was to decline an offer of marriage from Lord Osborne, and much of the interest of the tale was to arise from Lady Osborne's love for Mr. Howard, and his counter affection for Emma, whom he was finally to marry'.[24]

We have no idea what was to become of Elizabeth and Penelope.

V

Being a teacher in a boarding school, as Emma says, was perhaps the only opening for unmarried educated girls at that time. There is an interesting conversation on this subject between two girls in Harriet Martineau's *Deerbrook* (1837), which is worth citing. Margaret's family is short of money and she consults her friend Maria as to what she can do to earn money:

> "Cannot you tell me of some way in which a woman may earn money?"
>
> ".... That question is easily answered. A woman from the uneducated classes can get a subsistence by washing and cooking, by milking cows and going into service .... by working in a cotton mill ... But an educated woman, a woman with the powers which God gave her, religiously improved, with a reason which lays life open before her, an understanding which surveys science as its appropriate task, and a conscience which would make every species of responsibility safe - for such a woman there is in all England no chance of subsistence but by teaching ...."[25]

But as Elizabeth pointed out, the young ladies who opted to teach in schools were often exploited and humiliated in various ways so that teaching was not regarded as honourable for women of gentle birth. In 1822, Maria Edgeworth, in fact, argued that teaching as a *profession* should be made more attractive and honourable:

> The reward ought to be such as to excite women to cultivate their talents, and their understandings, with a view to this profession. A profession we will call it, for it should be considered as such; as an honourable profession, which a gentlewoman might follow without losing any degree of the estimation in which she is held by what is called the world. There is no employment, at present, by which a gentlewoman can maintain herself without losing something of that respect, something of that rank in society, which neither female fortitude nor male philosophy willingly forgoes. The liberal professions are open to men of small fortune; by presenting one similar resource to women, we should have a strong motive for their moral and intellectual improvement.[26]

The only other profession available to women was that of a governess though for most people, including Maria Edgeworth herself, teaching was, for all practical purposes, no different from the profession of a governess, specially in the case of female children. Jane Austen's view of the profession of a governess is perhaps embodied in the reaction of Jane Fairfax in *Emma*, who is, on all accounts, an extremely beautiful, intelligent and elegant girl. Patricia Beer indeed calls her 'the one really gifted woman in the book'.[27] She is also the only person in the novel of whom Mr. Knightley has a high opinion. Jane, however, ultimately marries Frank Churchill who has serious flaws in his character and who in our eyes is a wholly unsatisfactory husband for her. Modern readers may ask why such a refined and beautiful girl would throw herself away like this. Arnold Kettle provides the answer when he says that however good, clever or beautiful Jane Fairfax may be, she is 'an unprovided woman with no prospects in life beyond those of earning her living as governess'.[28]

Jane's attitude to the profession of a governess comes out clearly in her reply to Mrs. Elton who presses her to immediately accept the position at Mrs. Smallridge's lest she should lose it:

> 'I am not at all afraid of being long unemployed. There are places in town, offices, where enquiry would soon produce something - offices for the sale - not quite of human flesh - but of human intellect.'
>
> 'Oh! my dear, human flesh! you quite shock me; if you mean a fling at the slave-trade ....'
>
> 'I did not mean, I was not thinking of the slave-trade', replied Jane, 'governess-trade, I assure you, was all that I had in view! Widely different certainly as to the guilt of those who carry it on; but as to the greater misery of the victims, I do not know where it lies'.[29]

It may be added that many upper-class people in that age did treat governesses as no better than slaves.[30] Indeed, for someone like Mrs. Elton, there might not have been any substantial different between slave-trade and governess-trade. Selma James also notices the sexual angle. The governess, she says, 'worked and lived in a Great House virtually at the sexual disposal of the wealthy master'. It therefore exposed her to "what is now called 'sexual harassment at work' ".[31]

Unlike Jane Fairfax none of Jane Austen's heroines faces the threat of working for a living. They are all gentlewomen and they invariably better their economic and social status - some of them very considerably - through marriage. They are, however, worried at the prospect of remaining unmarried, all except Emma. She is not afraid of 'being an old maid like Miss Bates', because as she says:

> I shall not be a poor old maid like Miss Bates; it is poverty only which makes celibacy contemptible. A single woman with a

> very narrow income must be a ridiculous, disagreeable, old maid! .... a single woman of good fortune is always respectable ....

She adds:

> I have none of the usual inducements of women to marry .... Fortune I do not want; employment I do not want; consequence I do not want; I believe few married women are half as much mistress of their husband's house, as I am of Hartfield.' (I.10).

Other heroines, however, are not as fortunate. They want fortune, employment and, in addition, a home which they can call their own. Hence they must marry and that too, as soon and as well as they can. Jane Austen mentioned in a letter that 'single women have a dreadful propensity for being poor - which is one very strong argument in favour of Matrimony.'[32] It is extraordinary, however, that a writer who is so conscious of the difficulties faced by unmarried women in her society should have given no thought at all to the question of jobs for women. Perhaps being the daughter of a Tory parson, she was herself too much of a gentlewoman to engage in the sordid task of earning her own living.[33] She was, of course, lucky in that one of her brothers provided her with a house after her father's death. But not all brothers in the age were as affectionate or considerate. Further, as Mary Wollstencraft pointedly stated, there was the wife of the brother who was determined to drive out the sister whom she regarded as an intruder in her family who was consuming the substance which naturally belonged to her children. Jane Austen was very lucky in her sister-in-law too but interestingly, just before her death, she wrote to Anne Sharp, a friend and, significantly, a spinster and a governess: "In short, if I live to be an old woman, I must expect to wish I had died now; blessed in the tenderness of such a Family, and before I had survived either them or their affection." (22 May, 1817).[34]

VI

The predicament of a girl who is mortally afraid of being 'single' and 'poor' is brought out by Charlotte Lucas in *Pride and Prejudice*. Her father is not, of course, a poor man but he has a large family to support - a family which also has other unmarried daughters. Hence she accepts Collins' proposal of marriage immediately after it has been rejected by her best friend, Elizabeth Bennet. Defending her decision, she tells Elizabeth:

> "I am not romantic, you know; I never was. I ask only a comfortable home; and considering Mr. Collins' character, connections, and situation in life, I am convinced that my chance of happiness with him is as fair as most people can boast on entering the marriage state." (Chapt. 22).

Her family, we are told, is -

> properly over-joyed on the occasion. The younger girls formed hopes of coming out a year or two sooner than they might otherwise have done; and the boys were relieved from their apprehension of Charlotte's dying an old maid. Charlotte herself was tolerably composed. She had gained her point, and had time to consider of it. Her reflections were in general satisfactory. Mr. Collins, to be sure, was neither sensible nor agreeable; his society was irksome, and his attachment to her must be imaginery. But still he would be her husband. Without thinking highly either of men or of matrimony, marriage had always been her object; it was the only honourable provision for well-educated young women of small fortune, and however uncertain of giving happiness, must be their pleasantest preservative from want. This preservative she had now obtained; and at the age of twenty-seven, without having ever been handsome, she felt all the good luck of it. (Chapt. 22).

Elizabeth Bennet, of course, is both shocked and disappointed by Charlotte Lucas' attitude to marriage. However, Charlotte knows that human beings do not live by high sounding ideals but have to compromise with reality. Most people in her society do not find anything wrong with this compromise and when she visits her, Elizabeth herself is surprised that Charlotte's compromise has succeeded so well.

Given the situation, Mrs. Bennet's reaction to Elizabeth's rejection of Collins' offer of marriage is understandable:

> 'But I tell you what, Miss Lizzy - if you take it into your head to go on refusing every offer of marriage in this way, you will never get a husband at all - and I am sure I do not know who is to maintain you when your father is dead. I shall not be able to keep you - and so I warn.' (Chapt. 20).

The Bennet estate, as we know, is 'entailed, in default of heirs male, on a distant relation'.[35] That distant relation happens to be Mr. Collins. With five daughters and only 5000 pounds as principal, Mrs. Bennet and her daughters would have, according to one calculation, only 50 pounds per annum per head. In a way, Mr. Collins is really making amends to his cousins by marrying one of them. Indeed, as Lillian Robinson has said, 'Stupid and pompous he may be, but his offer, on the material plane, is valuable nevertheless.'[36]

Further, unlike Charlotte, the Bennet sisters have no brothers with whom they might stay should they remain spinsters. Indeed, the first thought that comes to Elizabeth's mind on hearing of Lydia's elopement is that "Lydia has no brothers to step forward". (Chapt. 47). They have only an uncle in business but he too could not be too young and he has a family of his own. Moreover, none of the Bennet daughters has the slightest training or aptitude for any profession or business. They have been brought up as a gentleman's daughters - so much so that, as their mother boasts, they never enter the kitchen as Charlotte Lucas often does!

In saying the above, my purpose is not to suggest that Elizabeth should have accepted Collins' proposal of marriage. All I am trying to point out is that in Jane Austen we are not allowed to forget the economic facts of life. In many feminist circles marriage as an institution is often scoffed at. There was no dearth of scoffers in eighteenth century England too but in a society where there were no honourable independent means of livelihood available to women, marriage of almost any kind seemed their only refuge.

And yet Elizabeth Bennet rejected Collins' proposal of marriage without giving the slightest thought to the consequences. It is not that she is romantic or has any very high expectations in the marriage market. When Bingley and Jane finally come together, Jane, somewhat foolishly, tells Elizabeth that she wishes that "there *were* but such another man for [her]". Elizabeth half-seriously retorts: "If I have very good luck, I may meet another Mr. Collins in time" (Chapt. 55). She does not, of course, mean it. She is not the kind of woman who would marry a man who is "neither sensible nor agreeable" and whose company is so "irksome" that one has to invent excuses to avoid it.

Critics are puzzled as to why Jane Austen should be grimly realistic in her treatment of Charlotte Lucas but spare Elizabeth Bennet the cruelties of the marriage market and happily provide her with a dream hero as husband. The explanation obviously lies in the fact that Charlotte and Elizabeth have an altogether different approach to marriage and indeed to life itself. Moreover, Charlotte has very little to recommend herself - Elizabeth has. Charlotte merely needs a home and she accepts the first person - in this case Mr. Collins - who can provide it: Elizabeth's demands are different. She wants happiness in marriage and is prepared to wait till she meets the kind of man who can provide it. To interpret her happiness in terms of the Cinderella story, as has been done by D. W. Harding, is not fair to Jane Austen. She is presenting two types of women, one who is afraid of being crushed by circumstances and the other who is capable of conquering them. To do so, she needs not only courage and intelligence but also the capacity to fight against social oppression and, if necessary, to suffer. She is distinctly superior to all other women characters in the novel and is not a Cinderella but the heroine of a novel of social realism.

NOTES

1. *Ladies and the Mammies: Jane Austen and Jean Rhys* (Falling Wall Press Ltd., Bristol, England, 1982), p. 14.
2. *Jane Austen and the French Revolution*, (London, 1979), pp. 155-6.
3. Mary Astell, *Some Reflection Upon Marriage*, (1700), pp. 57-8.
4. Cited by Roger Thompson, *Women in Stuart England and America: A Comparative Study* (London, 1974), p. 35.
5. The quotation is taken from the abridged edition (London, 1977, p.40).
6. See Shirlene Mason, *Daniel Defoe and the Status of Women* (Eden Press Women's Publications, Montreal, 1978), p.83.
7. "A new Method for making Women as useful and as capable of maintaining themselves, as the Men are; and consequently preventing their becoming old Maids, or taking ill Courses", *Gentlemen's Magazine*, 9, 1739, p.525. Cited by Ruth Perry, *Women, Letters, And the Novel* (New York, 1980), pp. 29-30.
8. Cited by Bridget Hill ed. *Eighteenth Century Women: An Anthology* (London, 1984), p.129.
9. Mary Wollstencraft, *Vindication of the Rights of Woman* (1792), ed. Miriam Brody Krammick (Penguin Books, 1975), pp.157-8.
10. See Donald Greene, "Jane Austen's Monsters", *Jane Austen: Bicentenary Essays*, ed. John Halperin (London, 1975), p.271.
11. See Patricia Beer, *Reader, I Married Him: A Study of the Women Characters of Jane Austen, Charlotte Bronte, Elizabeth Gaskell, and George Eliot* (London, 1974), p.56.
12. Frances Beer, ed. *The Juvenilia of Jane Austen and Charlotte Bronte* (Penguin Books, 1985), p.16.
13. Ibid, p.16.
14. Ibid, p.16.
15. Ibid, p.85.
16. Q.D. Leavis, "A Critical Theory of Jane Austen's Writings," *Scrutiny*, X, 1941, p.74. Cited by Frances Beer, p.14.
17. Frances Beer, p.16.
18. *Women and Marriage in Victorian Fiction,* (London, 1976), p. 18.
19. Jean B. Kern, "The Old Maid, or 'to grow old and be poor, and laughed at'", *Fetter'd Or Free?: British Women Novelists 1670- 1815*, edited by Mary Anne Schofield and Cecilia Macheski, (Ohio State University Press, Athens, Ohio, 1986), pp. 201-210.
20. See Oliver MacDONAGH, *Jane Austen: Real and Imagined Worlds,* (Yale University Press, New Haven, 1991), p.39.
21. Ibid, p.41.
22. Ibid, p.39.
23. All quotations are taken from Margaret Drabble's Penguin edition of *Lady Susan/The Watsons/Sandition,* (1985), p.108.

24. Ibid, p. 152.
25. Cited by Anthea Zeman, *Presumptuous Girls: Women and Their World in the Serious Woman's Novel* (London, 1977), p. 45.
26. *Essays on Practical Education* (1822), i. p.414, cited by Hazel Mews, *Frail Vessels: Women's Role in Women's Novels from Fanny Burney to George Elliot* (London, 1969), pp. 177-78.
27. Patricia Beer, p. 50.
28. "Emma", *Jane Austen: A Collection of Critical Essays,* ed. Ian Watt (1963), p. 117.
29. In *Catharine*, an early juvenile piece, this is how the profession of a governess is described by the daughter of a clergyman who is now dead: "It was one so opposite to all her ideas of propriety, so contrary to her wishes, so repugnant to her feelings, that she would almost have preferred servitude to it, had choice been allowed her." Since no choice was allowed, "infinitely against her inclinations [she] had been necessitated to embrace the only possibility that was offered to her of a maintenance." (Frances Beer, p. 138).
30. Mary Wollstencraft wrote: "The few employments open to women, so far from being liberal, are menial, and when a superior education enables them to take charge of the education of children as governess, they are not treated like the tutors of sons." (cited by Valerie Grosvenor Myer, *Jane Austen* (London, 1980), p. 79).
31. *Ladies and Mammies: Jane Austen and Jean Rhys*, (Falling Wall Press, Bristol, 1983), p. 45.
32. Cited by Lloyd W. Brown, "The Business of Marrying and Mothering", *Jane Austen's Achievement,* ed. Juliet McMaster (London, 1975), p. 30.
33. As against this attitude, see Mary Hays' *Memoirs of Emma Courtney* (1796) whose heroine says (p. 55): "Cruel prejudice! Helpless women! Why was I not educated for Commerce, for a profession, for labour?" But Mary Hays was Mary Wollstencraft's friend and disciple and hence the difference in her attitude from that of Jane Austen.
34. Cited by Margaret Drabble (ed.) *Jane Austen: Lady Susan/The Watsons/ Sandition* (Penguin Classics, 1985), p. 20.
35. See Rachel M. Brownstein, *Becoming a Heroine: Reading about Women in Novels* (Penguin Books, 1984), p.96: "Elinore and Marianne Dashwood in *Sense and Sensibility*, Elizabeth Bennet in *Pride and Prejudice* and Anne Elliot in *Persuasion* are victims of the patriarchal law of entail, which prevents them from inheriting their fathers' houses, favouring selfish and obnoxious men like John Dashwood and Mr. Collins, and even scheming hypocrites like Mr. Elliot, over deserving young women."
36. Lillian S. Robinson, "Why Marry Mr. Collins?", *Sex, Class and Culture* (Indian University Press, Bloomington and London, 1977), p.186.

Chapter VII

Jane Austen on Marriage

Jane Austen's view of marriage can perhaps be better understood if we keep in mind the low expectations of women with regard to marriage in eighteenth century England. While all women were, of course, expected to marry and were taught the duties of a wife from their childhood, they were also warned not to have too rosy a picture of married life in their minds. Anna Howe, the most clear-headed girl in Richardson's *Clarissa Harlowe* (1748-9), says: "When I look round upon all the married people of my acquaintance, and see how *they* live, and what *they* bear who live *best*, I am confirmed in my dislike to the state". (IV. 477). (Italics Richardson's).[1] She also seems to subscribe to the view that marriage "dampens the personality, especially the female personality".[2] She describes the man-woman relationship in married life as fluctuating and says: "In short, how he *ascends* and how I *descend*, in the matrimonial wheel, never to take my turn again, but by fits and starts, like the feeble struggles of a sinking State for its dying liberty". (I.340) (Italics Richardson's).

Jane Austen herself is conscious of the pitfalls in the way of a happy married life. Her correspondence — as also her fiction — gives us the impression that she is perhaps almost afraid of marriage. Patricia Beer believes that Jane Austen "could not bear to hear about married bliss" and mentions her "fear, amounting to an obsession, towards the end of life, about childbearing".[3] It was not an unnatural fear. Quite a few deaths in child-birth had taken place in her own circle. We learn from her letters that when her brother

James' second wife, Mary, was expecting her second child, Jane Austen wrote to Cassandra: "Mrs. Coulthard and Anne, late of Manydown, are both dead, and both died in child-bed. We have not regaled Mary with the news". After the baby was born, she wrote: "Mary does not manage matters in such a way as to make me want to lay in himself ... things are not in that comfort and style about her which are necessary to make such a situation an enviable one". Two other of her sisters-in-law were to die later as a consequence of repeated child-bearing; and once, hearing of another pregnancy in an already large family, she drily noted, "I would recommend to her [Mrs. Deeds] and Mr. D the simple regimen of separate rooms". Shortly before her death she wrote to Fanny, "Mrs. Clement too is in that way again. I am quite tired of so many children". When she believed that her other elder niece, Anna Lefroy, was expecting her third child within three years of marriage, she wrote, "Anna has not a chance of escape ... Poor Animal, she will be worn out before she is thirty?"[4] Lloyd W. Brown cites her letter to Fanny Knight: "Oh what a loss it will be when you are married. You are too agreeable in your single state, too agreeable as a Niece. I shall hate you when your delicious play of Mind is all settled down into conjugal and maternal affections". Her advice to Fanny is to marry late and not begin "the business of Mothering quite so early in life" so that she "will be young in constitution, spirits, figure and countenance, while Mrs. Wm. Hammond is growing old by confinements and nursing".[5]

All this does not mean that Jane Austen was against marriage. As we learn from her letters, she felt disappointed when her relationship with Tom Lefroy was cut short by his aunt. This was a most suitable match for her. Tom, a recent graduate of Trinity College, Dublin, currently reading law at the Inns of Court in London, had come to stay with his aunt in the neighbourhood of the Austens. They danced a few times at private balls and he also visited her at her house. Realising that he was taking too serious an interest in Jane Austen, a girl with small fortune, the aunt immediately sent him to London and put an end to what might have blossmed into a deep relationship and perhaps a marriage. They were both nearly of the same age, about twenty years, and the match was approved by Cassandra and other members of the family. Though Jane tried to laugh it off, yet the fact that the aunt intervened on account of her small fortune left a permanent scar on her mind. It is no wonder that the hardships of girls with small fortune became the dominant theme in almost all her novels. We also know Jane Austen's one-day engagement to Harris Biggs. Why she accepted a young man who was just a boy and six years her junior and why she broke off the engagement within 24 hours are puzzling questions. But about one thing there is no doubt; Jane Austen would have readily accepted a serious offer from an appropriate suitor. She was certainly not averse to marriage.

It is, of course, true that like most sensitive women, she too was quite concerned about the risks that women took in child-birth in that period. The situation was quite desperate from the women's point of view. As a social historian, Wallace Notestein, has said, in seventeenth century England, women "spent the years from eighteen to forty-five in the business of bearing children. That meant that they were unwell much of the time. If they survived the perils of child-birth, and illness that followed frequent pregnancies, they bore eight to fifteen children (including child-births). ... John Donne ... had twelve children by his wife in sixteen years of their married life, she dying at thirty-three".[6] The situation did not change very much in the eighteenth century too as is clear from what Roy Porter says in *English Society in the Eighteenth Century* (1990): "Women's letters harrowingly chronicle the fatigue, ill health and premature ageing they suffered as they repeatedly grew full-bellied." He mentions the case of Lady Bristol, who married at the age of nineteen and at thirty-nine she had her last pregnancy, having produced twenty children, few of whom lived to grow up. "Lady Bristol's fertility was exceptional", Roy Porter says, "but many women dreaded the child-birth treadmill".[7]

And yet this fear has not prevented women from marrying in almost any age. Incidentally, as Meenakshi Mukherjee has pointed out, Jane Austen herself belonged to a family of eight, and in her novels the Heywoods have fourteen children (*Sandition*), Catharine

Moreland's parents ten (*Northanger Abbey*) and the Prices of Portsmouth at least nine (*Mansfield Park*), while Emma's sister Isabella has five children in seven years (*Emma*) and Musgroves have an unspcified number of "boisterous boys" and "chattering girls" other than the three older ones who figure prominently in the novel, *Persuasion*.[8]

I

It is, of course, difficult to generalise; but it is fair to say that the ideal of a happy marriage among the English gentry in the eighteenth century was based on "strong physical attraction, mutual esteem, and steadfast companionship. Upon esteem rested the other two. Without it attraction became lust, and companionship could never develop".[9] This ideal was not always attained. Perhaps man was more to blame for this than the woman. Dr. Gregory in his *A Father's Legacy to His Daughters* (1774) described the position fairly correctly:

> A man of taste and delicacy marries a woman because he loves her more than any other. A woman of equal taste and delicacy marries him because she esteems him, and because he gives her that preference. (p.83).

The point that Dr. Gregory is making is that men do not attach much importance to the intellectual and moral qualities of women, but their choices are largely determined by a woman's physical beauty. Women, on the other hand, cannot take the risk of falling for a man simply because he is physically and sexually attractive. They will accept him only when they are convinced that they have won his respect. It is not without significance that when Elizabeth Bennet realizes that she loves Darcy and would gladly accept him as her husband, Jane Austen breathlessly describes her state of mind: "She *respected*, she *esteemed*, she was grateful to him, she felt a real interest in his welfare". (*Pride and Prejudice*, Chapt. 44).

It is worth mentioning that most women novelists in the

eighteenth century also laid much greater emphasis on mutual esteem as a suitable basis for marriage. Sarah Fielding's Octavia in *The Lives of Cleopatra and Octavia* (1757) is prepared to "live single" if she cannot find "the object of my inclinations, and whose disposition would make an artful behaviour on my part totally needless to obtain good Usage or to secure his *Esteem*" (pp. 148-9).[10] A character in Sarah Scott's *A Description of Millenium Hall* (1762) pertinently asks: "which is more desirable, his esteem or his courtship?" She then gives an answer which is eminently sensible: "if you really love him, you can make no comparison between them: for surely there cannot be a greater suffering than to stand low in the opinion of any person who has a great share of our affections." (p.125).[11] In the Preface to *The Advantages of Education* (1793), Jane West says:

> I do not choose to hold up matrimony as the great desideratum of our sex: I wish them to look to the general *esteem* of worthy people and the approbation of their own hearts, for the recommense of their merit, rather than to the particular addresses of a lover. (I:p. 3-4).[12]

She says elsewhere:

> How poor ... is the woman's boast, who is conscious that she rather gratifies the vanity, than charms the heart of the husband. (p.115).[13]

Male writers, on the other hand, seem to attach much less importance to mutual esteem. As Paula Backscheider says: "Defoe insists upon similarity of temper, age, social status and piety. (cf. *Conjugal Lewdness*, 1727: 213-28, 252-72). He may portray a kind of lasting love as he does with Moll Flanders and Jemmy, a satisfying marriage as he does with Jack and his fourth wife, a deep affection and continued enjoyment of conversation as well as sex as he does with Roxana and the Prince, but he does not show us the development of mutual esteem."[14]

Fielding and other eighteenth century men novelists are also deficient in this respect. In theory, of course, Fielding declares that:

> "esteem and gratitude are the proper motives to love, as youth and beauty are to desire, and, therefore, though such desire may naturally cease, when age or sickness overtakes its object: yet these can have no effect on love, nor ever shake, from a good mind, that sensation or passion which hath gratitude or esteem for its basis." (*Tom Jones* (1749, Book VI, Chapt. 1).

But in his novels, like Defoe, Sterne, and Smollett, he also emphasizes women's sexual attractiveness rather than the gradual development of mutual respect and affection. In Richardson's novels too mutual esteem between men and women is not a central theme. It is, however, not safe to generalize. In Thomas Holocroft's *Anna St. Ives* (1792), the opinion is expressed that love between man and woman should lead to "*the friendship of marriage*". (Italics Holocroft's). "Surely, if it be not friendship", we are told, "according to the best and highest sense in which the word is used, marriage cannot but be something faulty and vicious."[15]

II

In 1700, Mary Astell had already stated that the only suitable basis for marriage is friendship: "He who does not make friendship the chief inducement to his choice, and prefer it before any other consideration, does not deserve a good wife, and therefore should not complain if he goes without one" [*Some Reflections Upon Marriage*) (1700), (p.18)]. In eighteenth century England, however, most men were attracted either by a woman's money or by her beauty and these precisely are the motives for marriage which Mary Astell rejected. In her *Reflections*, she declared: "There's no great Odds between [a man] Marrying for the Love of Money, or for the Love of Beauty; the Man does not act according to Reason in either case, but is govern'd by irregular Appetites" (p.25). It is these "irregular appetites" which determine many of the marriages in

Jane Austen. One such marriage is clearly that of Mr. Bennet in *Pride and Prejudice*. "Had Elizabeth's opinion been all drawn from her own family", Jane Austen tells us,

> she could not have formed a very pleasing picture of conjugal felicity or domestic comfort. Her father *captivated by youth and beauty*. (Italics mine), and that appearance of good humour, which youth and beauty generally give, had married a woman whose weak understanding and illiberal mind, had very early in their marriage put an end to all real affection for her. Respect, esteem and confidence had vanished for ever, and all his views of domestic happiness were over-thrown." (Chapt. 42).

The description of the Bennet marriage makes it clear that for Jane Austen a happy marriage is one in which there is "real affection", "respect, esteem and confidence" between husband and wife. The Bennet marriage clearly lacks almost all these elements. It would, however, be wrong to blame Mrs. Bennet alone for this. She is from a typical eighteenth century family where girls got no proper education and where the general standard of culture was rather low. Mr. Bennet, however, is an educated man and a 'gentleman', as Elizabeth claims with pride, but he makes no attempt to make the marriage succeed. Elizabeth indeed

> had never been blind to the impropriety of her father's behaviour as a husband. She had always seen it with pain; but respecting his abilities, and grateful for his affectionate treatment of herself, she endeavoured to forget what she could not overlook, and to banish from her thoughts that continual breach of conjugal obligation and decorum which, in exposing his wife to the contempt of her own children, was so highly reprehensible.

After she fails to persuade him to put some check on Lydia's conduct lest her "disdain of all restraint", bring disgrace to the whole family, Elizabeth sees most clearly "the disadvantages which must attend the children of so unsuitable a marriage". She particularly feels "the evils arising from so ill-judged a direction of [her father's] talents; talents which rightly used, might at least have preserved the respectability of his daughters, even if incapable of enlarging the mind of his wife." (Chapt. 42).

Mr. Bennet clearly needed a wife who should have provided him with companionship but how can a man get such a wife if his motive for marriage is just physical attractiveness and sexual passion? In her *Reflections*, Mary Astell had claimed that only those marriages succeed where men are "guided by Reason and not by Humour or brutish passion."

The worst feature of the Bennet marriage is the harm that it does to the children. Mr. Bennet does take some interest in Elizabeth but is quite indifferent to his other daughters. Mrs. Bennet's influence on her daughters is, of course, disastrous. One daughter, Lydia, elopes with an adventurer, the other, Kitty, wishes to follow in her footsteps if given an opportunity, the third, Mary, desperately tries to cover up her emptiness through a show of learning. The father knows that they are "three very silly sisters" (Chapt. 41), but the mother encourages them and he does not care to intervene. Elizabeth and Jane alone escape the contamination but that is perhaps "because they have spent much time with their middle-class but virtuous, intelligent, well-informed and 'well-bred' aunt and uncle, the Gardiners - appropriate name for right cultivators of youth".[16]

The marriage of Sir Thomas Bertram in *Mansfield Park* is no better than that of Mr. Bennet. Here too the basic motive is physical attraction though the financial motive is not altogether absent: "Miss Maria Ward of Huntington with only seven thousand pounds, had the good luck to *captivate* (Italics mine) Sir Thomas Bertram of Mansfield Park .... and to be thereby raised to the rank of a baronet's Lady." (Chapt. 1). Such captivation does not last long and we discover that after some time Lady Bertram starts withdrawing into her own shell and 'in consequence of a little ill-health, and a great deal of indolence, gave up the house in town, which she had been used to occupy every spring, and remained wholly in the country, leaving Sir Thomas to attend his duty in parliament.' (Chapt. 2). 'To the education of her daughters', Jane Austen goes on to say, 'Lady

Bertram paid not the smallest attention. She was a woman who spent her days in sitting nicely dressed on a sofa, doing some long piece of needlework, of little use and no beauty, thinking more of her pug than her children, but very indulgent to the latter, when it did not put herself to inconvenience'. (Chapt 2). The children are left to the care of an aunt who encourages precisely those tendencies in their character which should have been suppressed. Hence one girl runs away from her husband's home with a wholly undependable lover, the other elopes with a worthless man and one of the sons wrecks his health through dissipation.

III

The fact that many marriages in Jane Austen are "bad or bleakly empty .... revealing different degrees of failed mutuality, non-reciprocation and myopic egotism or frivolous self- gratification",[17] serves as a warning to her heroines. They are anxious that their own marriages should be based on affection so that in their case, there is no dearth of reciprocation, mutuality, esteem and regard. To achieve such marriages, however, is not easy in view of the situation in which Jane Austen's heroines are placed. Anthea Zeman thus describes the situation:

> These are the girls whose marriage chances depended entirely on their personal attractions. They have no money; everyone knows they have no money. They are in the same ballrooms and assemblies as more fortunate girls, the acknowledged heiresses, which puts them in a singularly exposed position. Apart from the obvious fact that they will have fewer, and generally poorer, suitors to choose from, they are seen by the world as in *need* (Italics Zeman's) of a husband, as Mantraps prepared to do almost anything to secure a future and a fortune for themselves."[18]

Charlotte Lucas in *Pride and Prejudice* does after all demonstrate the truth of Zeman's statement. But none of Jane Austen's heroines gives the impression that she is in *need* of a husband and she is certainly not the kind of woman who would be prepared to do almost anything to secure a future and a fortune for herself. Indeed, she would have no respect for such women. All men in Jane Austen, of course, have the feeling that no woman can decline an offer of marriage, almost any kind of marriage. Even a sensible man like Mr. Knightley has to be snubbed by Emma: "It is always incomprehensible to a man that a woman should ever refuse an offer of marriage. A man always imagines a woman to be ready for anybody who asks her." (*Emma*, Chapt. 8). Unlike Charlotte, Jane Austen's heroines do decline offers of marriage and accept only the man of their choice.

In her juvenile pieces, it is true that some girls act almost in panic and they seem to be willing to do almost anything to secure a husband. We have met such girls in *The Three Sisters* and *The Watsons*. But Jane Austen's heroines have completely outgrown this phase and none of them acts in panic for fear of being an old maid. They recognize that husband-hunting lowers a woman's reputation. They are girls with intelligence and have the capacity to take their own decisions about their future. Their relations often embarrass them. Indeed, the greatest enemy of the Bennet sisters is their mother. But the girls act with dignity in almost every situation. Ultimately they determine their own future. A good example is that of Anne Elliot. She seems to have made the mistake of rejecting the one man whom she loved. She receives other offers but she rejects them. She spends seven long years of hopelessness but never loses her dignity. The conduct of her family members is often offensive but she never loses her balance and remains busy in whatever work she is required to do. Ultimately the man arrives and claims her. But it is not a Cinderella story. These girls have character and no Prince Charming can take them for granted.

At a time when most marriages were mercenary, these girls were at a clear disadvantage. It was, of course, a difficult period. The gentry was losing its power and status and the trading classes were gaining in strength. The gentry regarded a suitably arranged marriage as the surest way to get rich. Jane Austen is acutely conscious of this situation. Wickham in *Pride and Prejudice* shifts his attentions from Elizabeth Bennet to Miss King the moment he learns that Miss King's grand-father has died and she has inherited 10,000 pounds. Mr. Willoughby in *Sense and Sensibility* is genuinely in love with Marianne as he later confesses to Elinore, but a dowry of 30,000 pounds is too great a temptation and he deserts her for a wholly unsatisfactory wife. Darcy's cousin, Colonel Fitzwilliam, honestly and frankly tells Elizabeth Bennet that in minor matters he is as free as Darcy but "in matters of greater weight, I may suffer from the want of money. Younger sons cannot marry where they like". Elizabeth cannot help retorting: "Unless where they like women of fortune, which I think they very often do." Colonel Fitzwilliam between whom and Elizabeth a much deeper relationship could have developed, candidly confesses: "Our habits of expense make us too dependent, and there are not many in my rank of life who can afford to marry without some attention to money."

"Is this", thought Elizabeth, "meant for me?" and she coloured at the idea; but, recovering herself, said in a lively tone,

> "And pray, what is the usual price of an Earl's younger son? Unless the elder brother is very sickly, I suppose you would not ask above fifty thousand pounds."

He answered her in the same style, and the subject dropped. (Chapt. 33).

But this subject is only rarely dropped and in most cases dowry was a powerful motive for marriage throughout the eighteenth century and beyond. In the beginning of the eighteenth century, Mary Astell had bluntly stated:

> "What qualifications do they look after in a spouse? What will she bring?, is the first Enquiry: How many Acres? or how much ready coin?"[19]

The younger sons of Earls who married for money - like others who had done so - must have realized sooner than later that their marriage had failed to give them the kind of 'felicity' that can come only from love. As Lawrence Stone has pointed out, eighteenth century Englishmen by and large found this 'felicity' outside marriage. According to him, "throughout the eighteenth century, it remained quite common in upper-class circles for men of rank, position and quality, to keep a mistress or series of mistresses". The girls who, "in return for a fixed allowance, became the mistresses of noblemen and wealthy gentlemen," Stone says, "were nearly all women from well-to-do professional or merchant background whose fathers had gone bankrupt, and who found this virtually the only way of maintaining the standard of living to which they were accustomed".[20]

Jane Austen does not, of course, emphasise this aspect of contemporary life in any of her novels but there is no doubt that she is quite aware of the damaging impact of such a situation on girls' minds.

IV

Though Henny Tilney in *Northanger Abbey* tells Catharine that "man has the advantage of choice, woman only the power of refusal" (Chapt.10), Jane Austen's heroines enjoy much greater freedom. But love marriage in their social circle was not easy. Marriage was still a family affair and in any case most girls were not permitted by their parents to meet eligible young men privately. Elizabeth Bennet herself objects to Lydia's going out to private parties and expects her father to put restrictions on her movements. Girls from such families met young men only at public places, at dances, dinners, assemblies etc. In such circumstances, a girl could judge a man only by his appearance, his dress, his manners - all external features but appearances can be very deceptive. Elizabeth Bennet, as we know, is at first enchanted by Wickham; and whatever she may say, Emma at one stage is in love with Frank Churchil. Frank Churchil is not, of course, an altogether wicked character but Wickham is a real villain. But, as Jane Austen tells us, "his appearance was greatly in his favour" and he had a "very pleasing address". (*Pride and Prejudice*, Chapt. 15). He is "beyond" all officers of his regiment "in person, countenance, air and walk." (Chapt. 16). Elizabeth does not have it "in her nature to question the veracity of a young man of such amiable appearance as Wickham" (Chapt. 17). Indeed, he "must always be her model of the amiable and the pleasing." (Chapt. 27). Is it any wonder that Lydia should fall for him and elope with him?

Lydia indeed raises a larger question, namely, what should society do to train its young women to resist sexual attraction. Anthea Zeman has wisely said: "All [Jane Austen's] novels end with propitious marriages, but they are not manuals on how to get married. They are, far more, a series of guide books on when, how and in what frame of mind *not* to get married." (pp. 16-17).[21] Lydia had not learnt in what frame of mind *not* to get married. Nor had her mother taught her anything about it. Indeed she herself did not know it. She was constantly hunting for husbands for her daughters to the grave embarrassment of her two elder daughters.

In Jane Austen's times, it was a normal assumption of women that men are predators. As Jenni Calder has said: "All but the worthiest of them are liable to take advantage of women at the slightest opportunity.[22] How they should conduct themselves to resist these predators becomes almost the main concern of women in Jane Austen. One way of doing so is, of course, to cultivate a sense of personal dignity and self-confidence. Such cultivation, however, is possible only if women recognise that they can lead happy and useful lives on their own without all the while hankering after male approval and praise. Professions could have, of course, helped but in a society where no professions are available, they have to find pleasure and purpose in whatever work they like best. Anthea Zeman says that women "should, in the first place, take care of themselves, take themselves seriously." She adds that they should

> make sure they get exercise out of doors, and have a routine - a morning walk, needlework on hand, regular hours for practising music, arranging for obtaining new books, regular call-paying and charitable activity. Thus established, they possess

> dignity; they were people with employment, people who can be interrupted, not people who are waiting for something exciting to happen. This is their defence against the world. Girls without it - the Lydia and Kitty Bennets with their noses pressed against the window-pane as the officers pass by - are as defenceless as rabbits."[23]

But the real defence of women against the world finally is their own intelligence. Intelligence alone can serve as a shield against all male onslaughts on her honour or dignity. It also makes her self-sufficient. In the worst of circumstances, an intelligent woman can depend upon her inner resources. In the case of Jane Austen's heroines, it is true, religion and the traditional values prevalent in her society also provide them strength. The education that was provided to women in those times, though not of a very high intellectual order, did help to develop their moral sense. Indeed, the chief aim of education in that period was to inculcate in women virtuous conduct and cultured behaviour.

In this context, it is worth mentioning that Jane Austen rejected the fashionable view that a woman of culture should be proficient in music, dancing, painting, etc. It is no mere coincidence that most of Jane Austen's heroines are deficient in these superficial accomplishments. As Darcy is *Pride and Prejudice* says, women should not be content merely with these accomplishments but add to them "something more substantial, in the *improvement of the mind by extensive reading*." (Chapt. 8) (Italics mine).

V

In his open defence of Squire Western's elligible daughter, Sophia, Squire Allworthy in *Tom Jones* (1749) categorically declared that love was "the only foundation of happiness in a married state, as it can only produce that high and tender friendship which should always be the cement of this union." He went on to emphasize that he"would tolerate neither any use of parental compulsion, nor marriage motivated by lust for a beautiful person or by avarice for a great fortune or by snobbery for a noble title."[24]

All Jane Austen's heroines want this "high and tender friendship" to be the basis of their marriage. But they invariably marry men who are rich or, at any rate, prosperous enough to maintain their family in middle class style. If they marry like Fanny Price's mother, they will have to endure poverty and degradation. None of Jane Austen's heroines, including Fanny Price herself, would like to accept such a situation. Jane Austen's position is often summed up by critics in Lord David Cecil's words: "It was wrong to marry for money, but it was silly to marry without it."[25] Perhaps it is a somewhat cynical way of stating the exact position. It is not that Jane Austen's heroines keep both love and the man's financial standing in mind while accepting him. But they belong to a certain social circle and they usually marry within that circle or slightly above it. The only important point is that they must not become victims of penniless adventures under the influence of sheer romantic passion but keep their feet on the ground. Of course, they would prefer "a marriage of true minds *and* important social status and responsibility .... as wife of a landed gentleman or dedicated professional man"[26] but such a marriage cannot be made to order.

Jane Austen makes it clear, however, that none of her heroines would marry a man simply because he is rich. Indeed, they would not accept a marriage which is not based on love and deep affection. Fanny's case in *Mansfield Park* is perhaps the most instructive in this connection. Mrs. Norris describes her as "the lowest and last" (chapt. 23) and Henry Crawford thinks that she is "helpless, friendless, neglected, forgotten" (chapt. 30). Almost an orphan and brought up by her uncle, one would assume that she has no option but to accept almost any offer of marriage. And yet she too, like Emma, resents the arrogant assumption of men that "a man must be acceptable to every woman he may happen to like himself". (chapt. 35). Emma, of course, is an heiress and can dare to refuse almost any offer of marriage but Fanny is only a poor relation. But Jane Austen expects even a poor girl like Fanny to have a sense of self-respect. Unexpectedly, the only person in *Mansfield Park* who is able to appreciate Fanny's attitude to marriage correctly is Mary Crawford.

She tells her brother: "From my soul I do not think she would marry you *without love*; that is, if there is a girl in the world capable of being uninfluenced by ambition, I can suppose it is her." But Mary Crawford is also wrong when she adds: "but ask her to love you, and she will never have the heart to refuse" (chapt. 30). Fanny, however, does have the heart to refuse and tells her uncle: "I - I cannot like him, Sir, well enough to marry him." (chapt. 32). He accuses her of ingratitude but she is determined and hopes that his anger would abate with time and he would feel, "as a good man must feel, how wretched, and how unpardonable, how hopeless and how wicked it was, to marry without affection." (chapt. 32).

The view that marriage without affection is wretched, wicked and indeed unpardonable is also expressed in Jane Austen's letters. In a letter to her niece, Fanny Knight, Jane Austen says: "Anything is to be preferred or endured rather than marrying without affection...." In another letter, she is even more emphatic: "Nothing can be compared to the misery of being bound without Love, bound to one, and preferring another. That is a punishment which you do not deserve."[27]

VI

Recognising that even the most intelligent of women can make a mistake in showering her affection on a wrong person, Jene Austen demands that affection, too, must have a rational basis. Elizabeth Bennet, who is easily the most perceptive of Jane Austen's heroines, regards her sister Jane and Bingley an ideal couple precisely because their happiness is "rationally founded." (chapt. 55). This insistence on rationality in love has made critics question the spontaneity of love in Jane Austen. Lawrence Lerner, for instance, has said that marriages in Jane Austen "are famous, and so, of course, are her love stories, but how much of the passion of love do they express?" *Persuasion*, he claims, is the only novel in which Jane Austen seriously tried to express the experience of love; her careful skirting of it in all the others can be seen in the detached language of the proposal scenes." His examples of the proposal scenes - in *Pride and Prejudice* and in *Emma* - are quite telling. Darcy, he says, "expressed himself on the occasion as sensibly and as warmly as a man violently in love is supposed to do." In *Emma*, he claims, Jane Austen "simply surrendered to this awkwardness and deliberately laughed it off: 'What did she say? Just what she ought, of course. A lady always does'"[28]

But we need not make fun of this remark. In a traditional society where daughters from childhood have been taught what they should do and what they should not do, the girl knows how to respond to a man's overtures. She has been taught, almost without being made too much aware of it, the rules of conduct and she is thus capable of facing any situation as she should. Every traditional society lays down its own rules and the young men and women follow them. No questions are asked about the rightness or wrongness of these rules. But when they are violated, society either tries to cover it up or punishes the individuals in whatever way it suits it. When Lydia elopes with Wickham, everyone is shocked. This is the grossest social misdemeanour. But the family - its old members and one who is going to be its newest member - put their heads together and it is covered up through their marriage. Only Elizabeth is not satisfied. She knows that Lydia is too young and Wickham altogether unsuitable as a husband. "They must marry? And he is *such* a man?", she asks. But her father is right: do what the society expects.

The reason for Jane Austen's failure to express 'passion' is explained by Lawrence Lerner thus: "What Jane Austen most admired was the ability to resist impulse."[29] "Jane Austen really believed," he adds, "that every impulse must be submitted to the inspection of the judgement, and, if necessary, restrained; just as she really believed that happiness depended on virtue."[30] He concludes somewhat nastily:

> The heroes and heroines of Jane Austen will always feel as much gratitude - as much pity, as much indignation, as much love - as the occasion required. To them all we apply Aziz's complaint to Fielding: "Is emotion a sack of potatoes, to be measured out by the pound?"[31]

It is true that Jane Austen's heroines distrust sentiment and do not enter matrimony on impulse. It is a step that they take only after considerable thought. As Gary Kelley has said, Jane Austen's novels "clearly avoid, militantly avoid, we might say, the melodramatic, the sensational, the exotic, the intensely personal".[32] But Lawrence Lerner is in search of the intensely personal. That is why he is so dazzled by Marianne in *Sense and Sensibility* that he regards her as "the true heroine of *Sense and Sensibility*" and asserts that her true conquest is not "over Colonel Brandon but over the propriety in whose name the author puts her down."[33] Marianne's character, of course, is extremely attractive and quite often in the novel we admire her for defying propriety. One such occasion is clearly when she snubs Mrs. Ferrars. The tone of the novel would have greatly suffered if there were none in the novel to cut Mrs. Ferrars to size. However, we cannot also forget that Marianne acts foolishly when she falls desperately in love with the first attractive man that she meets and ignores Elinore's warnings. She does not realize, as Elinore does, that the world is not safe for young women and that they must never act in haste or without thought. And, of course, they need control over their feelings much more so at a time when they are getting deeply involved. It is lucky that Marianne had a sister like Elinore who brought her back from the brink of death through her love, care and devoted nursing.[34] We need not therefore have any difficulty in accepting Jane Austen's point of view and however attractive we may find the character of Marianne, we cannot treat her as the heroine of the novel.

Jane Austen may have been influenced in her outlook by contemporary events. After a somewhat tumultuous response to the French revolution in the earlier years. England was in a largely anti-revolutionary mood when Jane Austen came on the scene. On top of everything else, there was the war against France and even fear of a French invasion. All this encouraged conservative thinking and it is no accident that quite a few anti-Jacobin novels were published in England during this period advocating, among other things, traditional moral values of life. Jane Austen too is a conservative writer subscribing to such moral values. That even the most revolutionary writer in the age, Mary Wollstencraft, held views about love and marriage which are no different from those of Jane Austen need not surprise us. After all both were rational in their outlook and believed in the power of reason. Hence their advice to women was not to act on impulse and in the matter of marriage be guided by "friendship and respect, not love."[35] Some other contemporary writers too hold similar views. In her *Letters of Julia and Caroline* (1795), Maria Edgeworth shows how irrational and stupid some women's conduct can be: 'In vain, dear Caroline, you urge me to think; I profess only to feel'. Julia thinks that women's weaknesses make them more lovable: '... let us, Caroline, content ourselves to gain in love what we lose in *esteem*'.[36] In the prefatory remarks to her novel, *Coelebs in Search of a Wife* (1808), Hannah More summarised the contemporary ideal of love some years later:

> Love itself appears in these pages, not as an ungovernable impulse, but as a sentiment arising out of qualities calculated to inspire attachment in persons under the domination of reason and religion.[37]

That feelings should be under the control of reason, specially the feeling of love, however difficult it may be to do so, is not, therefore, something for which Jane Austen has to be singled out for condemnation as Lawrence Lerner does. It was the normal view of most writers in the eighteenth century. That it has a universal application is seen by what a character in Doris Lessing's *The Golden Notebook* (1962) says: "Sometimes, I dislike women, I dislike us all, because of our capacity for not-thinking when it suits us; we choose not to think when we are reaching out for happiness."[38] Eighteenth century novels are full of women who are seduced and abandoned by faithless men and who end tragically and most writers writing in 1790s recommend restraint and emotional discipline on the part of women and tolerance towards fallen women on the part of society. Such ideas are, of course, an offshoot of the view that women are rational beings - a view that was propounded both by revolutionary and conservative writers alike.

Most of Jane Austen's contemporaries would have agreed with Jane Austen's view that Wickham and Lydia in *Pride and Prejudice* would not be happy since "they were only brought together because their passions were stronger than their virtue" (Chapt. 50) and would have found Lawrence Lerner's view that though Lydia is foolish yet "in that sort of folly lies a kind of happiness"[39] as utterly unacceptable. They would have indeed approved of the advice that his virtuous friend in Charles Lloyd's novel, *Edmund Oliver* (1798), gives to the hero: "If you marry, marry from serious and well-grounded esteem, and not from love. I view your passion with interest as eliciting the powers of your mind; but Heaven grant that you form no connection while under its influence."[40] Such advice had much greater relevance for women than for men. They needed much more to understand that they must not form any connection when they were under the influence of passion but only after reason had resumed control over passion. It was believed - and is still believed in many circles - that women fall victims to passion much more easily than men, that their conduct is much more prone to be guided by emotion, that they need protection not only from others but also from themselves.

VII

While saying that she treated the marriage of Jane and Bingley as having a rational foundation, Elizabeth Bennet also claimed that it was so "because they had for basis .... excellent understanding .... and a general similarity of feelings and taste between them" (*Pride and Prejudice*, Chapt. 55). An excellent understanding does not, of course, necessarily depend on similarity of feelings and taste and Jane Austen does not always insist on such similarity. She has no sympathy, for instance, with the aggressive romantic notion of Marianne who confidently asserts: "I could not be happy with a man whose taste did not in every point coincide with my own. He must enter into all my feelings; the same books, the same music must charm us both." (*Sense and Sensibility*, Chapt. 3). As against this romantic notion of total identity, there is the altogether cynical view of Charlotte Lucas:

> "Happiness in marriage is entirely a matter of chance. If the dispositions of the parties are ever so well known to each other, or ever so similar beforehand, it does not advance their felicity in the least. They always continue to grow sufficiently unlike afterwards to have their share of vexation; and it is better to know as little as possible of the defects of the person with whom you are to pass your life." (*Pride and Prejudice*, Chapt. 6).

As against these extreme views, there are Elizabeth's eminently sensible and rational views: "She began now to comprehend," we are told,

> that [Darcy] was exactly the man who, in disposition and talents, would most suit her. His understanding and temper, though unlike her own, would have answered all her wishes. It was an union that must have been to the advantage of both; by her ease and liveliness, his mind might have been softened, his manners improved, and from his judgment, information, and knowledge of the world, she must have received benefit of greater importance. (Chapt. 50).

Jane Austen's normal view is that women must make a *rational* assessment of their feelings towards the man they want to marry and not allow themselves to be swept off their feet by romantic sentiment. In his review of *Emma*, Sir Walter Scott mentioned this distrust of romantic sentiment of Jane Austen and accused her of preaching the "doctrine of selfishness" and "calculating prudence."[41] Elizabeth Bennet, he said, decided to marry Darcy because when she saw Pemberley, "her prudence" began "to subdue her prejudice."[42] Prudence, of course, is a necessary virtue in a Jane Austen heroine but if Elizabeth Bennet married Darcy really for his wealth and to become the mistress of Pemberley, then she was not being prudent but mercenary. And yet at no stage in the novel do we get the impression that she is a mercenary character. Indeed, she is the only heroine in Jane Austen who raises the very important question of a moral distinction between prudent and mercenary motives in marriage. When her aunt, Mrs. Gardiner, accuses Wickham of being "mercenary" for deserting her and attaching himself to Miss King who could fetch ten thousand pounds, Elizabeth replies:

> Pray, my dear aunt, what is the difference in matrimonial affairs, between the mercenary and the prudent motive? Where does discretion end, and avarice begin? Last Christmas you were afraid of his marrying me, because it would be imprudent; and now, because he is trying to get a girl with only ten thousand pounds, you want to find out that he is mercenary. (Chapt. 27).

But obviously Elizabeth knows that Wickham *is* being mercenary in his conduct and in her reply, she is merely evading the issue. Her aunt, however, pursues the subject and the following conversation takes place:

> 'If you will only tell me what sort of girl Miss King is, I shall know what to think'.
>
> 'She is a very good kind of girl, I believe. I know no harm of her'.
>
> 'But he paid her not the smallest attention, till her grandfather's death made her mistress of this fortune! (Chapt. 27).

The point to be noticed is that Wickham *is* mercenary and that both Elizabeth and Mrs. Gardiner *know* the difference between the prudent and the mercenary and further that Elizabeth does not approve of Wickham's conduct but what can she say? She *does* want to condemn him but she feels embarrassed in doing so after her previous interest in him even after her aunt's warning. Hence her equivocation. But in Jane Austen, there is no equivocation. She does approve of prudent conduct but everywhere rejects mercenary conduct both amongst men and women. All the heroines are prudent in one form or another, and yet, significantly, none of them is even slightly mercenary. Jane Austen indeed despises women who are out to catch rich husbands. Such women are shallow, selfish and calculating, and all of them, in a smaller or greatest measure, are mercenary in one form or another - women like Isabella Thorpe in *Northanger Abbey*, Lucy Steele in *Sense and Sensibility*, Mary Crawford in *Mansfield Park*, Louisa Musgreve in *Persuasion* and Caroline Bingley in *Pride and Prejudice*. Darcy reflects the author's point of view admirably when he says: "There is a meanness in all the arts which ladies sometimes condescend to employ for captivation. Whatever bears affinity to cunning is despicable" (Chapt. 8). Jane Austen's own comment on Lucy Steele's conduct in *Sense and Sensibility* (Chapt. 50) is even more devastating:

> "The whole of Lucy's behaviour in the affair, and the prosperity which crowned it, may be held forth as a most encouraging instance of what an earnest, an unceasing attention to self-interest .... will do in securing every advantage of fortune, with no other sacrifice than that of time and *conscience*" (Italics mine).

VIII

Prudence in any case demands that women must not go by first impressions and must accept a proposal only when they have evidence regarding the man's inner nature. In a society where men can desert their wives at will and no protection is provided to them either by law or custom and where they can take nothing with them, neither any property nor even their children, their first anxiety is for a stable and secure relationship. Much more so if their families are not in a position to look after them. They, therefore, cannot be too impressed by outward polish. It is not without significance that Jane Austen was "suspicious of decadent court and aristocratic culture, especially its codes of amorous gallantry and coquetry."[43] This suspicion can be fully understood only if we recognise that what her women need is a sense of *security* which can be provided by men of steady principles and not by polished aristocratic rakes.

It may be added in this connection that Jane Austen deprecades the tendency of young girls to think in terms of perfect men as their life-partners. In a letter to her niece Fanny, she puts it wittily:

> "There *are* such beings in the World, perhaps one in a Thousand, as the Creature You and I should think perfection, where Grace and Spirit are united to Worth, where the Manners are equal to the Heart and Understanding, but such a person may not come in your way, or if he does, he may not be the eldest son of a Man of fortune, the Brother of your particular friend, and belonging to your own County."[44]

It is also interesting to learn from one of her letters that when Fanny asked her advice regarding a young man about whom she was not able to make up her mind as he was too religious and lacked wit, Jane Austen replied:

> "Wisdom is better than wit, and in the long run will certainly have the laugh on her side; and don't be frightened by the idea of his acting more strictly up to the precepts of the New Testament than others."[45]

It is a sound advice and all Jane Austen's heroines (whatever their contradictions) finally accept it.

It was to establish the general principle that wisdom is to be preferred to wit in man's character that Jane Austen introduced in each of her novels a young man who is witty and glamorous but otherwise wholly unsatisfactory as a life-partner. Most heroines at some stage feel dangerously drawn towards such a man but soon drop him in favour of a more stable relationship. Willoughby in *Sense and Sensibility* not only dazzles Marianne but also Elinore. Wickham in *Pride and Prejudice* dazzles the whole Bennet family and at one stage, Elizabeth herself feels confused about him. Frank Churchill in *Emma* also enters the novel as a Prince Charming and causes serious disturbance in Emma's placid world. Crawford in *Mansfield Park* almost wrecks whatever values the place stands for, though, mercifully, he fails to impress Fanny, the heroine of the novel. In *Persuasion* this role is played, somewhat ineffectively and clumsily, by William Elliot. These characters do, in one form or another, make some impression on the minds of the heroines, but finally the heroines choose safe life-partners who are men of steady principles and deep feelings though in some ways they are pedestrain and even dull. Tony Tanner describes them as "too serious, humourless, severe, haughty, perhaps a little pedantic, a little lugubrious (and - even if this is not articulated -) somewhat de-eroticised, prematurely middle-aged."[46]

Even though she is looking at the problem from the point of view of women in her times — and women too belonging largely to the middle or the lower-middle class — there is no doubt that Jane Austen shows an excellent understanding of the nature of marriage in general. It is interesting to see that Thomas Hardy in his novel, *Far from the Madding Crowd* (1874), also looks at marriage more or less from the same angle. The heroine in this novel, Bathsheba, is completely dazzled by Seargant Troy, who is very similar to Mr. Willoughby of *Sense and Sensibility.* He is 'uncommonly handsome' and otherwise so attractive that she marries him even though she knows so little about him that he is almost a stranger. She is saved by his death and finally she marries Gabriel Oak with whom, in the words of Carolyn Heilbrun, there is the "possibility of friendship and mutuality, rather than the glamour of romance."[47] Jane Austen understood this situation even better than Hardy. But as an eighteenth century novelist, she cannot let her heroines venture on such experiments as Hardy could. Heilbrun's comment on Bathsheba's finally accepting Gabriel Oak is very illuminating for our understanding of Jane Austen: "Bathsheba had to learn that men who do not exploit her are not therefore less manly-most women have still to learn it."[48]

IX

Jane Austen's women are clearly in search of "friendship and mutuality" and distrust relationship inspired by "the glamour of romance". This is perhaps best seen in *Sense and Sensibility*. In this novel, Jane Austen is seen rejecting the contemporary novel of passion to write the novel of moral and intellectual perception, and consequent ethical action. This perception and ethical action are best seen in the central characters of the two sisters in this novel. They clearly represent two different attitudes to marriage. Elinore's demands in marriage are clearly very modest and, in her circumstances, also very realistic. Through Elinore's character, Jane Austen raises the question of the need for "self-knowledge and self-mastery" in a heroine.[49] These qualities Elinore possesses in ample measure. Hence it is only after judging the character of the hero rightly that she accepts him even after he has been disinherited by his rich mother. As if deliberately, Jane Austen paints a rather dull picture of Edward Ferrars, the hero in this novel.

> He was not handsome, and his manners required intimacy to make them pleasing....he was neither fitted by abilities nor disposition to answer the wishes of his mother and sister, who longed to see him distinguished .... His mother wished to interest him in political concerns, to get him into Parliament, or to see him connected with some of the great men of the day... But Edward had no turn for great men..... All his wishes centred in domestic comfort and the quiet of private life. (Chap. 3).

The fact that this man loves Elinore and, further, that in his scale of values domestic comfort and the content of the life of a private citizen are placed so high should make him an ideal husband for Elinore whose values also fit in very well with his profession as a clergyman - a profession that was approved of neither by his mother and sister nor by Lucy Steele to whom, in a moment of weakness, he had got engaged. Elinore, of course, wholly approves of the profession of a clergyman. She believes that her marriage with Edward can be "a marriage of true minds."

Elinore's younger sister, Marianne, however, has an altogether different notion of marriage. Her ideal is not quiet domesticity but excitement and romantic passion. She is not too impressed by Elinore's choice and finds Edward too tame. There is "something wanting" in him, she tells her mother:

> his figure is not striking - it has none of that grace which I should expect.... His eyes want all that spirit, that fire, which at once announce virtue and intelligence. And besides all this... he has no real taste.... I could not be happy with a man whose taste did not in every point coincide with my own. O mamma! how spiritless, how tame was Edward's manner in reading to us last night. (Chap. 3).

She at last meets the man who satisfies 'her ideas of perfection' (Chapt. 10). Mr. Willoughby is not only "uncommonly handsome" but also possesses "more than common gracefulness". (Chapt. 9). Moreover, there is something "manly" (Chapt. 9) about his beauty and, the more her acquaintance with him grows, the more she is impressed by "his manners", "his pursuits, his talents, and genius" (Chapt. 9). Indeed, "his person and air were equal to what her fancy had ever drawn for the hero of a favourite story" (Chapt. 9).

This Prince Charming, however, is proved to be a thorough-going villain. Marianne is, of course, completely dazzled and overwhelmed by him but, as later events show, he is a man without conscience and can easily deceive innocent young women. He has already wrecked the life of another young woman who is soon going to be the mother of his child. At the first opportunity he deserts Marianne too, to marry Miss Grey who brings him a dowry of 30,000 pounds.

The question is often asked as to why Jane Austen thought it necessary to arrange Marianne's marriage with Colonel Brandon whom at one stage Marianne had described as "old enough to be her father".

Tony Tanner claims "that there is something punitive in the taming of Marianne and all she embodies.... It is as though Jane Austen had gone out of her way to show that romantic feelings are utterly non-viable in her society,"[50] that "the structure of society was more powerful than the structure of feeling in any one individual."[51] We may not like it, but is Jane Austen altogether wrong in her understanding of the contemporary situation? She is clearly suggesting that we are not living in an ideal world and that we should accept with grace an alternative to the ideal which in Marianne's case is a marriage, based on a sentiment no "superior to strong esteem and lively friendship". (Chapt.50). This basis is perhaps "less passionate and fulfilling" but it is certainly "comfortable, convenient, respectable."[52] The latter words are hateful in certain circles, yet how many marriages were sustained in Jane Austen or any other writer in eighteenth century or even later - or in life - by sheer passion and sexual attraction? Moreover, what are the options available to Marianne? This marriage is certainly to be preferred to her staying with her mother, going out for long walks with Margaret or alone, and doing some reading. We may add to this, occasional visits to Elinore to shake off her frustration and boredom. Marriage to a man of Colonel Brandon's sincerity is certainly to be preferred to such a barren life. Jane Austen's society would have wholly approved of her decision to marry off Marianne to the Colonel.

Jane Austen's rejection of Marianne's romantic point of view and acceptance of Elinore's sedate attitude to marriage is not to be scoffed at. That domestic happiness is dependent on steadiness of character in husband and wife rather than on ecstacy of romance is something that Jane Austen consistently emphasises. After Elizabeth's Bennet's feelings of dislike for Darcy are replaced by feelings of "respect and esteem" and indeed "gratitude", Jane Austen pauses in the midst of the narrative and defines two different modes of love:

> "If gratitude and esteem are good foundations of affection, Elizabeth's change of sentiment will be neither improbable nor faulty. But if otherwise, if the regard springing from such sources is unreasonable and unnatural, in comparison of what is on often described as arising on a first interview with its object, and even before two words have been exchanged, nothing can be said in her defence, except that she had given

> somewhat of a trial to the latter method, in her partiality for Wickham, and that its ill-success might perhaps authorise her to seek the other less interesting mode of attachment." (chapt. 46).

It is this "less interesting mode of attachment", then, which Jane Austen recommends as a suitable basis of marriage.

If Elizabeth Bennet, who is easily the most dynamic and the most perceptive of Jane Austen's heroines, is willing to accept what she herself describes as a "less interesting mode of attachment" in preference to passionate and exciting love, what shall we say of her other heroines, especially of Fanny, the heroine of *Mansfield Park*? The marriage of Fanny and Edmund is, of course, a very congenial and compatible one but Jane Austen makes it clear that it is not inspired by romantic or sexual love. Whatever Mary Crawford's faults - whether of "manner" or of a "tainted" mind (Chapt. 27) - the fact is that Edmund falls passionately in love with her. As he writes to Fanny: "I cannot give her up, Fanny. She is the only woman in the world whom I could ever think of as a wife" (Chapt. 44). Fanny is, of course, dear to him. But at no stage does she stir his blood. She recognises this fact though she herself is wholly committed to him and has loved him almost from the beginning. She broods over his letter and fears that his attachment to Mary is "an attachment" that would "govern his whole life." "Accepted or rejected," she says, "his heart is wedded to her for ever." (Chapt. 44). She can hardly hope that Edmund's passion for Mary would ever subside. But it does subside: though the process, as described by Jane Austen, sounds somewhat clumsy:

> Scarcely had he done regretting Mary Crawford, and observing to Fanny how impossible it was that he should ever meet with such another woman, before it began to strike him whether a very different kind of woman might not do just as well - or a great deal better; whether Fanny herself were not growing as dear, as important to him in all her smiles, and all her ways, as Mary Crawford had ever been; and whether it might not be a

> possible, an hopeful undertaking to persuade her that her warm and sisterly regard for him would be foundation enough for wedded love. (Chapt. 48).

Perhaps realizing that this foundation may not be strong enough, Jane Austen awkwardly adds:

> I purposely abstain from dates on this occasion, that everyone may be at liberty to fix their own, aware that the cure of unconquerable passions, and the transfer of unchanging attachment, must vary much as to time in different people. I only interest every body to believe that exactly at the time when it was quite natural that it should be so, and not a week earlier, Edmund did cease to care about Mary Crawford, and became as anxious to marry Fanny, as Fanny herself could desire. (Chapt. 48).

This change, of course, meant, in Jane Austen's words, that Edmund "should learn to prefer soft light eyes to sparkling dark ones." (Chapt. 48).

The marriage of Henry Tilney with Catharine Moreland in *Northanger Abbey* is also a sedate affair based on affection and not on passionate attraction for "sparkling dark eyes", At the end of the novel, Jane Austen says:

> though Henry was now sincerely attached to her, though he felt and delighted in all the excellencies of her character and truly loved her society, I must confess that his affection originated in nothing better than gratitude, or, in other words, that a persuasion of her partiality for him had been the only cause of giving her a serious thought. (Chapt. 30).

And, then, Jane Austen, somewhat gleefully and even mischievously, adds:

> It is a new circumstance in romance, I acknowledge, and

> dreadfully derogatory of an heroine's dignity; but if it be as new in common life, the credit of a wild imagination will at least be all my own. (chapt. 30).

Jane Austen need not give herself credit for this wild imagination. The fact is that in common life most marriages originate in nothing better than partiality shown by one party or another.

In Emma's marriage, love is there, and, of course, esteem and confidence. How passionate this love is becomes evident when Harriet tells her that Mr. Knightley might marry her. At this information, we are told, 'It *darted through her, with the speed of an arrow, that Mr. Knightley must marry no one but herself*!' (Chapt. 47). (Italics mine). One wonders whether it is her vanity which is hurt. Vanity is certainly hurt but love is also there and a deep affection.'

> Before being threatened with its loss, Emma had never known how much of her happiness depended on being first with Mr. Knightley, first in interest and affection. Satisfied that it was so and feeling it her due, she had enjoyed it without reflection: and only in the dread of being supplanted, found how inexpressibly important it had been. (chapt. 48).

She even thinks that she will be satisfied if Mr. Knightley stays unmarried in Highbury:

> Let him but continue the same Mr. Knightley to her and her father, the same Mr. Knightley to all the world; let Donwell and Hartfield lose none of their precious intercourse of friendship and confidence, and her peace would be fully secured. Marriage, in fact, would not do for her. It would be incompatible with what she owed to her father, and with what she felt for him. Nothing could separate her from her father. She would not marry, even if she were asked by Mr. Knightley. (Chapt. 48).

Of course, she does marry him and the feeling of Mr. Knightley for

Emma and of Emma for Knightley can certainly guarantee domestic harmony. As Gary Kelley has commented:

> "No doubt, Mr. Knightley will have much to do with his wife to keep her from her follies, just as Jane Fairfax will be kept busy with her too enthusiastic and impulsive husband; but then that is what marriages are for, among other things."[53]

It may be added that Emma's character is a highly flawed one. In this connection, Linda Hunt has made an interesting point. She claims that the central purpose of Jane Austen's novels is "to define, in fictionalized form, the ideal woman, either by offering an exemplary heroine or, sometimes, by showing the vicissitudes of an imperfect heroine who must learn to correct her errors in conduct and attain perfection before she can win a husband."[54] Perfection, of course, is neither possible nor desirable and in any case, as Jane Austen said in a letter to her niece, Fanny Knight: "Pictures of perfection, as you know, make me sick and wicked". (23 March 1817). But the heroines have to correct some of the serious errors in their conduct in order to become good wives. Emma has clearly to correct quite a few of the flaws in her conduct, the chief being her "insufferable vanity" and her "unpardonable arrogance .... to arrange everybody's destiny. (*Emma*, Chapt. 47).

XI

The most satisfactory marriage in Jane Austen, however, is the marriage of Elizabeth Bennet and Darcy in *Pride and Prejudice*. This marriage can perhaps be described as "aesthetically right, morally and humanely balanced, financially sound."[55] To believe that Elizabeth is marrying Darcy to become the mistress of Pemberley, as Sir Walter Scott unwisely thought, is clearly absurd. Nor can anyone doubt the genuineness of Darcy's affection for her. The special merit of this marriage, however, is that it is the only marriage in Jane Austen where there is complete *equality* between man and woman. This is not a minor point, though it is often ignored. In almost all Jane Austen's novels, the hero and the heroine are shown reaching a compromise which establishes the moral or intellectual dominance of one over the other. In *Northanger Abbey*, the hero is clearly superior. So also in *Emma* where Mr. Knightley and not Emma, however bright and sparkling she might otherwise be, finally dominates the tone of the novel. In *Mansfield Park*, however, the wisdom of the novel is embodied in Fanny. So also in *Sense and Sensibility* where we accept Elinore's point of view. In *Persuasion* too, the perception and intelligence of Anne Elliot are the guiding factors. In *Pride and Prejudice* alone, both Darcy and Elizabeth are equally to blame for creating the complications and finally both change and recover the understanding necessary for achieving a mature relationship.

The nature of this equality is best understood in the light of Elizabeth's father's remarks: "I know your disposition, Lizzy," he says, "I know that you could neither be happy nor respectable unless you truly esteemed your husband - unless you looked up to him as a superior. Your lively talents would place you in the greatest danger in an *unequal marriage*". (Italics mine). (Chapt. 59). Mr. Bennet is obviously talking of equality of talents and not of social status. Darcy is, of course, superior to Elizabeth in fortune for she has, in Mark Shorer's words, "no money, no family, no tradition .... nothing but her splendid intelligence."[56] But - and this is precisely the point that Jane Austen is making - why does a woman *need* anything else? And what kind of equality is it where we measure things in terms of money, family or tradition? Elizabeth Bennet at least attaches no importance to money, family or tradition as Jane Austen makes clear when she describes her first visit to Lady Catharine's house as Mr. Collin's house-guest.

> When they ascended the steps of the hall, Maria's alarm was every moment increasing and even Sir William did not look perfectly calm - Elizabeth's courage did not fail her. She had heard nothing of Lady Catharine that spoke her awful from any extraordinary talents or miraculous virtue, and the mere stateliness of money and rank, she thought she could witness

without trepidation. (Chapt. 29).

Jane Austen brings two individuals together, both equally blind to begin with and both equally repentant at the end, who finally recognise each other's value. What they give to each other is not only affection but also esteem, respect and confidence which Elizabeth's parents had failed to give to each other. Darcy needs to recognise that Elizabeth has as much right to have pride as he and Elizabeth has to recognise that Darcy's prejudice (against her family) is not without basis.

XII

Denis Donoghue has asked why Jane Austen's world should be "divided between charming scoundrels and dull saints. She must discriminate between the charm of Wickham and the vivacity of Darcy, between the force of Frank Churchill and the style of Knightley."[57] But Jane Austen does not fail to discriminate. Indeed she makes the point that her scoundrels are not really charming nor are her saints dull. Malcolm Bradbury rightly points out that "Birth and good manners are important in Jane Austen, but only when there is something behind them."[58] As Mr. Knightley reminds Emma, manners are a speciality of the French, not of the English. Frank Churchill thus may have manners but he is utterly heartless and it is Mr. Knightley and Darcy who have that "something behind" which makes them superior to others. The Wickhams and the Churchills are good enough only to flirt with and women in polite society may have to suffer them but surely they can make no contribution to domestic happiness which is what marriage after all means.

Angus Wilson is doubtful whether Darcy and Mr. Knightley would make good husbands. He is indeed not sure that Jane Austen's view of life is sufficiently positive to guarantee happiness in marriages. "Lizzy is so real and Darcy so unreal," he says, "that we cannot take the compromise seriously."[59] But this compromise is the essence of the novel. Elizabeth herself had seen the difference between Darcy's 'understanding and temper' and her own but recognised that 'he was exactly the man, who, in disposition, and talents, would most suit her'. (Chapt. 50). Gary Kelley has said that in her novels Jane Austen presents "the coalition of gentry and professional middle classes." Her own family, Kelly says, "had been moving steadily through the professions towards gentry status for two generations at least."[60] In *Pride and Prejudice,* Elizabeth's father represents the lower gentry - he is a landed "gentleman" - and Darcy represents the somewhat higher gentry but not the aristocracy. From the social angle, it is indeed a wholly satisfactory "coalition". From the artistic point of view it is enough to say that while Elizabeth is certainly more sparkling than Darcy, Darcy has solid qualities which more than compensate for his seeming incapacity to laugh at himself. Elizabeth's father too raises the question of great disparity between Elizabeth's "lively talents" and Darcy's pride. But Elizabeth reacts sharply:

> "I do like him," she replied with tears in her eyes, "I love him. Indeed, he has no improper pride. He is perfectly amiable. You do not know what he really is; then pray do not pain me by speaking of him in such terms". (Chapt. 59).

Angus Wilson also has some difficulty in accepting the compatibility of Emma and Mr. Knightley. Mr. Knightley, he says, is "pompous, condescending and a bore" and however "excellent" he may be as a landowner or as an employer - and however "thoughtful and tactful" as a "provider of apples for Miss Bates" - we do not know what sort of husband he will make "for Emma's untortured high intelligence". "What will she do all day while he is busy, healthily walking about in all weathers?"[61] he asks. The answer to Angus Wilson's last question, of course, is precisely the one that Jane Austen gave in another context: "just what she ought, of course. A lady always [knows]." Critics who have no experience of family life in a traditional society often talk of the boredom of wives in marriage. "As the Victorian age took shape," Jenny Calder tells us, "and as the walls closed in on the Victorian heroine and the

Victorian marriage, two features grew into dominance: stasis and boredom." Jenny Calder, however, recognises that "Jane Austen's heroines are not bored" and gives an excellent reason for this state of things:

> they may not always be useful, but they are usually busy. They know how to find pleasure in passing the time in what seem to them useful activities, needlework, sketching, music, visiting. In Jane Austen's novels languor and boredom, such as we find in *Mansfield Park*'s Lady Bertram, are a reflection of character, not of society.[62]

It is worth remembering that the society that Jane Austen represents is essentially a semi-rural society to which the concept of boredom is somewhat foreign. The men that the two heroines, Elizabeth Bennet and Emma Woodhouse, have married are land-owners and in their case, of course, there would be no dearth of activity for their wives. Darcy and Knightley are so much a part of "the resident *native* gentry" and are so "attached to the soil"[63] that their wives have to perform varied duties in looking after the welfare of their tenants and neighbours in the countryside. Darcy is not, of course, as native as Mr. Knightley who is -

> "known to every farmer and labourer from his childhood, frequently mixing with them in those pursuits where all artificial distinctions are lost, practising hospitality without ceremony, from habit and not on calculation."[64]

Darcy, after his marriage and his comparative deliverance from the snobbish hold of Lady Catharine, is also expected to perform his social role as squire with much greater ease. Elizabeth and Emma indeed are likely to be busier than Jane Austen's other heroines - three of them wives of clergymen and one the wife of a sailor. All these women are likely to lead very useful and purposive lives and the assumption clearly is that these marriages - as against the marriages of their parents and other members of the older generation (with the notable exception of the Crofts) are likely to be happy.

NOTES

1. The references from *Clarissa Harlowe* are from the Everyman Edition.
2. Lloyd W. Brown, "The Business of Marrying and Mothering", *Jane Austen's Achievement,* ed. Juliet McMaster (London, 1975), p.31.
3. Patricia Beer, *Reader, I Married Him: A Study of the Women Characters of Jane Austen, Charlotte Bronte, Elizabeth Gaskell and George Eliot* (London, 1974), pp.2, 4.
4. See Oliver MacDONAGH: *Jane Austen: Real and Imagined Worlds* (New Haven, 1991), p. 73.
5. Op. Cit., pp.27, 31.
6. Wallace Notestein, "The English Woman, 1580-1650", *Studies in Social History* (1955), edited by J. H. Plumb, p.90.
7. Roy Porter: *English Society in the Eighteenth Century* (Penguin Books, New Edition, 1990), p.27.
8. Meenakshi Mukherjee, *Jane Austen* (Macmillan, New Delhi, 1991), p.34.
9. Paula R. Backscheider, ' "I died for Love": Esteem in Eighteenth Century Novels by Women', *Fetter'd Or Free?: British Women Novelists 1670-1815,* edited by Mary Anne Schofield and Cecilia Macheski (Ohio University Press, Athens, 1986), p. 152.
10. Cited by Deborah Downs-Miers, "Springing The Trap: Subtexts and Subversions", *Fetter'd Or Free?*, p.313.
11. Cited by Paula R. Backscheider, Ibid., p.160.
12. Ibid., pp. 159-60.
13. Ibid., p.166.
14. Ibid., p.155.
15. Cited by Bridget Hill, *Eighteenth Century Women: An Anthology* (London, 1984), p. 87.
16. See Gary Kelly, *English Fiction of the Romantic Period 1789-1830* (London, 1989), p.127.
17. Tony Tanner, *Jane Austen* (London, 1986), p. 10.
18. Anthea Zeman, *Presumptuous Girls: Women and Their World in the Serious Woman's Novel* (London, 1977), p. 20.
19. *Some Reflections Upon Marriage* (1700), p.20.
20. Lawrence Stone, *The Family, Sex and Marriage in England 1500- 1800* (Penguin Books, abridged edition, 1977), p.329.
21. Anthea Zeman, pp. 16-17.
22. Jenni Calder, *Women and Marriage in Victorian Fiction* (London, 1976), p.16.
23. Anthea Zeman, pp.21-22.

24. See Lawrence Stone, p.188.
25. Cited by Lawrence Lerner, *The Truth Tellers: Jane Austen, George Eliot and D. H. Lawrence* (London, 1977), p.26.
26. Gary Kelley, p.114.
27. Cited by Lloyd W. Brown, p. 29.
28. Lawrence Lerner, *Love and Marriage; Literature and its Social Context* (London, 1979), pp. 25, 26, 27.
29. Lawrence Lerner, *The Truth Tellers: Jane Austen, George Eliot, D. H. Lawrence,* p. 137.
30. Ibid., p. 146.
31. Ibid., p.151.
32. "Jane Austen and the English Novel of the 1790s", *Fetter'd Or Free?: British Women Novelists, 1670-1815*, edited by Mary Anne Schofield and Cecilia Macheski, (1986), p. 295.
33. *The Truth Tellers,* p. 166.
34. See Sir Walter Scott's very perceptive comment on *Sense and Sensibility* in his unsigned review of *Emma* in *Quarterly Review*, March 1816: "The interest and merit of the piece depend altogether upon the behaviour of the elder sister, while obliged at once to sustain her own disappointment with fortitude, and to support her sister, who abandons herself, with unsuppressed feelings, to the indulgence of grief." (*Jane Austen: The Critical Heritage*, ed. B.C. Southam, London, 1968), p. 64.
35. See Alice Browne, *The Eighteenth Century Feminist Mind* (Brighton, 1987), p.158.
36. Ibid., p. 163.
37. Cited by Alice Browne, p.159.
38. Cited by Carolyn G. Heilbrun, *Reinventing Womanhood* (London, 1979), p.174.
39. Lawrence Lerner, *The Truth Tellers*, p.154.
40. Cited by Marilyn Butler, *Jane Austen and the War of Ideas*, pp.109-110.
41. *Jane Austen: The Critical Heritage*, ed. B. C. Southam, p. 68.
42. Ibid., p. 65.
43. Gary Kelly, *English Fiction of the Romantic Period, 1789- 1830*, p.112.
44. Cited by Rachel M. Brownstein, *Becoming a Heroine: Reading about Women in Novels* (Penguin Books, Harmondsworth, 1982), p. 139.
45. Cited by Christopher Gillie, *A Preface to Jane Austen* (London, 1974), pp. 16-17.
46. Tony Tanner, p.29.
47. "Marriage Perceived: English Literature 1873-1941", *What Manner of Women* (New York, 1977) ed. Mariane Springer, p.175.
48. Ibid., p. 175.
49. Gary Kelly, *English Fiction of the Romantic Period*, p.114.
50. Tony Tanner, ed. *Sense and Sensibility* (Penguin Classics, 1986), p.31.
51. Ibid., p.33.

52. P.J.M. Scott, *Jane Austen: A Reassessment* (London, 1982), p.102.
53. Gary Kelly, *English Fiction of the Romantic Period,* p.133.
54. "A Woman's Portion: Jane Austen and the Female Character", "*Fetter'd Or Free*", p.9.
55. Malcolm Bradbury, "Jane Austen's *Emma*" (1962), *Emma* ed. David Lodge (Casebook, 1968), p.218.
56. "Pride Unprejudiced", *Kenyon Review*, 18 (Winter 1958), p.81.
57. "A View of Mansfield Park", *Critical Essays on Jane Austen*, ed. B. C. Southam (1968), pp. 48-9.
58. "Jane Austen's *Emma*", *Emma* (Casebook), ed. David Lodge, p.222.
59. Angus Wilson, "The Neighbourhood of Tombuctoo: Conflicts in Jane Austen's Novels", *Critical Essays on Jane Austen*, ed. B. C. Southam (London, 1968), p.198.
60. Gary Kelly, *English Fiction of the Romantic Period*, p.111.
61. Angus Wilson, p. 198.
62. *Women and Marriage in Victorian Fiction*, p. 56.
63. See the quotation from William Cobbet in Tony Tanner, "Jane Austen and 'The Quiet Thing': A Study of Mansfield Park", *Critical Essays on Jane Austen*, ed. B.C. Southam, p.139.
64. William Cobbet, Ibid., p. 139.

Index